The Best of
"The Spirit of Medjugorje"

Volume II
1998-2004

Compiled by

June Klins

authorHOUSE®

AuthorHouse™
1663 Liberty Drive, Suite 200
Bloomington, IN 47403
www.authorhouse.com
Phone: 1-800-839-8640

First published by AuthorHouse 9/17/2007

ISBN: 978-1-4343-1755-1 (sc)

Printed in the United States of America
Bloomington, Indiana

This book is printed on acid-free paper.

Compiled by June Klins
Editor's declaration:

The decree of the Congregation for the Propagation of the Faith, A.A.S., 58,1186 (approved by Pope Paul VI on October 14, 1966) states that the Nihil Obstat and Imprimatur are no longer required on publications that deal with private revelations, provided they contain nothing contrary to faith and morals. The events of Medjugorje are presently under investigation. The editor and writers of the following works wish to affirm our readiness to accept the final judgment of the magisterium of the Church. A final decree of the Church will be made known once the apparitions cease.

Although the editor of this book and the previous editor of "The Spirit of Medjugorje" have made every effort to ensure the accuracy of information contained in this book, we assume no responsibility for errors, inaccuracies, omissions, or any inconsistency herein.

About the Cover

Designing a cover was the hardest part of creating the first book. I wanted the cover to reflect exactly what the "spirit" of Medjugorje is all about. It was on my way home from a Eucharistic Holy Hour where we had prayed 15 decades of the Rosary that the idea popped into my head: The "spirit" of Medjugorje is a spirit of peace, love and joy, and the way to peace, love and joy is to **live the messages** of Our Lady. The cover should be a collage representing the 5 things Our Lady is asking us to do – Pray with the heart, Bible, Eucharist, Confession, and Fasting. These are known as the "five stones" or "weapons against Goliath," a theme that runs throughout this book.

I felt that the cover of Volume II should reflect the same messages, but with different pictures. Although Volume I had Our Lady in the center, I chose the Risen Jesus for the center of Volume II to show that Our Lady brings us to Jesus. All of the pictures on the cover were taken in Medjugorje.

This book is dedicated to Our Lady, Queen of Peace, and to Her faithful daughter, Joan Wieszczyk, my predecessor, mentor and friend.

Table Of Contents

Acknowledgments

I am very grateful to the Holy Spirit for the inspiration to compile this book, to Our Lady, for Her loving guidance through this project, and to all the people who prayed for this book to become a reality.

I am thankful to Joan Wieszczyk for her sixteen years of loving service as editor of "The Spirit of Medjugorje," and for her blessing and support in the publishing of this book.

I am thankful to Tom Klins for supporting my pilgrimages to Medjugorje. If it were not for his generosity in funding my pilgrimages, this book would not exist.

I am very grateful to Carolanne Kilichowski, Martha Herron and especially to Louise Lotze for their help with the arduous job of proofreading.

I would like to thank Diana Stillwell, Carolanne Kilichowski, Kathy Longenecker, Mike Golovich, Louise Lotze, Carlotta Zuback, Joel Vidonish, Helen Bell, Jason Smith, Wendy Ripple, and Tom Klins for their photographs, and Brian Klins for his cartoons.

And, last but not least, I would like to thank all of those who consented to the re-publishing of their works in this book. I would like to pay tribute in a special way to Msgr. James Peterson, the spiritual director of "The Spirit of Medjugorje" newsletter.

Foreword
By Msgr. James Peterson

Over the last 26 years, there has been a unique series of heavenly apparitions with no parallel in history. It is true that the series of prophets in the history of the Hebrews is not matched anywhere else in human history. In them, over centuries, God was preparing a nation that would be earnestly monotheistic. Their preaching enforced the mission of one another.

In Mary's daily apparitions at Medjugorje, we have an earnest invitation to the seers, to those associated with them, and to all the world to pray and sacrifice for world peace.

This volume of Our Lady's messages carries a pattern of helping all of us to learn how to pray. Mary wants us to love prayer and calls us to develop deeper forms of prayer. She wants us to know what a responsibility we have when we realize that peace will come to our very fragile planet because of the seriousness we bring to self-discipline and prayer.

The messages included here are too important to be read once and thrown away or forgotten.

They are a treasury of insights we need to be aware of until the work is finished – either by our entrance into eternal life, or by arriving at the moment of Mary's Queenship of World Peace.

Introduction

My Story

My "fairy-tale" life crumbled to pieces in 1995 when tragedy befell my family. I took out the rosary I had from childhood, dusted it off and began to pray with it again. As She always does, Our Lady led me to Her Son and I began to attend daily Mass. I began to experience the peace that only God can give.

Then, on January 11, 1997, I became incapacitated with a strange condition that caused my hands and feet to go numb. After three weeks, the numbness went into a burning sensation that was excruciating. I missed work, could not drive and was virtually house-bound, as my symptoms baffled doctors, including even those at the renowned Cleveland Clinic. Then in January of 1998, my mother's friend sent her a medal of Our Lady of Medjugorje for me. I thought this was very generous of her to give me something so special, especially since she lived far away and had never even met me. I wrote her a note of thanks the next day, but it was not until a week later that I realized that there were no words adequate enough to express my gratitude.

Five days after I had received the medal, I found the answer to my problems on the Internet. As I had suspected all along, my problem was a hormone imbalance. That day I began using a topical cream purchased in a health food store and the healing process began that very night. By the end of the week I was able to walk up and down every aisle in the grocery store, something I hadn't been able to do in a year. I knew that the Blessed Mother had pointed me in the right direction, especially when I realized that the day my mother gave me the medal was January 11, exactly one year to the date after my problems began.

Soon I was feeling well enough to begin planning a trip to our son's graduation from basic training at Ft. Benning, Georgia in May. Since the graduation date was a few days after Memorial Day, we decided to make a little vacation of it and go to St. Augustine, Florida for a few days before going to Ft. Benning. We had never been to St.

Augustine before, but my parents and grandparents always loved it there, and my mother thought I would like the Marian shrine there.

On the Sunday before Memorial Day we visited the mission where the shrine is located. The shrine is called "Our Lady of La Leche," and is the oldest Marian shrine in the United States. When my husband, Tom, and I went into the shrine, I filmed everything inside. Then we walked around the rest of the mission grounds, taking in its beauty and historical significance and took pictures of the huge cross which stands at the place where the first Mass was celebrated in this country.

Later on that evening, it began to bother me that while I was in the shrine, I never lit a candle for my mother who was having a problem with her eyesight at the time, nor did I even say a prayer. So I asked Tom if we could go back to the shrine again before leaving for Georgia.

When we arrived at the shrine we were the only ones there. Soon a man and a woman entered the shrine. As I was lighting some candles, the man said to me, "Have you ever heard of Medjugorje?" I proceeded to tell them about the medal from my mother's friend. Then, the woman reached into her purse and gave me a gold medal with a beautiful picture of the Blessed Mother on it. She told me that this medal was from Medjugorje and it had been blessed by the Blessed Mother during one of Her apparitions. Then the man said that they had been given a special blessing when they were in Medjugorje that they could pass on. He said that this blessing lasts a lifetime, and asked me if I would like to receive the special blessing. He gave me the blessing, and said that I could pass it on to anyone, non-Catholics included. Then he told us about the time that the Blessed Mother appeared right there in the shrine when Vicka, one of the visionaries from Medjugorje, was visiting the shrine. He showed us his rosary that turned gold and told us that he video taped the sun spinning. He then said to me, "Don't be surprised if your rosary turns gold." Then he invited me to say the Rosary with them since the reason they were there was for their weekly prayer group. After we said the Rosary, he remarked that it was odd that only two other people had shown up that day, when they usually have 15 or 20. In hindsight, I think that it was all part of God's plan. For, if the others had all shown up, these people might not have ever spoken to us.

It was about an hour or two into our ride to Ft. Benning, when Tom said, "Take out your rosary, and see if it turned gold." I took it out just to appease him, and was shocked when I saw that my rosary did, indeed, turn gold. I was speechless as the golden links glistened in the brilliant sun. Over and over in my mind, I wondered why this happened.

After we got home from our trip, I started to look more seriously into going on a pilgrimage. For Valentine's Day that year, Tom had given me the bonus check he had received at work, and said that I could use it for my mother and I to go on a pilgrimage. By that point I was really on my way to recovery, and a pilgrimage was something we had wanted to do since before I had become incapacitated. In February I started sending for brochures and information on pilgrimages. We were mostly interested in Guadalupe, Fatima, Lourdes, and Betania. Tom thought it was too dangerous to go to Medjugorje at the time, so I did not even consider it. However, every time we would find a trip we agreed on, it was either full or cancelled. I spent most of my Easter vacation trying to find a pilgrimage. Then I gave up, because my mother caught a virus that affected her vision, and we didn't know how long it would last. I just felt it was not in God's plan for us to go on a pilgrimage that year.

After we came back from Florida and Georgia, though, my mother's eyes were improving, and so I began to look into it again. I got on the Internet, and found a pilgrimage to Fatima, Lourdes, Medjugorje, and Rome. I e-mailed and asked about it, and a woman named Sandy sent me the number of the travel agency. As I had suspected, it was full. I wrote to Sandy and told her to keep me informed of any future pilgrimages.

A few days later Sandy wrote and told me that the travel agency was going to try to see if my mother and I could go on just part of the trip. It never occurred to me that you could go on just part of a pilgrimage. That afternoon, a woman from the travel agency called and said, "Sandy and Father Ken are pressuring us to find two seats to Medjugorje for you and your mother." I could not believe my ears. I had never even communicated with Father Ken! I felt that we were supposed to go on this trip, even though we had never even considered going to Medjugorje in the first place. How could I say no? I felt more at ease about going there too because when we were at our son's graduation, I had read an article in the Army newspaper about how peaceful it was in Bosnia now. I called my mother right away, and when a man from the travel agency called back, he said he already had us booked on the flights. I hadn't even told them "yes" yet! I could not believe it, because the trip was only two weeks away!

If someone would have told me 6 months before that I would be traveling to Bosnia and climbing two steep mountains, I would have told them they were crazy. But with God all things are possible, and this was all part of God's plan for me. I did wonder though - why did I get invited to Medjugorje?

The mystery began to unravel our first full day in Medjugorje, when, during a talk of the visionaries, a man I did not know walked up to me and asked me why I was not taking notes. He said, "You are a teacher. You should be taking notes." I asked the man how he knew I was a teacher, and he said he didn't know, that I just looked like a teacher. You can bet that from that point on I took notes.

When I returned home and shared the stories of my pilgrimage with a lady at my church, she gave me a copy of "The Spirit of Medjugorje" newsletter and suggested that I write up my testimony and send it in to the editor, Joan Wieszczyk. So I did.

From that point on, I began to write in almost every issue of "The Spirit of Medjugorje," and at the Notre Dame Medjugorje Conference in 2000, Joan asked me if I would take over as editor if anything ever happened to her. I prayed about it for a few days and then told her "yes." I could never say "no" to Our Lady, as I recalled Her message of 6/5/86: "I wish you to be active in living and spreading the messages." Besides, I thought, in the two years that I knew Joan, she was never sick, not even with a cold or the flu. So, saying "yes" was really quite easy, because Joan was healthy and vibrant. In March of 2001, Joan asked me to join her staff as the co-editor.

The following year Joan suffered a heart attack. The newsletter was suddenly thrown into my lap. After Joan's surgery, she made a pilgrimage of thanksgiving to Medjugorje, where she prayed about her retirement. When she returned, she asked me to take over as editor. Seven years previous to that, I could not have found Medjugorje on a map, much less spell it! And now I was going to edit a newsletter about Medjugorje! Not to worry though, Our Lady was interceding...

When going through some boxes in a closet, I found an article I had cut out of the newspaper two years PRIOR to my first pilgrimage to Medjugorje. It was an article about Ivanka coming to our city. I have no idea why I cut it out, because I knew nothing about Medjugorje at the time, or who Ivanka was. I do not remember doing that at all. When I read through the article though, I found that the person who brought Ivanka to town was Joan – who would 2 years later become my mentor! Our Lady had the whole thing orchestrated right from the start.

In 2005 I published Volume I of *The Best of "The Spirit of Medjugorje."* The story of how that came about is in that book. This book, Volume II, just takes up where that one left off.

Although we continue to publish our newsletter monthly, there may not be a Volume III, since the majority of the issues after December, 2004, can be read on the Internet. I do realize, however, that not everyone has Internet access, so I will do whatever Our Lady and Her Son direct me to do. I am an unprofitable servant, and will do what I am obliged to do (Lk 17:10).

My Objective

My objective for publishing this book remains the same as the objective of our monthly newsletter and for Volume I – to **instruct** people about Our Lady's messages and to **inspire** them to live and spread the messages. I hope to be able to donate copies of this book to prisons, schools, libraries, etc. I also hope to be able to send the books to foreign countries. I want to help spread Our Lady's messages to the whole world.

Who Should Read This Book?

This book is for everyone. For those who do not know much about Medjugorje, it serves as an "extended beginner's guide." (We also publish a "beginner's guide" newsletter for those who know little or nothing about Medjugorje.) For those who have followed Medjugorje, it will serve as a "shot in the arm" to stir up that fire again.

How To Read This Book

This book should not be read in one sitting, but should be read a little at a time so to digest all that Our Lady is telling us.

The date at the top of each article is the issue in which the article was originally published. The articles are not in chronological order. I prayed to the Holy Spirit to help me compile and order all of the articles. I originally took all the selections to Medjugorje with me for the 25th anniversary of the apparitions and offered them up during an apparition to Ivan at the Blue Cross. Then after it was all compiled, after many changes, I took it with me to another apparition to Ivan, this time in Brunswick, Ohio. I also took it, as I do with the monthly newsletters, to Mass and Adoration and offered it up and asked if there needed to be any changes. Just as there are always changes to the monthly newsletter, so too there were a number of changes with this book.

My Prayer

I hope and pray that every person who reads this book will be inspired to live and spread the messages of Our Lady - messages of peace, love and joy. I will pray every day of my life for everyone who reads this book. Thank you for responding to Her call.

Chapter One:

All About Medjugorje

(8/04)
Special Edition – Beginner's Guide

Suppose you were told that you could have a glimpse of Heaven without having a near-death experience?

In the early 1980's, 17 year-old Vicka Ivankovic-Mijatovic and 10 year-old Jakov Colo, visionaries from the village of Medjugorje, in what is now Bosnia-Herzegovina, had such an opportunity. Vicka claimed, "Our bodies disappeared from Jakov's house. Everyone looked for us. It lasted 20 minutes in all." Vicka described the experience:

"One afternoon, I was with Jakov at his home and Our Lady came, telling us that She was going to take us to show us Heaven, Hell and Purgatory. Before we left, we were wondering how long the journey was going to take, whether we would go up, or down, or how many days we would be traveling. But Our Lady just took Jakov's left hand and my right hand and we went up. We could see the walls just moving aside, giving us enough space to go through. It took us just a moment, and we found ourselves in Heaven. Heaven is one, huge endless space. There is a special kind of light that does not exist on earth at all. We saw people dressed in gray, yellow, and pink gowns. They were walking, praying and singing together. We were able to see small angels circling around. There is a special kind of joy in Heaven. I have never experienced anything like that at any other time. Our Lady told us to see how overjoyed were all the people who were in Heaven.

"Purgatory is also one huge space, but we were not able to see people. We could only see darkness – an ashy color. We were able to feel the physical suffering of the people. They were shivering, and struggling. Our Lady said we need to pray for those people so that they can get out of Purgatory.

"As for Hell, there is one huge fire in the middle. First, we were shown people in normal condition before they were caught by that fire. Then as they are being caught by that fire, they become the shape of animals, like they have never been humans before. As they are falling deeper into the fire, they yell against God even more. Our Lady says that, for all those who are in Hell it was their choice, their decision to get there. Our Lady says for all those who are living here on earth who are living against God's commands, even here they are living in a kind of hell so when they are there, they are continuing just the same life as before. Our Lady says that there are so many who live here on the earth who believe that when this life is finished, everything is finished, but Our Lady says, if you think so, you are very wrong, because we are just passers by on the earth."

So how do we get in the door to Heaven? Jesus told us 2000 years ago, but for those who did not listen to Him, He sent His Mother, as the Queen of Peace to remind us and remind us and remind us.....

Since 1981 She has been coming to earth every day to tell us how to live so that we can enjoy eternal happiness and avoid eternal damnation. When will we begin to listen?

Apparition Hill

In the Beginning

Medjugorje is a small mountain village in the region of Bosnia, Herzegovina, the former Yugoslavia. This true story takes place in the Bijakovici section of Medjugorje.

On the afternoon of June 24, 1981, at approximately six o'clock in the evening, on the area of Crnica Hill known as Podbrdo, two young girls, Ivanka Ivankovic, age 15, and Mirjana Dragicevic, age

16, were returning home from a walk when they saw an incredibly beautiful woman. She didn't say anything to them but indicated with gestures to come closer. They were afraid to come near, even though they immediately thought Her to be Our Lady.

The next day, June 25, the two girls returned to the hill with four others – Vicka Ivankovic, age 16, Ivan Dragicevic, age 16, Maria Pavlovic, age 16, and Jakov Colo, age 10. A figure in white was calling them to come up the hill. The children were somehow transported in some mysterious way to a beautiful Lady who called Herself the "Queen of Peace." On the third day, She told the children that She was the Blessed Virgin Mary. On the fourth day, She appeared three times to the children. For priests, She gave this message: "May the priests firmly believe and may they take care of the faith of the people!" She told the children, "Do not be afraid of anything."

In a talk given on September 12, 1998, Mirjana recounted the first days:

And that day, June 24, 1981, I went out for a walk with Ivanka. It was the Feast of St. John the Baptist, and so that day no one was working. The two of us went for a walk below the hill that is now called the Hill of Apparitions, and we talked about ordinary things, the kinds of things young girls talk about. And in one moment Ivanka said to me, "I think Our Lady is on the hill." She said that very matter-of-factly. I said, "Well, She has nothing better to do than come to the two of us." Because I thought that was [an] impossible thing. And I returned home and left Ivanka there. And when I came to the first houses of the village, I felt a need to return to the place. I needed to see what she was doing. And when I returned, I saw Ivanka in the same place. And she said to me, "Look, please, I am begging you." And I looked and I saw a woman with a long gray dress and She was holding a child in Her arms. It was very strange because on that hill nobody ever went up there, especially with a child in their arms. The two of us just stared because all of our emotions were all confused within us. And in that moment, Ivan, one of the other visionaries, came also because that was the way he would normally walk to get to his home. I remember it like it was today. He was carrying apples in his arms and when he saw what the two of us were looking at, like every brave man, he dropped everything and ran. And then I said to Ivanka, "Who knows what this is; maybe it is better we leave also."

We returned home right away, and we told everyone that we have seen Our Lady but nobody believed us. My grandmother said, "Take a rosary and pray and leave Our Lady alone." I had the desire within me to be alone to pray. And so that entire night we spent in prayer, so that God could help us understand what was happening to us. And the next day Jakov and Marija were the only ones who said, "How lucky you are, we wish we could have seen Our Lady also."

And the next day we all found ourselves at the Hill of Apparitions without having called one another there. And with us came our parents or our uncles. I could say to you that it was probably the entire village gathered there because everyone wanted to see what was happening to the children. And we saw Our Lady in the same place, but this time She didn't have a child in Her arms. And that second day, June 25, 1981, is the first time we went to Our Lady, and that day many people from the village saw many signs from Our Lady, so they believed us because without them we could not have endured some of the stuff we endured later. I think that might have been Our Lady's plan, to help them understand that it was true. And in the former Yugoslavia it was not easy to be a believer but especially not easy to be a visionary.

After a few days, the army immediately encircled the hill, and they said if anyone would go up on the hill, they would go to jail immediately. And so, we had to have the apparitions in secret places, and many of the people in our village helped with this. And so, I think it was Our Lady who truly helped them to understand and believe we were speaking the truth because we needed their help. My parents at that time were in Sarajevo. My aunt felt a responsibility, and she called my parents. My aunt said, "Something is happening to her." And my mother got very scared and she said, "Well, what is it?" And my aunt said, "Well, she is saying she is seeing Our Lady." And my mother asked, "Is she normal?" And my aunt said, "Well, she looks the same as she looked before." And then my mom said, "Well, then she is speaking the truth."

According to the visionaries, the Lady, known in Croatian as Gospa, has been giving messages to the seers and to the world ever since that day. To date She has given thousands of messages. At first the messages were almost daily, later they were just on Thursdays. In January of 1987, Our Lady told the seers She would begin to give messages to the world on a monthly basis, on the 25th of each month. Though there are thousands of messages, there are 5 primary ones. The basic messages consist of peace, prayer, conversion, fasting, and faith.

The Visionaries

Vicka Ivankovic-Mijatovic – Vicka is the oldest of the visionaries. She was born September 3, 1964, in Bijakovici, and comes from a family of 8 children. Her prayer mission given by Our Lady is to pray for the sick. Vicka, her husband Mario, and young daughter & son live in the small village of Gruda, a few kilometers north of Medjugorje. In January of 1983, Our Lady began to tell Vicka Her life story. The information Our Lady dictated to Vicka over these two years will be published when Our Lady tells Vicka it is time. Vicka: "The only way to peace and love is prayer and fasting."

Mirjana Dragicevic-Soldo – Mirjana was born March 18th, 1965, in Sarajevo. Her prayer mission from Our Lady is to pray for all unbelievers. Mirjana graduated from the University of Sarajevo where her family lived. Mirjana, her husband Marco, and their two daughters live in Medjugorje. On August 2, 1987, Our Lady started appearing to Mirjana on the 2nd day of each month to pray with Mirjana for all unbelievers. Mirjana tells us that Our Lady defines "unbelievers" as those who have not yet felt God's love. She tells us that if we only once saw the tears in Our Lady's eyes for all unbelievers, that we would all begin praying intensely for this intention. Mirjana: "The Mass, the Rosary, and fasting, especially on bread and water only, can stop war, can change the natural law, particularly if they are done with great faith and great trust and great love."

Marija Pavlovic-Lunetti – Marija was born on April 1, 1965, in Bijakovici. Her prayer mission given by Our Lady is to pray for priests and consecrated people. She also prays for the souls in Purgatory. She has three brothers and two sisters. When the apparitions started, she was studying in Mostar, about eighteen miles away. She is the visionary to whom Our Lady gives the public message to the world on the 25th of each month. Marija, her husband Paulo and their four children live in Italy. She visits Medjugorje a number of times each year. Marija: "Fear comes from Satan. Those who trust the Lord do not experience fear."

Ivanka Ivankovic-Elez – Ivanka was born on July 21, 1966, in Bijakovici. Ivanka's prayer mission from Our Lady is to pray for families. Ivanka has one brother and one sister. Her Mother Jagoda, died in May 1981. When the apparitions first began, Ivanka asked the Blessed Mother about her mother. God has allowed Ivanka to see and speak to her mother, who is in Heaven, five times over the years. Ivanka and her husband Raico and their three children live in Medjugorje. Ivanka: "People know whether they are living in God's will or not by how much peace they have. If they don't feel peace in their hearts, they know they are not doing the right thing. Those who are doing God's will have peace."

Ivan Dragicevic – Ivan was born on May 25th, 1965, in Bijakovici. His prayer mission given by Our Lady is to pray for priests and the youth of the world. There are three younger children in his family and although Ivan and Mirjana share the same last name, they are not related. Ivan, his wife Laureen and their three children reside half the year in Medjugorje, and half the year in Boston, MA. Ivan: "All prayer is pleasing to God. It is Satan who always tells us our prayer is not good enough, that we are not good enough. The least prayer is very much."

Jakov Colo - Jakov is the youngest of the seers. He was born on March 6, 1971, in Sarajevo, and was only 10 years old when the apparitions started. His prayer mission given by Our Lady is to pray for the sick. Jakov, his wife Annalisa and three children live in

Medjugorje. In the early years, the presence of the young fidgety boy among the group of seers is significant in terms of the authenticity of the apparitions. It was highly improbable that he would come to church for two to three hours of prayer every single day, in winter as well as in summer, year after year, simply to make believe that he is seeing the Blessed Virgin. Jakov: "We need to learn how to thank God because He gave us too much, and we do not understand that. We are constantly asking for more."

Editor's note: Pictures of the visionaries can be found in Chapter 2.

The Locutionists

Besides the 6 visionaries in Medjugorje, there are two locutionists (people to whom God speaks "with the heart," an experience which is known in the history of the Church as "locutio cordis" or inner locution). In December, 1982, Jelena Vasilj, 9 years old, began to hear Our Lady speak to her. In March of 1983, Marijana Vasilj (no relation), age 11, began to also have inner locutions of Our Lady. The messages to these girls were similar to the visionaries. In March of 1983, Our Lady established and led a prayer group through Jelena. Our Lady dictated to Jelena consecration prayers and a prayer for the sick and recommended the reading of Matthew 6:24-34 every Thursday.

Editor's note: The consecration prayers can be found in Volume I.

Official Letter to Pope John Paul II

The following letter was written by Fr. Tomislav Vlasic to Pope John Paul II on December 2, 1983. Fr. Tomislav Vlasic's letter was the fulfillment of Our Lady's urgent request of him. It is the official letter of the former pastor of St. James Church in Medjugorje to Pope John Paul II about the events in Medjugorje. It reports on the revelations that Mirjana received in 1982 and entrusted to Fr. Vlasic on November 5, 1983. The letter reads as follows:

After the apparition of the Blessed Virgin on November 30, 1983, Maria Pavlovic came to me and said, "The Madonna says that the Supreme Pontiff and the Bishop must be advised immediately of the urgency and great importance of the message of Medjugorje." This letter seeks to fulfill that duty.

1. Five young people (Vicka Ivankovic, Maria Pavlovic, Ivanka Ivankovic, Ivan Dragicevic, and Jakov Colo) see an apparition of the Blessed Virgin every day. The experience in which they see her is a fact that can be checked by direct observation. It has been filmed. During the apparitions, the youngsters do not react to light, they do not hear sounds, they do not react if someone touches them, they feel that they are beyond time and space. All of the youngsters basically agree that:

"We see the Blessed Virgin just as we see anyone else. We pray with her, we speak to her, and we can touch her."

"The Blessed Virgin says that world peace is at a critical stage. She repeatedly calls for reconciliation and conversion."

"She has promised to leave a visible sign for all humanity at the site of the apparitions of Medjugorje."

"The period preceding this visible sign is a time of grace for conversion and deepening the faith."

"The Blessed Virgin has promised to disclose ten secrets to us. So far, Vicka Ivankovic has received eight. Marija Pavlovic received eight. Jakov Colo, Ivan Dragicevic and Ivanka Ivankovic have each received nine. Only Mirjana Dragicevic has received all ten."

"These apparitions are the last apparitions of the Blessed Virgin on earth. That is why they are lasting so long and occurring so frequently."

2. The Blessed Virgin no longer appears to Mirjana Dragicevic. The last time she saw one of the daily apparitions was Christmas 1982. Since then the apparitions have ceased for her, except on her birthday (March 18, 1983). Mirjana knew that this would occur. According to Mirjana, the Madonna confided the tenth and last secret to her during the apparition on December 25, 1982. She

also disclosed the dates on which the different secrets will come to pass. The Blessed Virgin has revealed to Mirjana many things about the future, more than to any of the other youngsters so far. For that reason I am reporting below what Mirjana told me during our conversation on November 5, 1983. I am summarizing the substance of her account, without word-for-word quotations: Mirjana said that before the visible sign is given to humanity, there will be three warnings to the world. The warnings will be in the form of events on earth. Mirjana will be a witness to them. Three days before one of the admonitions, Mirjana will notify a priest of her choice. The witness of Mirjana will be a confirmation of the apparitions and a stimulus for the conversion of the world. After the admonitions, the visible sign will appear on the site of the apparitions in Medjugorje for all the world to see. The sign will be given as a testimony to the apparitions and in order to call the people back to the faith.

The ninth and tenth secrets are serious. They concern chastisement for the sins of the world. Punishment is inevitable, for we cannot expect the whole world to be converted. The punishment can be diminished by prayer and penance, but it cannot be eliminated. Mirjana says that one of the evils that threatened the world, the one contained in the seventh secret, has been averted, thanks to prayer and fasting. That is why the Blessed Virgin continues to encourage prayer and fasting: 'You have forgotten that through prayer and fasting you can avert war and suspend the laws of nature.' After the first admonition, the others will follow in a rather short time. Thus, people will have some time for conversion. That interval will be a period of grace and conversion. After the visible sign appears, those who are still alive will have little time for conversion. For that reason, the Blessed Virgin invites us to urgent conversion and reconciliation. The invitation to prayer and penance is meant to avert evil and war, but most of all to save souls. According to Mirjana, the events predicted by the Blessed Virgin are near. By virtue of this experience, Mirjana proclaims to the world: 'Hurry, be converted; open your hearts to God.'

In addition to this basic message, Mirjana related an apparition she had in 1982, which we believe sheds some light on some aspects of Church history. She spoke of an apparition in which

Satan appeared to her disguised as the Blessed Virgin. Satan asked Mirjana to renounce the Madonna and follow him. That way she could be happy in love and in life. He said that following the Virgin, on the contrary, would only lead to suffering. Mirjana rejected him, and immediately the Virgin arrived and Satan disappeared. Then the Blessed Virgin gave her the following message in substance: *'Excuse me for this, but you must realize that Satan exists. One day he appeared before the throne of God and asked permission to submit the Church to a period of trial. God gave him permission to try the Church for one century. This century is under the power of the devil; but when the secrets confided to you come to pass, his power will be destroyed. Even now he is beginning to lose his power and has become aggressive. He is destroying marriages, creating divisions among priests and is responsible for obsessions and murder. You must protect yourselves against these things through fasting and prayer, especially community prayer. Carry blessed objects with you. Put them in your house, and restore the use of holy water.'*

According to certain Catholic experts who have studied these apparitions, this message of Mirjana may shed light on the vision Pope Leo XIII had. According to them, it was after having had an apocalyptic vision of the future of the Church that Leo XIII introduced the prayer to Saint Michael which priests used to recite after Mass up to the time of the Second Vatican Council. These experts say that the century of trials foreseen by Leo XIII is about to end.

Holy Father, I do not want to be responsible for the ruin of anyone. I am doing my best. The world is being called to conversion and reconciliation. In writing to you, Holy Father, I am only doing my duty. After drafting this letter, I gave it to the youngsters so that they might ask the Blessed Virgin whether its contents are accurate. Ivan Dragicevic relayed the following answer: 'Yes, the contents of the letter are the truth. You must notify first the Supreme Pontiff and then the Bishop.' This letter is accompanied by fasting and prayers that the Holy Spirit will guide your mind and your heart during this important moment in history.

Yours, in the Sacred Hearts of Jesus and Mary, Father Tomislav Vlasic Medjugorje, December 2, 1983

Editor's update: As of this writing (4/13/07), two of the other visionaries have received the tenth secrets. Ivanka received her last daily apparition on May 7, 1988. Our Lady told Her she would have an apparition once a year on June 25, the anniversary of the apparitions. Jakov received his last daily apparition on September 12, 1998. Our Lady told him he would receive an apparition every year on Christmas Day. Vicka, Ivan and Marija have received nine secrets. Also, Our Lady visits Mirjana every second of the month to pray with her for the conversion of non-believers.

Vatican Statement

"We bishops, after a three-year-long commission study accept Medjugorje as a holy place, as a shrine. This means that we have nothing against it if someone venerates the Mother of God in a manner also in agreement with the teaching and belief of the Church. Therefore, we are leaving that to further study. The Church does not hurry."

His Eminence Cardinal Dr. Franjo KUHARIÆ, Archbishop of Zagreb

(Glas Koncila, August 15, 1993)

It is likely that the Church will not continue its investigation into Medjugorje until the apparitions of Our Lady cease. His Holiness, Pope Urban VIII stated: "In cases which concern private revelations, it is better to believe than not to believe, for, if you believe, and it is proven true, you will be happy that you have believed, because our Holy Mother asked it. If you believe, and it should be proven false, you will receive all blessings as if it had been true, because you believed it to be true." (Pope Urban VIII, 1623-44)

In June of 1986, Pope John Paul II said, in response to a group of twelve Italian bishops seeking pastoral advice on people making pilgrimages to Medjugorje, "LET THE PEOPLE GO TO MEDJUGORJE IF THEY CONVERT, PRAY, CONFESS, DO PENANCE AND FAST."

Little Known Fact about Medjugorje

In 1986 the U.S. State Department became very interested in what they were hearing about Medjugorje. The U.S. Ambassador to Yugoslavia at that time, David Anderson, was told to send political officers to investigate the rumors of apparitions. Reporting back to Anderson the two political officers stated, "You're not going to believe this, but there is something going on there." (The State Dept. information are excerpts from an upcoming book called *Medjugorje Investigated* by Michael Kenneth Jones. For more information visit Michael's website, www.medjugorjeusa.org .)

Editor's note: The book is now available from the above mentioned website.

The Five Stones

Father Jozo Zovko, who was the pastor of St. James when the apparitions began, speaks often about what he calls "the weapons" or the "the five stones" against Goliath. They are: prayer with the heart, especially the Rosary; Eucharist; Holy Bible; monthly Confession; and fasting.

It is important to approach each of these slowly, so not to get discouraged. When Our Lady first appeared to the children, She asked them to pray the "Peace Rosary, " which is the Creed and 7 Our Father's, 7 Hail Mary's, and 7 Glory Be's. Later She had them pray the 5-decade Rosary, and then worked up to the 15-decade Rosary.

Our Lady asks for frequent attendance at Holy Mass. It might be good to first start by going a day or two during the week, then work up to every day if possible. Our Lady always says that when given the choice of going to Mass or to one of Her apparitions, one should always choose Holy Mass.

To read the Bible, one need not read a whole book or even a whole chapter daily. Even a sentence or two in the morning and in the evening is beneficial. We need to be constantly fed with the Word of God to fight the good fight.

As for monthly Confession, Our Lady told the visionaries that there is not a person on earth who does not need to confess monthly.

Fasting is the most difficult of the five. Fasting means that we give up something that we like and offer that sacrifice to God. Our Lady asks that we fast weekly on Wednesdays and Fridays. One can give up sweets, coffee, cigarettes, alcohol, television, etc. But, Our Lady stresses that the best and most powerful fast is on bread and water. Great graces come from fasting and it can help with situations in your life that seem hopeless. Because it is so hard to fast, one should always pray for the grace to be able to do it. Again, one should work up to it, starting perhaps by giving up eating between meals, then one day of bread and water, and finally two days of bread and water.

The Fruits of Medjugorje

"You will know them by their fruits. Grapes are not gathered from thorn bushes nor figs from thistles, are they? So every good tree bears good fruit, but the bad tree bears bad fruit" (Matthew 7:16-17).

There have been many physical healings through Our Lady of Medjugorje since 1981. The parish office reports that as of 2001, there were 445 documented reports about miraculous physical healings. David Parkes, Rita Klaus, Char Vance, Artie Boyle, and Tom Rutkoski are just a few of the people who have received a physical healing that defied medical science. Each of these people, in recorded testimony, also had spiritual healings as well, and do not hesitate to emphasize that, given the choice of a physical healing or a spiritual healing, they would take the spiritual healing.

It would take hundreds of books to contain the testimonies of the spiritual healings and conversions that have taken place through Our Lady of Medjugorje in the last 24 years. More than a few members of the clergy have also had healings as well, including a priest who had left the priesthood and returned 17 years later through Our Lady of Medjugorje. (His story is in Chapter 3 of this book.)

Organizations which reach out to the homeless, poor and orphans have been created by people upon returning from Medjugorje. Gospa Missions in Evans City, PA, the Mission of Mercy in Buffalo, NY, St. David's Relief in Mesquite, TX, and His Work in Progress in Yardley, PA, are just a few of the many fruits of Medjugorje.

Many priestly and religious vocations have been fostered through Medjugorje. Fr. Donald Calloway, Fr. Ed Murphy, Fr. Ljubo Kurtovic and Fr.Miro Sego are just a few of the many religious vocations which have been fostered through Medjugorje. "A good tree cannot produce bad fruit, nor can a bad tree produce good fruit" (Mt 7:18).

Joan Wieszczyk and David Parkes

A Medjugorje Pilgrimage
By June Klins

Before June of 1998, Medjugorje was never in my travel plans. I was afraid that it was dangerous, that I would not like the food or the experience of staying in someone's home, and that I would be bored. Nothing could be farther from the truth in every case. I will be eternally grateful to the travel agent who booked me on the plane to Medjugorje without my having agreed to it! I never experienced such peace in my life, the food was wonderful, the people were so hospitable and joyful that I did not want to leave, and I was never bored for even a second. There is much to do, including climbing two mountains – Apparition Hill and also Cross Mountain, where a large cross was built in 1933. Ana Shawl who takes pilgrims to Medjugorje testifies: "No matter how many times people come to Medjugorje, it's the same as when you go to visit your mother. There's always something more, there's always more conversations with her, and no two conversations with our mothers are the same. That's the way I feel about being there. I know we have our Mother in Heaven wherever we are and She is always close to us, but I think there is something so special about coming to Her little Medjugorje – two mountains, rocks, vineyards and a church. To make the trip is difficult, but once there, most everyone has difficulty coming home. Like during the Transfiguration with the apostles – they wanted to pitch tents to stay there, they never wanted that vision to end."

Pilgrims enjoying food and fellowship

Signs and Wonders
By June Klins

On my first trip to Medjugorje I was very excited because it was anniversary time and I expected to see a lot of miracles. I had heard that the sun spins like it did in Fatima and that some people see "gold dust" or the cross on Mt. Krizevac light up or disappears mysteriously. Well, after four trips there, I have never seen any phenomena like this, even while people standing right beside me were witnessing these things. Many people have miracle photos they took in Medjugorje. These signs and wonders are gifts that are given to certain people for a reason only God knows. On my first

16

pilgrimage, I randomly picked up five stones on Apparition Hill. I later discovered that four of the stones had images on them. One has the face of Jesus with a fetus above His head, and the other three have Our Lady with Baby Jesus. I wondered why I got these stones. I certainly did not need them to believe. I carry these stones, which seem to have a pro-life message, in my purse and show them to people at any opportunity. The scriptures tell us that the gifts we receive should be shared with others.

What is the purpose of these signs and wonders? To get our attention! Jesus performed miracles from the very beginning of His ministry on earth. The miracles were a means to an end. Once Jesus got their attention, He could work the real miracles of changing hearts. The same is true in Medjugorje. The "miracle of the sun" is to show that God exists and then to point us to the real "miracle of the Son," Jesus in the Holy Eucharist. Those who go to Medjugorje must be on guard not to focus too much attention on the signs and wonders, at the risk of ignoring the abundant graces available in Medjugorje through a conversion of heart, the real sign and wonder at Medjugorje.

(2/00)
Mary's Messages
By Joan Wieszczyk

It's been over 18 years since Our Lady first appeared to the six visionaries of Medjugorje. These apparitions continue till this day. She is still appearing to three of them on a daily basis. Our Lady comes with an important message. She comes like never before in history.

The parish of St. James in Medjugorje is part of an important role. It is seen as a model for the whole world. It is a management of spirituality, drawing people from all nationalities. St. James truly is an apostolic church. This church with its twin towers is one of the devotional points in Medjugorje.

In Medjugorje, Our Lady is constantly calling people who have strayed away from God. She tells us that "God exists." We are to put Him in the first place in our lives.

If you notice, She always completes the end of Her messages by saying, "Thank you for having responded to my call." The word "call" intones a sense of calling to do something. Medjugorje is a school where we receive "something to feed our hearts." Our Mother is grateful because we are ready to do this and therefore, She thanks us. Yes, She thanks us for living Her messages.

What is the message? We know lots of incidental facts and stories about the visionaries, etc. We know of the graces of Medjugorje, but what is actually the message? She has been coming with the same message for over 18 years. She appears daily. On Mondays and Fridays, She often comes twice a day. Since 1981, Our Lady has been meeting with the prayer group on the mountain on these two days.

In order to receive the message, you must have a messenger. That messenger is Our Lady. She repeats Her messages over and over again, such as "pray, pray, pray."

She never gets tired. She loves us more than our earthly mother.

Medjugorje is very important in the eyes of Our Lady. That is why when you go there, you receive "special graces." She tells us that this is a time of grace in the world. She wants to convert the whole world to a complete transformation. Everyone is invited! Each one of us has an important role to play in "a great plan for the salvation of mankind. You are not able to comprehend how great your role is in God's design" (Jan. 25, 1987).

We have a great mission to fulfill. In order to understand the plan, we must pray. If we do not pray, we cannot understand or save the world. "I have appeared to help save humanity. I need you. I desire that through you the whole world will get to know the God of Joy."

Medjugorje is a place of joy. The visionaries have joy. This joy has to be contagious. I always said that the people who live the message of Medjugorje are joyful people! These people know that Our Lady is with them. They need not fear, for when you are living the messages, you are in good hands.

We need to live the messages now. The world is in great danger because people reject God. The do not have any real sense of His presence.

Mary cries about the youth of today, about priests, about the Holy Bible (we have forgotten to use it) and about peace.

Peace is not just the absence of war. Peace is harmony, unity between man and God. Peace is to receive God in your heart; Christ is in your heart. There is no peace without the Eucharist.

Our Lady says, "People live in darkness. They do not know the truth." Yes, the whole world is in darkness. We have to be a light. We can only bring light into the world by accepting Jesus as the answer. That is the reason Our Lady comes, to lead us on a path to Jesus. When Our Lady appears to the visionaries, She begins with the words, "Praised be Jesus." Our Heavenly Mother teaches us to always praise Jesus. We can praise Him by our prayer.

First Message – Prayer

Prayer is the only way to save the human race. If we do not pray, the race will not be saved. If you do not know how to pray, don't worry, just pray. Ask Our Lady to help you pray. She says to take your rosary beads. Hold onto them. It will be a sign to Satan that you belong to Jesus and Mary. Pray and consecrate yourself and your loved ones to the Sacred Heart of Jesus and the Immaculate Heart of Mary. Start prayer in your family. Make it into a prayer group. Go and pray in front of the Holy Eucharist.

Second Message – Fasting

Mary recommends us to fast twice a week, on Wednesdays and Fridays. To be fully purified, She asks us to fast on bread and water. But, take a step at a time. Give up something else if you cannot fast on bread and water. For example, give up TV. The spirit of prayer is lost and the communication is gone after you watch TV. You cannot tell Jesus, "I do not want to sacrifice." That is what the world is saying. Tell Him that you would like to participate and carry your cross and accept your sacrifice. Keep this in mind on Wednesdays and Fridays.

Third Message – The Holy Bible

Read the Holy Bible every day. In order to live the Bible, we have to read the Bible. Make sure that your Bible is placed in a prominent place in your living room, a visible place. Only in the Holy Bible are the pure messages from God. God speaks to you directly, now, in the presence of the Bible. There is a message for you every day. Fr. Jozo tells us to "kiss the Holy Bible, kiss the Word of the Lord." No wonder Our Lady recommends the reading of the Holy Scriptures.

Fourth Message – Reconciliation

Mary has said entire parts of the Western Church would be healed if people would go to monthly Confession. If you do not go to Confession, your conversion will be very difficult. Confession should be a joy. For many pilgrims, that joy has come alive by making a good Confession while in Medjugorje. Pray for your priests that they be inspired confessors. It is up to us whether we have good or bad priests. We are the ones who make up the Church. We are the live Church.

Fifth Message – The Eucharist

Mary cried because we have no respect any more. The Holy Eucharist should be the center of our conversion.

If you live these 5 messages – Prayer, Fasting, Reading the Holy Bible, Confession and the Holy Eucharist, holiness will sprout in you. Then you will have nothing to fear.

Our purpose in life is to become holy, not through our own strength. Therefore, overcome all sin through love. Live love inside of our hearts. This is holiness. Remember, our goal in life is to overcome sin. Be the reflection of Jesus Christ in the world, now, in the new Millennium.

St. James

(7/01)
St. James
By Joan Wieszczyk

July 25 is the feast of St. James. This is the name of the church in Medjugorje. On this date, the parishioners have a big solemn celebration. Last year the solemnity began with a procession. In the park, the former pastor, Fr. Ivan Landeka, presided at a Eucharistic celebration which included a large number of faithful – villagers and pilgrims.

The parish of Medjugorje was established in 1892. The parishioners decided to take St. James as their patron.

The church was built in 1897, and was severely damaged by an earth tremor in 1937. The remains are located in the circle park next to the shrine.

The building of the present church began in 1939, and was discontinued during the war in 1940. They began working on it once again in 1963. It was completed and blessed in 1968. For such a small countryside, the church was unusually large. It has twin steeples and a seating capacity for around 650. No one knew why

21

such a big church was built. Mary told the visionaries that it was in God's plan. Millions of pilgrims have come and are still coming.

Now the church of St. James is too small, so they had to build an outside gazebo onto the back of it to accommodate all the pilgrims. Who would have dreamed that the patron saint of St. James Church would also become the patron saint of pilgrims?

(2/98)
In the Beginning...

On this sixteenth anniversary of the apparitions at Medjugorje we feature an interview with Marinko Ivankovic given to Sean Conroy for the "Medjugorje Herald" at his home in Bijakovici on Aug. 16th, 1996, and we are grateful to Dragon Zovko for translating this conversation.

SEAN: Can you recall Marinko, clearly fifteen years later, of Our Lady appearing on Podbrodo Bijakovici on June 1998I?

MARINKO: Yes, I was working as a mechanic in a body shop in Mostar, on the morning of June 25th, 1981, going by car with my wife Dragica who worked in Citluk. We gave a lift to Marija and Vicka Ivankovic who were going to school in Mostar. After we passed the church in Citluk, Marija who was sitting behind me said, "We saw Our Lady last night." I slowed down the car, I turned around and said, "Who saw Her?" "Vicka," she replied. I questioned Vicka who was sitting next to Dragica about who saw Our Lady first. She answered Ivanka Dragicevic, Milka Pavlovic (Marija's sister) and myself. She gave me every detail as to how it happened and what She looked like. They were walking down by the crossroad (beyond the big Belgian building that is there now) when they saw Her about 500 meters on the side of Podbrodo. I told Vicka when I return home I will go and ask Ivan, for I will be able to believe him more than you or a hundred girls.

Ivan confirmed everything that Vicka told me. Right away I believed. That was the second evening Our Lady appeared. I was told it was fifteen minutes to seven She was to appear, but She appeared one hour earlier. When I got to the cross-roads, the visionaries were coming down from the mountain. Ivanka's grandmother was waiting for her beside the road. Ivanka and Mirjana were walking downhill together. I came towards them and said, "Ivanka why are you crying so much?" She started hugging her grandmother, and said, "I asked Our Lady about my mother," (who died a short time before the apparitions) and She said, "Do not worry about your mother, she is with Me in Heaven, but you should obey and listen to your grandmother." The grandmother was Ivanka's father's mother. Marija said she asked Our Lady to give us a sign as no one would believe what we had experienced. Our Lady had placed Her hand over the watch on Mirjana's hand. Where the number twelve on the watch is normally, was now at the spot of number nine. Being a mechanic myself, I found that very interesting, for if a person were to change the watch like that, the key in the mechanism would have to be broken, but everything was working perfectly.

SEAN: You were the first person to tell a priest about what was happening?

Marinko: When I saw I could not stop Ivanka crying I felt it better to contact a priest, for he may be able to explain to her what was really happening. When I arrived by car at the rectory, I found two nuns standing outside. I asked if Father Jozo is there, they said, "No." With that, Father Zrinko came and said what do you need. I told him – six children have reported seeing Our Lady yesterday which was the 24th, and again this evening the 25th, and one of them is crying a lot. I thought you should see them and try to console them – talk to them and find out if what they are saying is true. Then Father Zrinko said, "Marinko, let those who have been gifted by God let them see, those who do not see is OK." As I left him I felt very disappointed and discouraged. I could not understand why he would not go with me. Note (Ivanka, Mirjana, Vicka, Ivan, Jakov and Marija were those who saw Our Lady on the 25th. Milka and Ivan Ivankovic were not there.) On the third evening June 26th, I went to exactly the same spot from where the visionaries had seen Our Lady the two previous evenings. I was present when the visionaries said, "Look at the light, look at the light." The third time they said, "Look, it is Our Lady." I was asking where, because I was willing to see. They showed me the direction and at that particular time about 300 people were at the spot on the side of Podbrdo where

She appeared on the two previous evenings. The visionaries said it is above them a little down to the South, a different place. We started climbing Apparition Hill. Vicka was carrying a glass with holy water that her grandmother Vida gave to her. As it was raining they were not climbing fast as it was very slippery especially for Mirjana who was born and raised in Sarajevo and had no experience of hill climbing. I took the holy water from Vicka to carry it for her. I was looking at Ivan because he was the first to reach the spot. The rest of the visionaries were 20 meters ahead of me as we all joined Ivan. I asked, "Where is Our Lady?" I asked if She was standing and they said no, but standing on one gray cloud and She was not touching the earth. Vicka said to me Our Lady is looking at you and She is smiling. I asked about the holy water I was carrying for her. She took the glass, and with her hand she sprinkled the water with the words, "If you are Our Lady stay with us, if not go away." I asked Vicka if Our Lady is still here. She replied, "She is still looking at you and still smiling." I had already asked the visionaries why Our Lady is here and what She wants from us. At this moment I repeated the same question. I said did you ask Her and they said, "No, why don't you ask Her?" Our Lady responded to their question, "I came because there are so many good believers here. I also want you to bring about reconciliation among the people." One man, Dunka from Bladvica, who was present, said to the visionaries, "Ask Our Lady to give us a sign so we too can understand." Simultaneously the visionaries said, "Blessed and do not see." (Blessed are they that believe and do not see?...Ed.)

SEAN: Would you tell me how your wife Dragica happened to be the first person to tell Father Jozo about the children seeing Our Lady?

MARINKO: Dragica was working on June 27th. A heavy piece of metal fell on her hand and she also broke her leg. They took her to the hospital in Mostar, and before they entered, they met Father Jozo who I believe was visiting his sick mother. He asked Dragica what had happened to her. "Nothing serious," she replied. Then she said to Father Jozo, "Where have you been? You should be in Medjugorje, for the Madonna has appeared there." He asked her who told her that, and she said the children (five or six of them) have

24

seen Our Lady for the past three evenings. Father Zrinko doesn't seem to believe it, so you should go and see for yourself she said. That is how it was.

SEAN: You might tell me about the day there was no apparition on Podbrdo.

MARINKO: On July 1, 1981, the visionaries were taken from the village by Metica and Lubica Vasilj, to Cerno. That was the day we had no apparitions on the hill and no Mass in St. James Church. Those two people saw the gray cloud that was above the 30,000 people on the Hill of Apparitions. People came down before the visionaries in Cerno. On the way they were stopped by Father Jozo Zovko and they told him they asked Our Lady that She come to the church for the apparitions: There was a misunderstanding with some people, for they thought Our Lady would come only three more nights.

SEAN: Did Father Jozo tell the visionaries to ask Our Lady to come to the church for the apparitions?

MARINKO: No, it was the Communists who wanted the people to go to the church and not to be up on Apparition Hill.

SEAN: When did Father Jozo Zovko become pastor of St. James parish in Medjugorje?

MARINKO: It's a long story. All the region, the county of Citluk, had one parish in the Village of Gradnici. A few years before the old church of St. James was built in 1892, people from the five villages (Medjugorje, Bijakovici, Melitina, Vionica and Surmanci) sat down together and decided to split from the parish of Gradnici. The remains of the old church can be seen from the walls of the roundabout as you leave the grounds of St. James church. It was agreed then that the parish office would be built across the road which was Medjugorje, while the church was in Bijakovici. That church built in 1892, started to fall apart in 1932 because its foundations became weak because the concrete was so poor. The parishioners made a decision and agreed they should start digging up the ground around the old church to build a church of the same plan that is St. James Church today. It was also agreed that every stone from the old church would be used in the new one, and while Mass was being said the people would stand up. There was a misunderstanding and the people of Medjugorje wanted the church built where St. James is today. There were a lot of arguments between the people of Bijakovici and Medjugorje about it. From 1936 to 1939 before the Second World War started, they built the stone walls that you see today of St. James. Everything remained that way up to 1965, for the Communists in the former Yugoslavia did not want to give permission to build churches. In 1968 St. James Church was consecrated and the first Mass was said. There was about three and a half thousand people in the Medjugorje parish back in 1936.

SEAN: What changes have you seen over the past fifteen years?

MARINKO: No doubt, Sean, you have seen many changes since you came to Medjugorje in 1984. The first three years I think were something special for each of us in the parish and villages around. Each experienced a special strength, that God had given them, that led to a strong conversion. At five o'clock in the evenings ninety per cent of the people who were working in their jobs and daily duties in the fields finished work and went to church every evening. I must say, from fifty to a hundred people from my neighborhood would climb the Hill of Apparition, saying the Rosary and singing songs to Our Lady. When the Mass was over you could see the people were so happy going back to their homes singing songs of praise to Our Lady.

One thing is most important, I can't be sure as to the year. Father Radovan Petrovic, the pastor who finished the building of the church, would say the eleven o'clock Mass on Sundays in thirty minutes and the people were happy with the short Mass. Father Luka Susac and Father Jozo Jolic, who followed him as pastors of St. James, had Mass on Sunday which lasted on hour and the people accepted that. But when Father Jozo Zovko came, his Masses would last one hour and twenty minutes. People started talking and whispering in the church, "We should send him away." When Our Lady came, Father Jozo used to lead the Rosary, celebrate Holy Mass and say five more mysteries of the Rosary after Mass. All took about three hours. He used to say to the people, "All is finished, let us go home now." But people wanted to stay longer in church, the same people who wanted him removed from the parish when he came first because his Mass was longer by twenty minutes than the previous pastor.

SEAN: Have you seen Our Lady?

MARINKO: No.

SEAN: Have you touched Her?

MARINKO: Yes, the first time about twenty days after the apparitions started. Our Lady invited the visionaries at eleven o'clock at night to Apparition Hill where She normally appears to them. About thirty or forty people from the neighborhood joined them. When we got to the spot, the visionaries stood before the small wooden cross (where the largest aluminum one is today) and made the sign of the cross. At that time I was beside the visionaries, my head down and my eyes closed when something told me to look up and open my eyes. I looked at the sky, it was falling apart, like opening up. A very fast white light was falling down in front of us. I said, "Look at the light." With that, about ten voices said the same thing. When the light finally arrived at the wooden cross in the hole in the front of the visionaries it was as if a big balloon had exploded with thousands of stars all different colors of red, blue and yellow. One little girl Zdenka started to cry. At the same time Marija Pavlovic said, "Peace, Our Lady is with us. Kneel down all of you and Our Lady will pray with us." At the moment I cried because of the happiness inside myself. I never experienced prayer like that before. We prayed together for about thirty minutes. After that, the visionaries said, "Our Lady said you can stand up, for She is inviting you all to touch Her if you wish." They all moved forward to touch Her. I believe at that moment I touched Our Lady. One of the visionaries said, "Someone stood on Our Lady's veil and She is gone."

The second time was on the feast day of Our Lady of the Angels, in the field between Medjugorje and Cilici. The visionaries told us, "The Madonna will allow all who wish to go to Her and touch Her." As they led the people to Her one by one, they would say, "Now you are touching Her veil, Her head, Her hand, Her dress. This lasted for about fifteen minutes, until the Madonna departed. Just then Marija cried out, I ran to her and asked, "Why are you crying?" She left us, for one part of Her dress was dirty, for some of the people who touched Her were sinners. The most important experience I had that evening was when Vicka and Jakov said to me, "Our Lady blessed you and kissed you."

SEAN: Before Our Lady came were you a prayerful man?

MARINKO: I was taught every day, in the morning you greet Our Lady with the sign of the cross, by saying the Angelus and the Glory Be, the same thing at noon time when the church bells rang, ninety nine per cent of the people stopped work and said the Angelus and prayed for those who had died. At seven o'clock in the evening the bell would ring. We called it 'Hail Mary'. That prayer would last fifteen minutes. We also had prayers for the sick, the Hail Holy Queen and the prayer of St. Anthony. I attended Mass on Sundays and feast days. Before the apparitions, I was often thinking, "Did that really happen with Jesus what is written down?" You could say I was doubting. After Our Lady came, I really had no doubts about anything written down in the Holy Gospels. It is interesting to note – before the apparitions started, there was never any evening Mass in St. James Church. It was always 8 A.M. and 11 A.M. on Sundays and feast days, and 7:30 A.M. on weekdays. We did not start having Mass in the church for sometime after the apparitions started there. For usually after the apparitions, Father Jozo would ask the visionaries to tell the people what Our Lady was saying. The visionaries did not feel like doing that. Only Vicka talked about it.

SEAN: Had you every any doubt about the apparitions?

MARINKO: None whatsoever. Many people came here out of curiosity, many came because they had different needs. I know people who came to my home who fasted and prayed a lot, no doubt something is leading them, probably faith.

SEAN: The war brought changes?

MARINKO: Yes, which is a great pity. I feel sad that the young people from the parish did not accept Our Lady's messages the same as we did of my generation fifteen years ago. That is my greatest concern.

SEAN: Would you like to see a church built on Podbrdo?

MARINKO: I would be a most happy man when a church is built on Podbrdo in honor of Our Lady. I do not believe it will be built until after Our Lady leaves the permanent sign.

SEAN: Thank you, Marinko, for sharing with us in such detail those wonderful happenings fifteen years ago, without any notes I must add.

MARINKO: Anyone who is interested in what happened in the early days could wake me up at three o'clock in the morning. I will be ready to tell them what exactly happened. That is something I have put first in my life, that something no one can take away from me.

Note: Marinko Ivankovic is no longer at the center of events in Medjugorje.

Marinko was born in Bijakovici in 1943 and he still lives there, being a mechanic by trade. When the young visionaries needed counsel and direction outside their own families, it was to this man that they turned, and there is no doubt that next to the six visionaries themselves, Marinko Ivankovic is the single most important witness to the amazing events in Medjugorje that year and his statement to Father Svetozar Kraljevic is one of the most basic documents we have on the beginnings of the Medjugorje phenomenon that has stirred the Catholic world.

Medjugorje Herald, Ireland

Cross on Cross Mountain

(9/99)
Celebration of the Exaltation of the Cross

The celebration of the Exaltation of the Cross will be held also this year on the first Sunday after the Nativity of Mary, that is, on September 12th.

This is an occasion to introduce all of you, who intend to come on pilgrimage to Medjugorje for that feast, to a short history of Cross Mountain and the cross erected on it. About one kilometer from the Church of Medjugorje, as the crow flies, rises the Cross Mountain, interconnecting with the Hill of Apparitions and the church to form a triangle. At its peak (520 meters above sea level) the pastor of that time, Fr. Bernardin Smoljan and the parishioners in 1934 erected an 8.56 meter high reinforced concrete cross. On it are inscribed the words: "To Jesus Christ, Redeemer of the human race, as a sign of their faith, hope and love, the pastor Fra Bernardin Smoljan and the parish of Medjugorje erected [this cross]. From every evil deliver us all, O Jesus." On the back side of the cross in memory of the 1900th anniversary of redemption are inscribed the dates "33 –1933".

Inside the cross itself the builders embedded relics from Rome obtained especially for that occasion, a small piece of the cross which Christians venerate as the cross on which Jesus Christ was crucified, the largest part of which is preserved in the church of the Holy Cross of Jerusalem in Rome. The cross was completed on March 15, 1934. From then on the custom arose of celebrating Holy Mass in honor of the Exaltation of the Cross every year at the foot of the cross on the Sunday following September 8th, the Nativity of Our Lady.

The Cross Mountain does not attract so many pilgrims because of natural beauty nor because of the significance of the cross that is erected, but only because a great number of people confirm that after the start of the Medjugorje apparitions they saw various signs of light and others signs on Cross Mountain. They all related them to Our Lady's apparitions and to the message of the Medjugorje apparitions – peace between God and man, and peace among men. They understood that the cross is central to Our Lady's messages and that the way to peace leads through the cross. Indeed a great many have found peace and their way to God on that mountain. In their pilgrimage devotion and practice they have included the veneration of the Cross. While climbing that difficult path to the Cross on Cross Mountain, pilgrims pray the Way of the Cross. For that there are fifteen bronze reliefs with Our Lady's image portrayed in each one placed along the path. Our Lady accompanies Jesus and us as well on life's way of the cross.

Information Centre "Mir" Medjugorje, www.medjugorje.hr

(5/04)
Medjugorje: the Continuation of Fatima
By Carolanne Kilichowski

Medjugorje has many similarities to Fatima. The main message of Fatima, as well as in Medjugorje, reflects the Gospels and shows the way for everyone to return to our Father's house.

Our Lady spoke in Fatima of Mass and Confession on the first Saturday of the month to make reparation. In Medjugorje, Our Lady expects even more, as She calls us to monthly Confession and daily Mass, if possible. She also expects us to pray the Rosary more often.

In Medjugorje, Our Lady asks us to pray with the heart, requesting all three mysteries. In Fatima She only asked for five decades.

In Fatima, Our Lady requested penance, but in Medjugorje She is very specific, asking us to fast each Wednesday and Friday. She states that the best fast is one of bread and water. Remember little Francisco going without water and giving up his lunch to someone else in order to do penance for sinners. He was so worried about others going to Hell.

The geographical areas are also similar in that it is mountainous and not the easiest to get to. They both have sheep grazing. I imagine even the roosters are crowing in both places!

Often people speak of how in Lourdes there was one visionary, Bernadette. In Fatima three, two girls and a boy, and now in Medjugorje, it has doubled to six, two boys and four girls.

Marija Pavlovic, has been receiving messages for the world since March 1, 1984, in Medjugorje. As Communism was collapsing leaving confusion in the world, Yugoslavia itself was involved in a violent civil war.

Fatima had its warnings of world punishments if Our Lady's requests were not taken to heart. Medjugorje also has come in the name of the Eternal Father, to warn the world of impending chastisements. Once again, She brings a plan to prevent the doom She sees possibly coming. For almost twenty three years our beloved Mother has asked us to pray with the heart, fast, read the Bible daily and know the Word, confess once a month and to, most importantly, make the Eucharist the center of our lives.

Could World War II have been prevented if more people followed the message of Fatima? Few had responded to the prophetic warnings of Mary. Could coming chastisements be averted now if we follow Our Lady's recipe for conversion for peace in Medjugorje? Are we doing all that we possible can to obey our Mother? Certainly evil is more prominent than ever! We must listen and put into action all that our Mother is requesting. We are also called to daily sacrifices.

I challenge you – Examine your heart today and meditate on how you have responded to the call! If you need help, choose a prayer partner and ask each other for help. If you start sliding, ask your partner to give you extra penance to make up for what you did not do. Be honest with each other and obey the penance. It will help you to attain a tougher self- discipline and therefore help you in attaining your goals. When I read the story of Fatima I admire Francisco, as he was an example to Jacinta and Lucia. We must all be examples to each other, to encourage and to constantly strive to "live the message." We must first "live the message" in order to give it to others. It will be all worth it when you will be standing at the gate of Heaven looking at Jesus as He says, "Welcome, My child, My Mother has told Me all about you."

"I call all of you, dear children to pray and fast still more firmly. I invite you to realize through the secrets I began in Fatima may be fulfilled. I call you, dear children, to grasp the importance of my coming and the seriousness of the situation. I want to save all souls and present them to God. Therefore, let us pray that everything I have begun be fully realized. Thank you for having responded to my call" (8/25/91).

Editor's note: Carolanne lives in Hamburg, NY.

Statue of Our Lady of Medjugorje at Fatima Shrine in Lewiston, NY

Chapter Two:

The Visionaries

(6/02)
Visions and Sainthood
By Joan Wieszczyk

The 6 visionaries of Medjugorje play a major role in spreading the messages of Our Lady. They have been given a huge responsibility. At times, they left their homeland and traveled to distant countries giving talks and witnessing about the apparitions. When they are in Medjugorje, they meet with pilgrims and explain the messages that Our Lady gave them. These messages are important because they are of the Gospel. The Blessed Mother wants everyone to know them and practice them now, at this special time of grace. She is preparing us to meet Her Son.

People are very curious about the supernatural. They want to see or touch the person who is, and who has been, having apparitions.

When in Medjugorje or at a conference, wherever a visionary is present, people tend to put them on a pedestal. They seem to forget that they are humans like you and I. Although they are humble and devout, seeing Our Lady doesn't make them a "saint."

We had the privilege of having Ivanka (one of the Medjugorje visionaries) speak at our parish. After her witness, we invited her and the guests for a social in the school cafeteria. People kept trying to touch her, pushing her so much that we had to separate her from the crowd, and she had to depart. She did not want to be treated as someone extraordinary. She and the other visionaries are not divine. Just as you and I have to follow the way of holiness, so must they strive for "sainthood."

Many people who experience supernatural events are quickly made "saints" by those who don't understand their faith and the ways and world of God.

Marija Pavlovic, the Medjugorje visionary who relays the monthly message to the world says, "It's not easy when people think you are a saint and you know you're not. Journeying on the path of holiness is difficult for me too, just as it is for everyone else. It is not always easy for me to love, fast or pray, and I don't feel that I've made it just because Our Lady has appeared to me. I'm called to sanctify myself as a woman, wife, and mother! Some even treat me as a clairvoyant and ask me their future!"

It is true that the visionaries of Medjugorje have seen Heaven, and some have seen hell and Purgatory. Since Mary has shown them the various supernatural dimensions, they must go out and witness what they have seen. They must apply the Blessed Virgin's teachings to their own lives. Their witness should make others fall in love with Her.

Being a visionary is not an easy task. They have been examined over and over so that the non-believers might believe, and those of us who believe, would believe more.

The visionary Ivan told us that he was attending the "School of Mary." She is his teacher. The Blessed Mother has been teaching him daily in Her apparitions, Saturdays and Sundays included. It has been over 21 years and he still has not graduated.

Our Lady of Medjugorje is the teacher of us all. It is through the visionaries that we get to know what She is asking of us. She wants everyone to help Her spread Her messages throughout the world. They are messages of Jesus, and the world needs them. We are very important to Her. She has said, without us (you and I), Her plans cannot be fulfilled. That is why the visionaries relay the messages to us. We must relay them to others. Just as the visionaries are told to live the messages, and to give good example, so must we be converted daily.

How blessed we are to have the presence of Our Lady for such a long time. She is our Queen and also our Mother, who understands, who loves, who suffers, and gives us hope. As long as She continues to appear, there is hope; and as long as we continue to follow Her messages, we need not fear, because Her messages are messages of PEACE.

Peace and Love are the same; Love comes from Peace and Peace from Love!

The problem is that we don't know how to love. That is the reason Our Lady has been appearing on earth so long, to teach us to love. Therefore, the mission for both, visionaries and us, is "to overcome every sin with love."

37

A "saint" is the one who "lives love within himself." It is our Christian duty to strive to become holy, to become "saints." If we live the messages of Medjugorje, we are living the seeds of holiness. We are on the road to sainthood. Until then, we are not yet "saints."

(2/99)
Special Missions of Each Visionary

Mirjana attended the Chicago Marian Conference in September, 1998. During the conference, she shared the following thoughts:

"Each of us six visionaries has a special mission in these apparitions. Our Lady chose me to pray for unbelievers (those who do not yet know the love of God). Vicka and Jakov pray for the sick, Ivanka prays for families, Marija prays for sisters, priests, and souls in Purgatory. Ivan prays for young people and priests.

"We visionaries are no more privileged than any of you. For Our Lady, we are all the same. She chose us so that through us She can send the messages, but She has chosen all of you. Because to whom would we give these messages if She hadn't called you also? Because we are all Her apostles.

"Our Lady always says, 'Do not talk about the secrets...pray.' One who experiences Mary as their Mother and God as their Father should have nothing to fear. I always say to people that we don't need to be like Fr. Petar, the priest to whom I will reveal the secrets. He always says to me, 'Come to confession to me, and at least tell me one of them right now!'

"I can tell you this, that Our Lady's heart will conquer. I want to tell you that I have heard about lots of different apparitions, some here in America, where reportedly Our Lady is talking about some horrible time to come where there are going to be floods and all kinds of disasters. And I always say, with a full heart, that that's not truly Our Lady speaking, because Our Lady is our Mother, and She loves Her children, and it is not Her desire that people love Her because they fear.

"That is not true faith. She changes us with Her smile and with love. And so we don't need to fear anything, but we need to place our lives in Her hands. We must not think about what will happen tomorrow. Our Lady desires that we think about what is going to happen now, in this moment, because who amongst us can say in ten minutes we will be alive. Our Lady desires that every second of our lives we're prepared to return to God."

The Medjugorje Star

(6/04)
Interview with Marija Pavlovic-Lunetti
By Bernard Gallagher

A stop for lunch at the Hilton Park Services on the M6 was an opportunity to meet and talk with the visionary Maria Pavlovic-Lunetti during her brief visit to England in March, 2004.

The United Nations has declared this year, International Year of the Family. Has Our Lady said anything about this?

Marija: No, not up to now. But you know, Our Lady has said from the beginning of the apparitions that the most important thing for families is to put God in the first place in our lives, and She says that the first prayer group needs to become our own family, and in our parishes after that. Also, we visionaries, now that Vicka is married, are all with families, and I think Our Lady is calling all of us in a special way through the family.

You must know of many parents who worry about their children who lose faith during their teen years and stop going to Mass. Have you any words of hope or encouragement to give these people?

Marija: Our Lady always says pray and become an example with our own life. She really asks, what is in Holy Scripture, to be salt of the earth and light of the world. I think in this way we become testimony for all our children, and also for people who work with us. Our Lady also asks us to wear and carry in our pockets, holy objects like medals and rosary beads, as signs that we belong to Our Lady and Jesus.

Often, a partner in a marriage, after a "conversion" experience in Medjugorje, returns home and begins to try and convert their husband or wife, and other members of the family. Sometimes it creates difficulties. Resentment and frustration can creep into the relationship. Has Our Lady ever given advice for these situations?

Marija: No, but I think it is better when a husband and wife go together to Medjugorje, so the experience is deeper and more beautiful and it becomes easier to begin to pray together. And also I think it is good, if possible, that the whole family decide to go all together, as they do when going on vacation to a seaside. It is a good opportunity for the family to be renewed and Our Lady is sure to help to bring new spirit into the family. I see many families that have never prayed, begin to pray together after going to Medjugorje.

It is also said that those who give their lives to Our Lady come under a lot of pressure from the enemy. Is there any truth in this?

Marija: True! I always say, when we are with God, Satan is not happy! Always when we work for peace. Today, peace is destroyed by murder and terrorism, as we have witnessed recently in Spain. Our Lady says we must become those who bring peace.

Our Lady has given you a special mission to pray for the Holy Souls...

Marija: No – for priests – for the consecrated! But I love praying for the Holy Souls also. Many people do not know that when we pray for the Holy Souls they become our friends. But Our Lady asked me particularly to pray for all the people who are consecrated in a special way to God.

For people who, for whatever reason, cannot go to Medjugorje, how can Medjugorje come to them?

Marija: I thank God that thanks to you, and thanks to all the people who spread the message of Our Lady, it can come in this way. For example, one month, at the invitation of my parish priest, I went to Brazil. At one church I met a man who had never been to Medjugorje, but he knew and really lived all Our Lady's messages. He said: "I choose the way of holiness for my life and my family. We love little in our families, so we try to live Our Lady's message and live love and peace in our own family." This was just as when Our

Lady said: "I want you to live Paradise here." It is really beautiful. So I see many people and many families live the message because of the way Our Lady uses people to spread Her message. And this also is very beautiful.

The tears of a mother can touch all hearts. On the third day of the apparitions you witnessed Our Lady weeping in front of a dark cross when She called for peace and reconciliation. This must have had a dramatic effect on you?

Marija: You know, exactly 10 years after this apparition when Our Lady wept, the war began in Croatia. When Our Lady cried, we did not understand; that the reason was for peace. It was also at this time She gave us a sign when She said that through fasting and prayer, wars could be stopped. But in some way we did not understand or believe that Our Lady was trying to help us. It was as if the situation had become relaxed. But after 10 years our inner peace changed with the horrible destruction of people and their homes, fighting and no peace. Then we understood Our Lady's tears and Her words about fasting and prayer.

The Medjugorje Message, UK

Marija and Ivan in St. James Church in Medjugorje

(1/00)
Ivan Speaks In Our Area
By Joan Wieszczyk

When a visionary from Medjugorje speaks, you can be sure of a huge crowd in attendance. People look forward to seeing and hearing them. They are hungry for the message, the message of the Gospel. This was no different in Chautauqua, New York and in St. Mary's, Pennsylvania, when Ivan Dragicevic, the eldest male visionary from Medjugorje, came.

I have heard him speak many times before, both in Medjugorje and in the United States. I was very impressed with how well he can speak English, even though he still uses an interpreter. In any form, he gets the message out. After all, he is an ambassador for Our Lady. I would like to share with you some of his message, which was given to us this past October.

Ivan: On the first day, Our Lady was there waiting for us and with Her hand She was telling us to come closer. She was smiling and She had the Baby Jesus in Her arms.

On the second day, we went up the hill and saw Her. She approached us and put Her hands on our heads and She started to speak Her first words, "Dear children, I am with you and I am your Mother. Don't be afraid of anything."

Then Vicka asked Her, "Who are you?" She said, "I am the Blessed Virgin Mary, the Queen of Peace. And I come, dear children, because my Son is sending me so that I can help you. Dear children, Peace, Peace, Peace!"

"Peace has to come between God and man, and peace has to come among men. Dear children, today's world is in danger and it is threatened to destroy itself and that is why I came because I want to help you and I want to lead you to the path of peace."

To be with Our Lady these 18 years means to be in Mother's School – in this school where Mother is teaching, in the school of Love, in the school of Prayer. That is a big school.

All these 18 years, through me, (I am only an instrument in God's hand), She speaks and gives messages – messages to the whole world because She is the Mother of all of us, because She loves all of us.

Dear friends, there are many crises in today's world and the biggest crisis is the crisis of faith in God. That is why She is constantly calling.

It is very hard to be with Our Lady everyday and talk to Her everyday and then come back and live on earth. I would love for everybody to see Our Lady. I always ask, "Our Lady, why don't you show yourself to everybody? Everybody would believe You. And I would not have to give this speech. Then I would have more private time." But She wanted it this way. She put Her fingers to me and chose me. That is a big joy and also a big responsibility. For whom God gives a lot, He always asks a lot from him. Believe this.... Blessed are those who did not see, but they believe.

Our Lady comes as the Queen of Peace. She comes from the King of Peace. She comes because She wants to take us to the way of Peace. She wants to take our hand and take us to God. But Our Lady says, "Dear children, if there is no peace in a man's heart, there is no peace in the world."

"That is why, dear children, do not talk about peace, but live peace. Do not talk too much about prayer, but live prayer. Live prayer in your heart. Live prayer in your families. Make prayer groups in your communities. Be a live church." That is what Our Lady wants.

Our Lady comes because She wants to bring joy to all of us. She wants to heal the simple human heart today. She never gets tired to call us to peace, conversion and prayer. She is very concerned about our salvation and that is why She calls us so much. She is never tired and is very patient with so much love.

She says, "Dear children, I am always with you. I am with you, and I want to help you so that peace can come. But, dear children, I need you because only with you, I can establish peace. That is why, dear children, decide for good and fight against evil and against sin."

Our Mother speaks very simply and repeats and never gets tired. She did not come to bring us fear. She did not come to frighten us with anything. She did not come to talk about darkness. She did not come to talk about the end of the world. She comes as a Mother of Hope. She wants to bring hope in today's tired world, in today's

43

tired family, in today's tired Church. She wants to bring hope and the light of hope and love.

Many people suspect today that some terrible things will happen in the year 2000, in the new millennium. Many others believe those people that something will happen. They already have started to prepare for that. They put food and water in their cellar and basements. But I have to say one thing. Our Lady does not speak any of that. She is constantly calling us to prayer. We have to be careful today about the prophets in this world, earthly prophets – those who prophesy and say a lot of things. But we have to have strong faith and we have to pray. We have to decide for God. What should we be afraid of? The Gospel says that we can move mountains if we have strong faith. We have the responsibility to do this. Our Lady is calling us because She wants to take us all into the new millennium – expecting from us more peace in the world, in the families, and among youth, more forgiving, more love, between parents, mothers, fathers, between parents and their children, so that every family becomes a prayer group. So that we go to Holy Mass, confess, go to Holy Communion, pray the Rosary, read the Bible, and involve other people. That is what Our Lady is expecting of us – not fear and not fright.

She is a mother. She is a mother who wants to teach us. She wants to warn us of things that aren't good, and lead towards good, always showing us good.

In every message She has given us in these 18 years, She is telling us, "Dear children, that is not good, do not believe that. Dear children, that is not your place, so later on you can accept my message."

How many times has She said, "Dear children, I love you."? It is very hard to talk about love that Our Lady has for us. In one message She says, "Dear children, if you knew how much I love you, you'd jump with joy."

She carries all of us in Her heart. She puts us all in Her heart. All messages She gives to us, She gives to the whole world. There are no special messages for a special country, or any special religion or nationality. We are always, "My dear children." She never says, "Dear Americans," or "Dear Italians," or "Dear French," etc. There are no privileges. She's a Mother of us all. We are all important to Her. No one is rejected. She does not look at the color of skin. She is a Mother. A Mother together with Her Son wants to renew this world. She says, "Dear children, come to me. You're tired and I will give you rest." Like Jesus says in the Gospel, "I will give you water." The water today in this world where you live is especially dangerous, in the world of all crises.

Our Lady is always calling us to leave sin and evil. There is a lot that is destroying today's humanity. How many crises are in the world today? How many divorces? How much alcohol and drugs? How many young people live in the streets? Those are the children that left their parents. Many of them left because they were from destroyed marriages and they did not have any love. They went to the street because they wanted to find their own joy, thinking that maybe they will find it. Then they find evil, they find drugs. Dear friends, family, today is a holy thing, like a priest is a holy thing, like sacrament is a holy thing. That is why Our Lady calls for families to pray so much. Peace in the families. Our Lady says, "Dear children, peace is a gift that God wants to give you. Open yourself to that gift and pray for that gift of peace. Open yourself to the Holy Spirit. Dear children, come back to God. Put God first in your life."

Our Lady asks each of us to open our own doors to our own hearts and do what we can. Don't look for mistakes in others. Do not criticize others. Don't look for the garbage in someone else's house and not see and clean your own. Or look in your own garden and see how many weeds are there. That is why Our Lady asks so much, so that we first start to work on ourselves. Our conversion is a process and a program for our life. We have to convert and change every day. Our Lady says, "Dear children, if your conversion is going to be holy and perfect, you always need to pray."

As I said before, She calls us to the Holy Mass. The Holy Mass should be the center of our life. At one meeting together with Our Lady, She says, "Dear children, if you were to decide today to come to me or to go to the Holy Mass, dear children, do not come to me. Go to the Holy Mass."

Conversion, Confession, pray the Rosary and kneel in front of the Cross, to read the Gospel and the Bible. That's what She wants.

She tells us to not let the Bible be just a decoration in our families and houses. Let that Word of God live in you. That is spiritual food in your life. Thousands of times She repeats the message, "Pray, pray, pray." And She still did not get tired. She never gets tired because She wants good for us. She loves us. You mothers know how many times you said to your children, "Be good. Don't do that." How many times did you repeat that? Thousands and thousands of times, and you still don't get tired. That's how our Mother is. She never gets tired and She knows that we are not perfect. She wants us to correct our mistakes, day by day, through prayer. That's why She calls us to pray especially with our heart and with love. Pray with our whole being so that prayer is a meeting with Jesus and a conversation with Jesus. So our prayer is a joy.

People ask me, "What does Our Lady say? How long should we pray?" Our Lady says, "Dear children, pray for so long until your prayer becomes joy." For prayer to have joy, you have to want to pray. It is the same as you want to talk to someone on the telephone. First you must pick up the receiver. When you take the receiver means to decide to pray, decide for God. Then when you dial the numbers means enter into prayer. In that prayer, you give everything to God so that you can receive from God. To God and to Our Lady, every prayer is dear, when that prayer comes from our heart. That is why prayer is the soul part of our faith and the most beautiful flower.

That's why prayer is a school. Through these 18 years, Our Lady is calling us to this school. Dear children, do not forget in the school of prayer there is no weekend. Everyday you have to attend the school of prayer. Dear children, if you want to pray better, you have to pray more. To pray more is a personal decision and to pray better is a grace. This grace is given to those who pray more.

Many people today say that they don't have time to pray. But our Lady says, "Dear children, there's not a problem with time. The problem is love." Because if someone loves someone, they will always find the time. And if they don't, they won't.

That's why She asks us to pray so much in depth. Dear children, with prayer, you can bring back joy, peace and love. With prayer, our family can grow spiritually. Our Lady wants to awaken us in the spiritual coma we are in, and take us back to peace. She says,

"Dear children, if you are strong, the Church will be strong too. If you're weak, the Church will be weak too, because you are the live Church."

Our Lady also calls the priests to speak simpler. When they speak to us, they should speak in simple words so that we can understand and live by what they preach. So they preach the living word of the Gospel.

Tonight, at the meeting with Our Lady where you were present, I would like to describe this meeting (apparition) with the words I can use to describe it. Our Lady came very happy. She greets us all at the beginning with the greeting, "Praised be Jesus, my dear children." After that She prayed above all of us with Her hands above us. She blessed us all then I recommended all of you and your needs and your families. Then She said, "Dear Children, I am very happy today to be together with you. I would like especially to call you to pray for the conversion of sinners these days. Pray this, dear children. Do not get tired to this prayer. Thank you for answering my calls."

And after that, Our Lady spoke to me. We then prayed together, the Our Father and Glory Be to God. Then She left in the Sign of the Cross and light, with the greeting, "Go in peace, my dear children." This is the most important thing of tonight's meeting. It's very hard to describe this meeting with my words.

I see Our Lady as I see you today. I talk to Her as I talk to you now. I can touch Her. She has a gray dress, white veil, blue eyes, rosy cheeks, black hair. She is on a cloud. She has a crown of stars. The beauty of Our Lady is very hard to describe in words.

One time I asked Our Lady, "Why are You so beautiful?" She said, "Dear children, I'm beautiful because I love. Dear children, if you love, then you will be beautiful."

I hope you will answer Our Lady's call and accept Her messages – messages of Peace, Conversion, Prayer, strong Faith, Love and Hope. So we can help build a better world. A world that is good for God's children.

So let this meeting tonight with you and me be a beginning of a spiritual renewal. When you go back to your homes, continue in that spiritual renewal in your families and with your children.

Jakov and translator

(1/04)
Reviving the Message: Fasting and Prayer
By Sean Bloomfield

As the world journeys into the year 2004, many are plagued with uncertainty about what the future holds. Thankfully the Blessed Mother is still here to guide us.

When the Medjugorje apparitions began, few could have imagined that Our Lady would still be appearing in such frequency to three of the six visionaries, let alone any of them. Even so, Marija, Ivan and Vicka continue to greet Her daily.

Jakov Colo, the youngest seer, stopped having daily apparitions on September 12, 1998, after he received all ten secrets from Gospa. He sees Her now once a year on Christmas Day. In the spirit of Christmas, Our Lady has given Jakov some important wisdom that involves every person on the planet.

I stayed with Jakov in 2001 to film and interview him for my first Marian video, "Medjugorje in the New Millennium." I was pleasantly surprised by his responses to my questions concerning people of other faiths. "Our Lady is calling everyone to conversion, not just Catholics," Jakov told me with a serene, almost angelic smile. "God is one and He is for all. And Our Lady always comes as a mother. She is a mother to all." I pondered this with intrigue. To me, the fact that Our Lady is reaching out to people of all faiths and cultures was one reason that I initially believed in Medjugorje. It felt nice to hear Jakov confirm this. "Our Lady loves each and every one of us in a special way," Jakov added knowingly. "And She would be very happy if each individual came closer to Her, so they can experience the love She has for each and every one of us."

In speaking with Jakov and observing his daily routine, it is impossible to deny the authenticity of the apparitions. This dedicated husband, father and visionary lives the messages and constantly promotes the importance of fasting and prayer.

During a recent talk to pilgrims in Medjugorje, Jakov asserted: "Many ask why it is important to fast. But if Our Lady has been inviting us for the past 22 years to fast, then it has to be important. It's not that difficult to fast as many people think. It's just a little thing we can do, a little suffering, but when we fast and we suffer a little, we have to do it out of love and in silence. No one around us should know we are fasting."

Nevertheless, he knows how difficult it is for most people to adopt Our Lady's requests into their daily routines. During the interview, Jakov admitted: "When Our Lady called me to these messages, I thought 'There's no way I can ever accept this.' I did pray before but it was not the way I pray now. I didn't feel it then like I feel it now. But I understood one thing: in order to accept everything that Our Lady is calling us to, we need to open up our hearts and surrender to Her completely."

That's exactly what Jakov did, and today he is a living example of Our Lady's graces. His pleas echo those of the Blessed Mother: "You have forgotten that through prayer and fasting you can avert wars and suspend the laws of nature." Now, more than ever, it's time to revive the Medjugorje message and let it carry us safely into the New Year.

Editor's note and update: If you would like more information on Sean's videos "Medjugorje in the New Millennium," "The Fruits of Mary," "Miracles of Medjugorje" and "Medjugorje, the 25th Anniversary," you can visit Sean's website at www.MedjugorjeVideo. com or call(toll-free) 1-877-211-8018, or write to Sean Bloomfield Productions, P.O. Box 3035. Tequesta, FL 33469.

(2/02)
Vicka Shares Insights about Lent

Many times we see Lent as a time when we make sacrifices and practice self-denial by giving up coffee, alcohol, chocolate, cigarettes, TV, or whatever we are overly attached to. But we must renounce those things out of love for Jesus and Mary, and be careful not to do it for our own glory. Often we wait for the end of the forty days, only to drink again, to watch TV again, etc. This is not the right way to live Lent!

Yes indeed, Our Lady asks us for sacrifices, but She does so all the time, not just during Lent. During Lent, we must offer to God all our desires, our crosses, our sickness and suffering, so that we may walk with Jesus, walk with Him toward Calvary. We should take to heart to help Him carry His cross because He carries His cross for all of us, asking Him, "Lord, how can I help You? What can I offer You?"

I don't mean that He cannot carry His cross, but when we join with Him from the heart, then it becomes a very beautiful thing. I don't refer to Him when I need Him only, but I walk with Him when He most needs me, during His suffering for us.

Many times, when we have a cross we could offer Him, we instead pray this way: "Lord, please remove that cross from my shoulders, it's heavy, I can't take it. Why is this cross given to me and not to someone else?" No! This is not the right way to pray! Our Lady says we should rather tell Him: "Lord, I thank you for this cross, I thank you for the great gift You are giving me!"

Very few are the people who understand the great value of the cross and the great value of the gift of our crosses when they are offered to Jesus. We can learn so much through this gift of the cross! In this time of Lent, we must understand from the heart how much Jesus loves us all, and we should walk by His side with great love. We should try to be united with Him in His passion. This is the sacrifice that is expected from us.

Let's walk this way, and then when the day of Easter comes with the Resurrection, we won't look at the Resurrection from the outside, but we will also be resurrected with Jesus, because we will have become free from within, free from ourselves and all our attachments. Isn't this a beautiful thing? We will be able to live His love and His Resurrection within ourselves!

Every single cross has a reason. God never sends any cross without a motive, a meaning, and He knows when He will remove that cross from us. At times of suffering, let's thank Jesus for this gift and also tell Him, "If you have another gift for me, I am ready. But right now I am begging for Your strength in order to have the courage to carry my cross and go forward with You, Lord!"

I remember how the Gospa spoke to me about suffering when She said: "If you knew the great value of suffering!" This is really a very great thing! And then it all depends on us, afterwards, to be ready for this or not. It all depends on our "Yes" to Jesus. It takes our whole life to learn this and go forward. Each morning, when we wake up, we can start our day with God. Our Lady does not ask us to pray the whole day long, but to put prayer in the first place, to put God in the first place, and then perform our works and go ahead in all the aspects of our life, visiting sick people, etc.

When we do a charitable work without prayer, it's not valuable. The same way, when we pray and do not act in a charitable way, it is not valuable either. Those two things – prayer and charity – work always together. And then, step by step, we go forward.

The Medjugorje Star

(7/03)
Ivanka's Mom
By Sister Emmanuel

Ivanka was the first of the 6 visionaries to see the Lady. On June 24, 1981, she was out walking with Mirjana in the hamlet of Bijakovici, along the path which runs at the foot of the hill of Podbrdo.

The following day, she was also the first to ask the Lady a question. Ivanka's mother had died 2 months earlier. "She is happy, she is with me," the Lady answered.

Some time later, on Ivanka's birthday, Our Lady surprised her by appearing with Ivanka's mother. The young girl was struck by her mother's beauty. She was much more beautiful than ever before! And this would not be a one-time surprise, for it happened 5 times! On June 25, 1991, the Gospa returned again with Ivanka's mother. Ivanka could hardly believe her eyes. When she saw her mother, she was even more beautiful than before. Amazingly beautiful!

Why had her mother changed? Marija Pavlovic gives us the answer. When the Gospa showed her Heaven and the intense happiness of the elect, She explained that in Heaven, saints grow in happiness. This crescendo in their happiness is linked to God's infinite greatness. God is so great that we will never cease discovering Him. Each time we discover a new aspect of His greatness, our love grows. As our love grows, our beauty increases. That was the reason why Ivanka's mother appeared even more beautiful when she came the second time.

"I am beautiful because I love," the Gospa once told Jelena Vasilj, who was absolutely amazed at Her beauty. "If you want to be beautiful, love!" It must be that in Heaven nothing could possibly be static. Love implies the ever-changing movement of exchange, as within the Holy Trinity. So, Heaven is full of activity!

Another experience related by Marija also illustrates this movement quite well. While the visionaries were praying before the Gospa, Marija noticed that the face of Our Lady was changing, becoming more and more joyful. It was as though the least prayer from Marija filled Her with new joy. The beauty and splendor of Her face grew with each new joy. It became more and more radiant. Then Marija asked, "Why are you more beautiful and joyful when I pray?"

"It is because with each Ave you say my joy increases."

Little by little, Marija was also flooded with the joy of Mary.

Even on this earth, we can start to live this crescendo of happiness within our hearts. Each prayer from the heart opens the heavens above and lets us in. Do you want to look beautiful? The Gospa gives you the recipe. And no cosmetics compete with Hers.

*Used with permission. **Medjugorje, The 90's**, copyright 1997, Children of Medjugorje*

Mirjana and her translator Miki Musa

(4/04)
Excerpts from Mirjana's Talk to Pilgrims in October, 2000
By June Klins

At the beginning of Mirjana's talk, she testified that on 8/2/97 Our Lady came to pray with her for unbelievers and has continued to do this on the second of the month ever since. She admitted that she didn't know how long this would continue. "Each one of our prayers wipes away the tears Our Lady has in Her eyes for unbelievers," Mirjana said. "Love them, but do not judge or criticize them."

Occasionally there is a public message on the second of the month. Mirjana repeated the message of 9/2/00 for those who had not heard it: *"I invite you to open your hearts and let me enter your hearts so that I am able to guide you. Be My apostles."*

Mirjana told a cute story that illustrates how important it is for parents to be a good example for their children. She said that when her daughter Marija was about 2 years old she hadn't told her about the apparitions yet because she thought she was too young to understand. Then one day when Marija was playing with a friend, Mirjana heard the friend say, "My mom is able to drive a car." Marija kept silent for a moment and then said, "That's nothing. My mom talks to Our Lady every day!"

During the question and answer period, someone asked Mirjana if Our Lady has ever brought anyone other than Baby Jesus with Her, such as any of the saints. Mirjana answered: "No, never, but we had a special experience once, one day at the beginning. We had a particularly difficult day because that was a time of Communism still. That morning the police took us for questioning and after that, we were taken to the psychiatric ward of the hospital and they told us we would be kept there because we were crazy. About midnight, they took us back to the house and when we got home we had an apparition, and when Our Lady came we started to cry. And we were able to see just the head of Jesus on the right side. We were able to see Our Lady as a human, but Jesus was more like a statue or an image. Our Lady said, 'Look at the One Who gave so much for the faith. Just compare that with the little you are suffering for the faith now.' After that we never saw anything like that again."

Mirjana said that many people ask her about the secrets, so she offered this advice: "Whoever feels God is our Father and Our Lady is our Mother should not be afraid of anything. Only unbelievers have fears. Being human, we are always talking about the future and the secrets, but Our Lady is telling us to do the opposite. Our Lady is teaching us to be ready to go to God every moment. We should not be talking about what is going to happen in the future. It is going to be God's will, whatever happens."

In answer to a question about the Church's position on the apparitions, Mirjana answered that she feels that the Pope believes in the apparitions because in 1987, when she was in Rome, she spent ten minutes with him, and he told her, "If I were not pope I would already be in Medjugorje confessing."

(1/02)
Medjugorje Visionary Jakov Colo

Our Lady appeared daily to Jakov Colo, youngest of the six Medjugorje visionaries, from June 25, 1981, to September 12, 1998, on which day Our Lady revealed to him the tenth secret. She has promised to appear to Jakov every year on Christmas.

Q: Many ask why the apparitions are lasting so long.
A: I think it is the wrong question. We should all give thanks to God for these 20 years of Our Lady's love towards us. Through this we can see how much She wants to save us and lead us to Jesus.

Q: Can you tell us something about the secrets?
A: People ask us about the secrets and think that they are something to fear. But we should only concern ourselves with one mystery, and that is our life. How are we living it? How do we accept God? Are we doing everything that God expects from us?

Q: What does God want to say to us through Our Lady?
A: Just look around and see how today's world is in crisis and without God, especially now in 2001, when many abnormal things have become normal. Our Lady is coming to us so that we may begin to seek the true value and goal of our life, and that is God.

Mir Peace Letter

(8/00)
Ivanka

The missionary Ivanka Ivankovic Elez, who has received all 10 secrets, sees Our Lady annually on June 25th of each year. Mirjana and Jakov also have 10 secrets and have annual apparitions, Mirjana on March 18th (her birthday) and Jakov on December 25th. Vicka, Marija (receives the monthly messages) and Ivan have only 9 secrets, therefore, according to their testimony, still have daily apparitions.

On the occasion of Ivanka's last daily apparition, which was on May 7, 1985, Our Lady confided to Ivanka the 10th secret. Our Lady told Ivanka that for the duration of her entire life, she would have an apparition once a year on the anniversary of the apparitions.

Thus it was also this year on June 25th. Ivanka had it in her family home. Present were her husband and children. The apparition lasted 7 minutes and was very joyful. According to Ivanka, the Gospa (Blessed Mother) was happy and spoke to her about the 6th secret. Our Lady gave the following message:

"I introduce myself as Queen of Peace and I call you once again to peace, fasting and prayer. Renew family prayer and receive my blessing."

Ivanka then came to the USA and spent most of the month of July, 2000, giving talks on the message of Medjugorje.

Ivanka – 19th anniversary

Q: Is it hard for you to wait a whole year to see Our Lady again?

A: Every day I am preparing myself for this moment, and now I could cry and laugh at the same time.

Ivanka and her husband

Q: What do you see when Our Lady comes?

A: Before Our Lady appears I see the light three times, then I see the most beautiful image of Our Lady and everything else disappears.

Q: Was anyone able to paint what you see?

A: None of the paintings come even close to the beauty and radiance of Our Lady.

Q: Can you tell us anything about the secrets? Many people are afraid.

A: I can only say about the sign that will appear here in Medjugorje when the time comes. This sign will be for those who do not believe. Those who live according to the commandments of God have no reason to fear.

Q: There are so many people here for the anniversary; does it bother you and others?

A: Our Lady is so glad when more people gather here to pray with Her and with us. The more prayers, the less evil in the world. This should make us all feel good.

Q: What would you like to say to people in the USA?

A: Parents should teach their children about God and pray with them.

Mir Peace Letter

(5/03)
Interview with Medjogorje's New Mother, Vicka
By Denis Nolan

Yesterday (4/14), after an absence due to the birth of her baby, Vicka took up again her place "back at my stairway." She told us several weeks ago that being able to go back to her spot would bring her "a big joy!" "You see, I am happy with my family, with my daughter, but I also want to say that being with the pilgrims is a great joy, a joy that fills my heart – giving them the messages of Our Lady, and being able in my turn to give others the love that Our Lady has given to me..."

Vicka on her stairway

Question: Vicka, last year we came to see you and interview you. You were not married then. Now you have more than a year of marriage behind you. What would you tell the young people especially, about family life?

Vicka: I can see that, today, young people are a little afraid of changing their lives, for the life they lead is very convenient, you see, since they can do whatever they want, being single. I would tell them to trust themselves more. For example, for me with my husband, as a family, I feel very good, really very good! And I want to tell all of them that they should no longer be afraid, but instead open themselves and listen, for God calls each one of us. We should be ready to hear what He wants and then choose a path. Today young people are in great confusion and they live in a very difficult time. This is why Our Lady is asking, "Pray for the youth, pray for your families!" We also have a little 2-month old daughter, whose name is Marija-Sofija. For us it's a great joy. She is life, great joy, a big fruit that the Lord has given us. And, with my husband, we are thanking God for such a beautiful gift! You know, we are ready. If the Lord made a gift, He can make more, so we are ready to welcome them with our hearts wide open!

Question: What do you feel in your heart for your little girl, a new love? This is all new for you!

Vicka: This can't be explained! When she was born, I could not believe it! It is something very big, bigger than you! So you try to touch, to see, and ask in yourself a million things and you tell yourself, "See how great God is!" With this small fruit, you can see how God creates, how He has created this new creature, how He is making this gift for you, how great His love is! While these thoughts are going through your mind, your love grows. Later, each time you see the child move, move her hands, it is always something new for you. Then you feel a great love, a great joy, something you just can't explain.

Question: We saw that after the baby's birth, you remained out of sight for 40 days, without talking to the pilgrims, without being seen. Is this a Croatian tradition?

Vicka: Yes, you know, not going out in public is our tradition. When a woman gives birth to a child, she must stay at home during this time. But people can come to visit, my parents, my sisters, my friends, to help (which is normal) and to bring their wishes, etc., according to our customs. Now, a few months have passed and little by little the time has come for me to go out.

Vicka then gave some practical advice from Our Lady's school in Medjugorje that will help us live Holy Week....

Question: About Confession, what do you have to say?

Vicka: Our Lady recommends that we go to Confession once a month. She says, "Do not go to Confession only because you have sins. Also ask the priest to give you advice to be able to move forward."

Question: There are people who think they do not need to go to Confession. They say they do not see their sins, they have not done anything wrong, or they address God directly.

Vicka: In that case, drop the matter. One should not force anyone. When someone talks like this, let's not discuss with them. Our Lady does not want such discussions. She prefers that we simply pray for these people. Our prayer and our example may touch these hearts.

But when you speak, you make them go away. It is preferable to keep quiet and to wait for the right moment. The Lord knows how to reach them, little by little.

Question: Don't the young people need to hear us speak?

Vicka: When I say "no words," I mean "not too many words!" When people talk too much, it gets heavier, it drives people away, and there isn't any fruit. If a youth or a child asks me a question, I am ready to answer them with all my heart. When they do not ask anything, it is better to remain quiet, not to say anything.

Question: What did Our Lady teach you about the connection between Confession and going to Communion?

Vicka: You see, sometimes we rush in for a quick Confession and we say, "There, I committed this sin, that sin, etc," but it is obvious that we have not prepared ourselves. If you are not really ready, if you are hiding something, or else you are fighting inside yourself, you will not come out liberated. When you go to Communion afterwards, you are not able to feel a deep joy. But when you free your heart from everything and you know that the Lord has forgiven you (He gave the priest the power of absolving your sins), you believe and then your heart is free! So, when you go to Communion, you can feel Jesus who comes to your heart, alive! Our Blessed Mother said, "Holy Mass is the most important moment, a holy moment! And at this moment Jesus comes to us alive!" When we are in church, She asks that we go take Jesus with no fear, nor excuses.

Question: How should we use our imagination while praying?

Vicka: It all depends on you! We so often think that prayer is an obligation, something that we should do. But Our Lady says that prayer should be a joy! If joy does not come in prayer, time goes by, you are not doing anything and it does the opposite. I am going to repeat what Our Lady said, since I can't find a better example than the one She gives with the vase of flowers: an example taken from nature. When we go out to a park or to the mountain, we see nature and all the things that grow, these are truly gifts of God. And the Gospa says, "All of you have a vase of flowers in your houses. Each day you pour a few drops of water in these flowers and you can see how these flowers develop and become pretty roses. In the same way, when, each day, you put two or three prayers with the heart in your hearts, you can see your hearts grow, like these flowers. When we stay 2 or 3 days without putting water in the flowers, we can see that these flowers disappear, they no longer exist." And Our Lady said, "But, when the time of prayer comes, you so often say, 'Today I am tired, I can't pray, I will pray tomorrow.' But the next day comes, and then the day after, and you say the same thing. So our prayer moves further away from us every day and our heart wanders away. Just as a flower cannot live without water, you cannot live without the grace of God. Prayer with the heart cannot be learned nor studied in books. Prayer with the heart can only be lived, from day to day, by moving forward."

Children of Medjugorje, www.childrenofmedjugorje.com

(1/03)
Jakov Colo on Thanking God
By Sean Patrick Bloomfield

Meeting Jakov Colo, the youngest visionary in Medjugorje, is like experiencing the growth of a boy to a man in a matter of seconds. One part of your mind recalls images of the first days of the apparitions: sandwiched among the five other visionaries, all of them kneeling tall and stoic in their older bodies, you had to look closely to see his tiny face peeking over the altar. That was Jakov, his eyes as round as Communion hosts, staring in awe at his Heavenly Mother.

Today, it's not hard to see the same little boy in the face of Jakov the man, although now he is in his early thirties, married, and has three beautiful children of his own. Being the most recent visionary to receive all ten secrets from Gospa, Jakov only sees Her now once a year, on Christmas Day.

Jakov with his translator

Jakov and his family live permanently in Medjugorje, in the same part of the village where he grew up. His only income stems from hosting occasional pilgrims in the guesthouse that adjoins his own home.

I was fortunate enough to stay with Jakov at his home in Medjugorje last year, while filming my documentary video "Medjugorje in the New Millennium." I had expected a challenge to get this infamously shy visionary to open up while on camera, but instead he delighted me with a smiling interview and in-depth answers to all of my questions.

"What did we forget today?" Jakov asked me once during the interview, through my interpreter Maria. I remember thinking to myself: Is he talking to me? I even checked to make sure I hadn't forgotten to take the lens cap off my video camera!

Finally, Jakov continued: "We forgot to thank our God. We are constantly asking something of Him. But we need to start thanking Him, beginning with the small things. You could say, for example, thank you God for this beautiful day today. Or, thank you God for all the people in my life."

Just then, Jakov's children ran past us, happily chasing a butterfly. Jakov smiled as he saw them, then he continued, "But at the same time, you need to begin to thank God for all the crosses that He gave to us. When we receive a small cross, we usually ask, 'Why are you giving this to me?'"

I remember how hard it was to maintain my objectivity as a filmmaker when Jakov spoke about crosses. In that instant, I began thinking of all the times I had whined to God whenever a minor burden came my way. "We need to learn how to thank Him," Jakov continued, "because God gave us too much, and we do not understand that. We are constantly asking for more."

When the interview was over, Jakov shook my hand and went to round up his kids. But I didn't get up. I just sat there, my camera still running, as I stared at the crucifix on the wall of Jakov's living room.

"Thank you, God," I said, and a tear streaked down my face. "Thank you for this moment."

Editor's note and update: If you would like more information on Sean's videos "Medjugorje in the New Millennium," "The Fruits of Mary," "Miracles of Medjugorje" and "Medjugorje, the 25th Anniversary," you can visit Sean's website at www.MedjugorjeVideo. com or call (toll-free) 1-877-211-8018 or write to Sean Bloomfield Productions, P.O. Box 3035. Tequesta, FL 33469.

(7/04-12/04)
Mirjana's Question and Answer Session

This was a continuing series we featured on Mirjana's question and answer session at the National Conference on Medjugorje at Notre Dame University on 5/30/04. (They were not written in any particular order.) Mirjana answered these questions in English with very little help from her interpreter.

Q: After the secrets have taken place, what will life be like on earth?

M: This is a secret! What I can only tell to everybody is don't be afraid – put your life in the hands of Blessed Mary and God and Jesus, and live normal. Don't think about these things. In life will be only God's will. Look at us visionaries. We know everything and we're living normal lives. We have children. Some visionaries are pregnant. We're not thinking about this. We must pray and try that every day, in every moment, in our lives, God will be in the first place. And don't be afraid of anything because God is your Father.

Editor's note: Mirjana laughed a bit when asked this question because the day before she had asked people not to ask about the secrets because as she said, "Secrets are secrets."

Q: In 1984, the Blessed Mother said it was Her 2000ᵗʰ birthday, and many historians claim that the Nativity of Our Lord occurred in the year 3 or 4 B.C. So Mary, then, would have been 12 or 13 years old. I was wondering if you could make any comment on when the Nativity of Jesus occurred.

M: You know, in the Bible we do not know much about Blessed Mary. We asked Blessed Mary, can She tell us something about Her- Her life- about everything that happened in Her life. She gave Her story to Vicka, Ivanka, and myself and we know everything exactly- how it happened in the beginning. And when the secrets are starting to be revealed, this will be the time to give this story to all who are interested. For now, only we know when. But, it is not as I read in some books that there will be a book of Blessed Mary's life. No, it will be a few pages about the life of Blessed Mary. And when I will give you all these things, you will know everything- when Jesus was born, how this happened – everything.

Q: Mary said that Her real birthday is August 5, but the Church recognizes September 8 as Her birthday. Is the Church going to change?

M: (laughing) Vicka, Ivan, Marija, and Jakov received this message of Blessed Mary that She said that Her birthday is not on the day we celebrate it (Sept.8), that it is a different date (Aug.5).

But we can compromise. Blessed Mary is a woman and She wants two birthdays! I would love two birthdays too!

Q: Has the Blessed Mother spoken about silence in regard to prayer?

M: She asked for family prayer. She asked for Rosary in the family. She asked for 7 Our Father's, 7 Hail Mary's and 7 Glory Be's with the Creed. And if you do these things you will feel the need to talk with God, to have meditation, and to have silence with God.

Q: Is there any book that you particularly recommend for people to read to learn about the Blessed Mother?

M: To learn about the Blessed Mother, to learn about Holy Mass, how to have Holy Mass with the heart, how to pray the Rosary with the heart, I always recommend the books of Fr. Slavko Barbaric. These are the books that I like because with simple words, he is showing you how to be in everything with the heart.

Editor's note: In an informal survey done with the Medjugorje internet prayer group last year, Fr. Slavko's book "Pray with the Heart" was rated one of the top 10 books about Medjugorje.

Q: What do you think is the most important part of Mary's messages?

M: LOVE- only love. That is what She wants us to feel for each other. She wants us to see brothers and sisters in everybody. She said one time that we cannot say we are Catholic, that we are believers, if we cannot see Jesus in everybody. I know it is difficult, but She said to do this. What She asks of us, and for me, the same, it is difficult. And when I'm praying, I always think, "Help me because it is so difficult to see Jesus in everybody." But this is what She wants – that we feel love for everybody, and that we feel everybody as our brothers and sisters. And She is coming every second of each month to tell us that we must pray for our brothers and sisters, not for us, because She said one time, "I know all your wishes. I'm reading your heart. Please help me. Pray for those who don't feel love of God yet. Pray for your brothers and sisters." It is love because, if, for example, you're walking on the street, and you are so sad, and for you it is doomsday, and you see one person who you don't know, and she is giving you a smile, you will feel better. And this is what Blessed Mary wants from us – small things – that we are ready always to listen to somebody, to give a smile to somebody, to have time for our neighbors, families, children, husbands, wives. This is what She wants from us.

Ivan in Ohio

(9/04)
Sanctity or Insanity?
By Peggy Golden

Six years ago, I had the opportunity to travel to Medjugorje and stay with Ivan, his wife Laureen, and their daughter Kristina. I secretly anticipated experiencing first hand one of the miracles of Medjugorje…I was familiar enough with what was happening there…the sun spinning, rosaries were turning gold, and pilgrims were seeing images of the Blessed Virgin. The possibilities were endless. I learned, however, that these would not be the true miracles of Medjugorje for me…that our God, who we believe to be omnipotent, is certainly capable of spinning suns, changing rosaries, and allowing our Blessed Mother to appear if He desires, but there was more.

Instead, I learned through the everyday examples of a man and his family, other visionaries, their parish, St. James, and their entire community, what it means to have a simple intimate relationship with Jesus. This is the REAL miracle of Medjugorje that I was privileged to experience...that individuals, families, and large groups altered their lives completely to spend time with God in daily prayer and regular celebration of the sacraments.

Since Ivan's teenage years, he has committed himself daily to living out God's perfect – yet somewhat difficult- will for his life. Because of this, he seems to be depicted as either a saint or someone whose sanity is in question. My experiences indicated otherwise.

Ivan greeted us on the bus with his wife with such a warm smile and welcome. Throughout our stay, Ivan cooked breakfast for us and ate meals with us. He prayed with us. He played soccer with his daughter. He climbed Apparition Hill and described what those first few days were like in June of 1981. He rolled his eyes when he was frustrated with a suggestion from his wife. He prayed with his family. He shared his clothes with pilgrims whose luggage never arrived. He prayed with his prayer group and thousands of others. He stayed up until 4:00 AM to watch those lousy Chicago Bulls win another championship. He attended Mass and sat in a back row. We sat on his porch and laughed with his wife as we imagined a business venture...the first McDonald's in Medjugorje including "happy meals" with the visionaries as collectible figures! We prayed with him in his home chapel during the daily apparitions. He patiently answered for the 8 millionth time what the Blessed Virgin looks like. And only once, in my opinion, did he ever error in judgment ...when he suggested I should arise early every morning and make breakfast for my husband!

And so my experiences indicate otherwise...It was neither sanctity nor insanity. It was about a man trying to bring about God's kingdom of love on earth in a small way. Because of Ivan's example, other people have come to experience the love of God more personally. Because of Jesus, we too are blessed with the same capacity and the same responsibility as Ivan: to give steadfast, inexhaustible love to God and others.

Since returning from Medjugorje, I have NEVER gained strength of inner peace from reflecting on a spinning sun or gold rosaries. Instead, I reflect on Ivan's example of prayer and his example of love for God and Our Lady, his wife and 3 children, his family, his community, and the whole world. He is a beautiful example to me of God's real love for all of us and His desire to be intimately entwined with us through prayer in our everyday lives.

Editor's note: Peggy is from Painesville, OH.

(1/00)
How Our Lady Appears
By Marija Pavlovic

Before Our Lady appears, we see a light three times; then She comes and says, "Hvaljen Isus!" (Praised be Jesus), which is a customary greeting among Catholics in Croatia. We answer: "Navijeke, Amen!" (Forever, Amen!) Then we receive the messages from Our Lady. If She doesn't give us any messages, we recommend the sick to Her. We pray and intercede on behalf of the pilgrims who come to Medjugorje. Our Lady starts: "Our Father..." and we continue, "Who art in Heaven...," then we ask Her for Her blessing. And Our Lady says: "Go in God's Peace!" After that, She leaves us. Whenever Our Lady is leaving, we see a heart, the sun and the cross.

On holy days, She is specially dressed in a gown interwoven with gold. Otherwise, She wears a gray dress with a white veil. Above Her head, we see a wreath of stars. When Our Lady talks, Her arms are extended; and when we pray with Her, She folds Her hands. The expression on Her face is also interesting. Sometimes She's happy, sometimes sad. When Our Lady talks about sin, She's sad. When She appears, it seems like She's coming from a distance. We wish to live every day for that moment, when Our Lady comes...for those five or six minutes.

Medjugorje Herald

Vicka

(5/04)
Interview with Vicka, February, 2004
By Sr. Emmanuel

The village is quiet during these winter months. For many pansion owners and the visionaries, less pilgrims means more time spent with family around the wood-burning stove. This past month, a woman from China stayed in Medjugorje, with my community. She mentioned that she thought it must be easy for the visionaries to discern what God wants of them. "When you see Our Lady every day," she said, "you know how to follow the right path. But for us, how are we to know the will of God in our lives and how can we be sure not to be mistaken?" I took a chance that Vicka would have some "winter time" to spend with us and would share some insights of hers. She welcomed my friend very kindly. Because she radiates such a heavenly joy and love, one may think she can give a magic recipe for peace! Well, she did draw a clear line to happiness, but indeed nothing magic!

Vicka spoke directly to my friend without even one question being asked. She said, "People who think they are clever and intelligent will do things according to their own plans and not care about

God's plan. Because of pride, they fail and face many difficulties in achieving their goals and in seeking God."

--In my case, I follow my own plans, yes, because of pride, but also because I want to know what will come step by step?

Vicka: You know, many people say they want to do the will of God, but actually, when they have to choose a way, they choose what they like most, what brings them pleasure. But one cannot do the will of God some of the time and at other times follow one's own feelings! Many say, "Lord, show me the way," but deep in their heart they have not yet made a strong decision to put God in the first place. They keep going back and forth with Him, and then they lack peace. After a while, they are stuck with no way out, and they find themselves in great pain. Then they cry to God saying: "Lord, why have you allowed this to happen to me?!" Unfortunately, these people have created their own problem! But God is merciful. When you follow Him again, He will work everything out for you. When you start with a strong decision to fulfill God's plans for your life, then God sees your good will and He gives you everything! God is always ready to give! And if you have missed the right path, He is always ready to take you back in His arms and to console you! But all this time spent going the wrong way and then returning to where you started, see how much time you've lost? You have no time to lose! All you have to do is to ask for the thing you need and then be open to receive God's graces. People just do not ask God for it. There is in every person's heart, God. Everyone knows somehow that God exists but some people avoid thinking about it and they deny it.

--Is it not right to follow our feelings? Aren't our feelings from God too?

Vicka: You have to see God's will first so that you have inner security and peace in your heart! When you have fear in your heart, you cannot feel right. You are not in harmony within yourself and you cannot trust your feelings. Seek first to be happy with yourself, to love yourself. When something is from God, you feel great joy, peace and harmony within you. When you feel fear, confusion and anguish, that is something from the enemy. If it is God's will, there will be problems, yes, but He will smooth out the way for you. When it is God's will, God will give you everything you need, problems and difficulties will finally go.

--That sounds so easy for you!

Vicka: You have to do it step by step, don't think of something big. It doesn't happen overnight! Usually, the most difficult part is the start. You have to start slowly to understand and to listen to God's will. Day by day you are learning to listen to God's will. You will find God's graces working for you. You'll receive God's graces when you follow God's will. There are times that God wants to test you to see if you are truly willing to follow His will. God wants you to choose. Sometimes you have struggles among other attractions and alternatives. God has given everyone a great gift: a free will, a freedom, he wants you to choose and to use your free will. God does not want to force you into anything. Sometimes we fail and choose the wrong things. God is merciful and God knows. As long as we have the good will to follow Him, God will help us.

--How can we win over those feelings that trouble us?

Vicka: Don't be afraid of anything, just renounce them and give them to God. You cannot pray if you let those troubles in. You know, Satan is always trying to trouble our hearts. We have to be aware of him, of his actions, and not let him work in our hearts. He will introduce worries and fears and he will disturb you in many ways. But all this, just give it to God and accept his peace! People do not realize how much He wants to give us, how much He loves us! You don't need to be afraid of anything.

Children of Medjugorje, www.childrenofmedjugorje.com

(5/01)
Medjugorje Seer: Parents, Take Your Children To Church

By Jakob Marschner

"Children need to experience the Church as their home," says Medjugorje visionary Jakov Colo who had daily apparitions of the Virgin Mary for more than 17 years. During lectures to pilgrims on Friday, both he and his fellow visionary, Ivanka Elez, also urged parents to pray with their children from very early on in their lives.

MEDJUGORJE, March 15th – Parents should take their children to church, even though they know that the children might start crying or otherwise have a hard time being silent during Mass. By keeping the children from the church out of concerns of what others in the congregation might think, the children are deprived of a most needed sense of relationship with the Church, Medjugorje visionary Jakov Colo advised pilgrims during a lecture on Friday.

Jakov, who had daily apparitions of the Virgin Mary until September 12, 1998, and now has a yearly apparition on Christmas Day, urged people in the church to accept that children are children, and that children sometimes cry. Keeping them away is a mistake, he underscored.

"It is very important to take children to the Holy Mass. They need to experience the Church as their home. They need to understand that it is important to go," said Jakov.

"When I was in the United States, it surprised me a lot to see people turn around when a child started crying during Mass. A child is a child. It happens, and it should not be enough of a reason to keep them away," he added.

The visionary also emphasized the importance of teaching prayer to children from very early on in their lives. By making prayer a daily routine in the family, the children will gradually learn that prayer is a joyful experience, said the visionary who was 10 years old when he saw the Virgin Mary for the first time. Jakov compared his own pre-apparition relationship with God to the one he now tries to teach his three children aged 6, 4 and 1.

"Before the apparitions I was never thinking about God and the truth that He exists. I went to Mass and I prayed, but I never felt as I feel now. I knew that God and Our Lady existed, but I never thought deeply about it," he said.

"Now I try to teach my own children from the beginning of their lives. It is very important that children are brought to understand these things from the beginning. Children understand a lot more than we think they do. It sometimes even happens that my oldest child is the one who suggests that we pray."

During her lecture to pilgrims on Friday, visionary Ivanka Elez also spoke about teaching prayer to children from the onset of their lives. Ivanka, whose daily apparitions ceased in 1985, has three children with a daughter of 13 as the oldest. She urged her listeners to make use of the fact that children of different age and personality also have different interests, and that this should be taken into account when teaching children how to pray.

"Some children want to play while they pray. Others want to draw or put colors on drawings while they pray. Parents can then ask them to make drawings of Jesus or the Virgin Mary during prayer. What is most important is that the children come to experience this love," Ivanka told the pilgrims.

While both visionaries said that making use of force cannot make children pray or go to church, Jakov suggested a better solution to a pilgrim who was sad that her children of age 17 and 20 have lost interest in living Christian lives.

"Pray for them and give them to Our Lady in prayer. And be an example for them," he said before going on to say that Medjugorje pilgrims are called to be an example for the world.

"The world is in need of experiencing the love of God. People need to see God in us; to see how God is working through us. That is the only way of being a true example of what Medjugorje is about. It is not important to come here to see us, the visionaries, or to look for signs. The biggest signs here are peace and conversion – people changing their lives," he said.

Indirectly answering Church officials and lay people who take the unusual duration of the apparitions as a sign against the authenticity of the Medjugorje apparitions, Jakov said that the question or objection is misapplied.

"We should never ask ourselves that question. What we need is to pay thanks to the Lord for sending His Mother to be with us so long. See how much He loves us: He loves us to the point of sending Her among us almost 20 years now," he said.

The visionary also took the opportunity to give a little pep-talk on fasting. From the beginning this discipline has been one out of five in the Virgin Mary's standard Medjugorje program for conversions to start and the world to grow better. The others are daily prayer, Mass and reading in the Bible, and confession of sins once a month.

"I have been fasting on bread and water every Wednesday and Friday since I was 10 years old. Fasting is not that hard. Many times we do things that we do not like to do, but we do it anyway although it is not all that important. On the contrary, fasting is very important. With prayer and fasting we can overcome everything," said Jakov.

Refusing to answer a question on the 10 prophetic secrets that are to be entrusted to each of the six Medjugorje visionaries (Colo and two others know all ten, whereas the remaining three seers have been told of nine such future events by the Virgin), the visionary preferred to emphasize that we are all in control of the future.

"We are in control of the future and capable of helping others if we allow God to live in us. Secrets are secrets, and you have to put the secrets aside," he said.

"Our secrets are our own lives. And how we choose to live them."

www.spiritdaily.com

Ivan

(9/03)
Interview with Ivan

The following is an excerpt from an interview with visionary Ivan Dragicevic by Damir Govorcin of "Catholic Weekly"while Ivan was in Australia in February this year.

CW: Can you describe what the Virgin Mary looks like?

ID: There aren't enough words to describe how beautiful Our Lady is. I could say that She has a gray dress, white veil, blue eyes, rosy cheeks, black hair, floats on a cloud, and a crown of stars. With every meeting with Our Lady, we always prepare with praying the Rosary, and we await Her coming. When Our Lady comes about 6:40 PM, but even before She comes, I can feel Her closeness in my heart. And then at that moment when I go to kneel, that is when Our Lady comes. When Our Lady comes I no longer see anyone in front of me, or behind me, I just see Her. Most of the time Our Lady comes joyful and at the beginning of Her arrival She always greets us with the greeting: "Praise be Jesus, dear children of mine." Sometimes She comes with angels, then after that greeting She prays over us with outstretched hands, She blesses us all with Her motherly blessing. She blesses any sacred objects that people have brought with them, then after that I recommend all the people who are at the apparition, all the sick, and those who have specifically asked for petitions. Then after that, I talk with Her. If She has a message She will give it to me – a message for the world, a message for priests, a message for families, a message for youth. Mainly the message Our Lady gives is for the whole world. As soon as I get the message I pass it on. I write it down straight away after the apparition, and then that message is sent to the whole world. Every time Our Lady goes after the end of the apparition, She always goes in the light of a cross with the greeting: "Go in peace dear children of mine." I see Our Lady three-dimensional; that means I see and talk to Her like I can with you. I can touch Her. If you ask me how old She is I say around 26 or 27 years old.

CW: You say you can touch Our Lady?

ID: I say I can touch Her if I want to, but I haven't. My children have. This was at Christmas time, when I lifted my children up and just looking at the reaction in my children's eyes when they were touching Her is difficult to put into words. My children – one is seven, one is three, and one is 16 months old – and you could see on their face the experience they had, that they lived. I didn't ask them about it because they are still young to describe this and how they felt. My children will be able to carry that gift and appreciate it.

CW: Are these the end times?

ID: No. We don't talk about the end of the world or the second coming of Jesus Christ. Our Lady didn't come to scare us; She doesn't come to talk to us about darkness. She is coming as the Mother of hope. She wants to bring a light into this world. She wants to bring us out of this darkness, and She wants to take us into a light and a new life. She wants to lift up this weary world, the weary families, weary young, weary Church. She desires to lift us up and strengthen us. She says: "Dear children, if you be strong, the Church will be strong. If you be weak, the Church will be weak. You are the living Church. Dear children, this world, this mankind has hope and has a future. But you have to begin to change. You have to come back to God."

CW: The Church has been under attack in recent times following the revelation of clergy sexual abuse. Has Our Lady shared with you her feelings on the matter?

ID: Our Lady hasn't said anything directly, but you can see Our Lady indirectly is calling us to pray specifically for this intention. Our Lady is always praying for Her children. Looking at the world not just with the priests, but looking at the crisis of the family. How many divorces there are, how many abortions, how many homeless children ... Our Lady is praying for all of this. That is why She came. She wants to tell us about the things that aren't good, and take us towards the good, show us what we have to do and that is to take Christ's gospel and live it. Return prayer to the family. Go to Mass, go to Confession, kneel in front of the cross, read the Bible in the family, forgive each other and love each other.

CW: In recent times, a lot of people have claimed that they see and speak to the Virgin Mary. Has Our Lady spoken about people coming as false prophets?

ID: Our Lady has never said anything about this, and I have never asked Her. A lot of people come to us and say that they see Our Lady. My position is that I can't say anything if Our Lady hasn't said anything. I would say to these people go and see your priest for advice.

CW: There has been criticism that the visionaries have made wealth from Medjugorje. How do you respond to this?

ID: All I can say is I will pray for these people. It's sad to say that there are a lot of people who think like that. It's nothing new, no surprise.

CW: There are people who suffer from a disease, such as cancer, and are in a lot of pain? Is it God's way of testing their faith?

ID: I meet a lot of people, especially the sick, on a daily basis. People come to me who are sick with cancer and all sorts of things. I always tell people, and I tell myself this, sickness no matter what type, we have to take and carry this as the will of God; that God is glorified through this. If it's God's will, He will make us better.

CW: *Can you describe Heaven and Hell?*

ID: Our Lady has showed me Heaven, but hasn't shown me Hell. She wanted to show me Hell, but I was scared. When I first saw Heaven, I was with Our Lady and I saw people walking, praying, singing, and they were wearing blue and white long robes. They were very happy. These people were, say, 35 to 40 years old. Heaven is a place without boundaries. I didn't see any fences. It is just its own special place. I was there for about three to four minutes. I can't describe Heaven's beauty. Remember what is said in the Gospel: "Eye has not seen, ear has not heard for those who come to know and love God."

CW: *Does it disappoint you and Our Lady that the Church has not given Medjugorje its full blessing?*

ID: No, I am not disappointed. The Church is always cautious. She follows. She asks and she is following the messages. I am praying for this intention. I wish to say what is said in the Gospel: "By their fruits you will know them."

CW: *What needs to be done to achieve peace in the world?*

ID: Peace in man's heart, peace in the family and then later that peace occurs. War always begins in man's heart and then it produces itself in other things. Every advice and wisdom outside of God is destined to fail. God has to be in the center, because only in God is peace. Whoever works with God goes towards peace and the world goes towards peace.

CW: *What do you see the role Medjugorje plays in the lives of people?*

ID: I believe Our Lady has touched so many in the world because She is a Mother. A lot of people, not just Catholics, have felt Her closeness. There have been lots of conversions in Anglicans, Protestants, and Methodists. They are all believers, but they were far away from their Mother. They came to realize that they must have a Mother. These people are praying the Rosary, going to Mass, reading the Bible. They have become big instruments in the hands of Our Lady and God. In today's world, we need these types of instruments. These people are going to carry Christ's word into this world. Today's world needs missionaries, and we are called to be missionaries.

CW: Tell me about yourself and your life.

ID: I don't like to talk much about myself, but in short my biography is this: I got married in 1994, and my wife is an American from Boston. We have three children – Christina, Mikaela and Daniel. We live in Medjugorje for six months and Boston for six months. In the winter we live in America because the kids go to school there. We live a type of life that our Lady is wanting from us. My life in the last 21 years has been a school, a school of peace, love and prayer. Everything that Our Lady has given, I want to bring into my family. I want to be a living sign – an instrument among men, a transmission – Our Lady, me, the world.

The Catholic Weekly, Sydney, Australia

(7/02)
Conversation with Ivanka Ivankovic-Elez

Q: Our Lady showed you Heaven and Purgatory. Can you describe them?

A: Heaven is the most beautiful place one can imagine, where you feel so much love and joy...In Purgatory I only saw gray darkness, and I heard prayers for help.

Q: Did you see anybody in Heaven besides Our Lady?

A: Once I saw baby angels and I saw Baby Jesus in Our Lady's arms at Christmas. Also I saw my mother in Heaven five times. My mother died two months before the apparitions started.

Q: How did you feel when you saw your mother?

A: I was very happy. I cried with joy.

Q: Did your mother look the same as you remembered her?

A: No, she did not look sick any more, and she looked more beautiful than when she was living on earth.

Ivanka

Q: Were you able to touch your mother?
A: Yes, when I saw my mother the 5th time, she hugged me and said, "My child, I am proud of you."

Q: What would you say to those who have lost loved ones?
A: Be glad for them, because they are in a better place. We are sad because we miss them, but they are free of suffering.

Q: How can we be sure that they are in Heaven?
A: If they lived according to God's commandments they will be in Heaven. If you are not sure, then you should pray for them and have a Holy Mass said for them, and you will see them in Heaven.

Q: Did Mary speak to more than one visionary at the same time in Medjugorje?

A: Yes, in fact, sometimes Our Lady would say different words to each of them at the same time. Also Our Lady appears to them at the same time even if they are not together. (Everything is possible with God.)

Q: I came back to church eight years ago. Is there a simple guide a simple retired soul like me can use to live by?

A: Somebody's prayers helped you to come back to church. If you can do the same for another person (or two) your mission on earth would be fulfilled.

Q: Is there any message of hope for us, who are unable to go to Medjugorje?

A: All that Our Lady is asking of us through the visionaries in Medjugorje is to live according to the teaching of Her Son, Jesus. We can do it in our own home.

Q: Is there hope for our dying parish?

A: Yes, begin prayer of the Rosary in your church with a few people. Our Lady will help you to wake up sleeping hearts.

Q: I struggle with discouragement and loneliness. Is there a message for me?

A: Yes, read Matthew, chapter 5.

Q: Why secrets? Is there frightening information about the future?

A: On the contrary, Our Lady in Medjugorje came to free us from our fears. She is teaching us how to live, how to talk to God with the heart, and obtain peace in ourselves and the world. Once we prepare ourselves, then we will be ready to hear and accept the Truth.

Q: How does Medjugorje fit into Lourdes and Fatima?

A: Our Lady appeared in Lourdes to one visionary in the morning. In Fatima, She appeared to three visionaries at noon. In Medjugorje, She appeared to the six in the evening and is still appearing. In one message, Our Lady said that She wants to complete the plans here in Medjugorje that She began in Fatima.

Mir Peace Letter

(10/00)
How Marija Receives and Passes on Messages

She described the process – in an interview – at the prayer meeting of Nov. 28, 1993, at the Palatrussardi in Milan. **You passed on special messages of the Madonna to the parish and to the world every Thursday from January 3, 1984 to January 25, 1987, and, from that date, on the 25th of each month only. What can you tell us about it?**

Yes, through me the Madonna gives these messages which She used to give Thursday and now every 25th of the month. She has said She gives these messages for all those who want to grow following the path of holiness. She has said that each of us is called to follow this path. However, the Madonna wanted, by means of these very simple messages, to call us to a very concrete life, to a very real path with God and the Church. In reality, the Madonna wanted to awaken us, to tell us how important we are for Her.

You have said more than once that you are convinced you have never made a mistake in passing on messages. How do you remember all the words, and how can you be sure to pass them on accurately?

Before passing on the message and writing it down, I say every time: "Let's pray." This is my assurance. If I don't pray, I lack confidence. When I pray I feel confident that I'm passing on the exact words. It can happen that at the end of the message, when I've already written it down, often it doesn't seem right. Once I began to cry and I said to Father Slavko, who is my spiritual guide, "I shall tell the Madonna not to give me the messages any more." But he said, "What's the matter? Isn't the message right?" Yes, the message is right, but once I've written it down, I can see that it isn't how the Madonna said it. At first the message seems so rich, so strong, so full. Then once it is written down it seems poor, empty...I can't explain it. They seem just words, and so I got upset and burst out, "That's enough, I can't pass on the messages any more." But then I understood: it is how you receive the message. Perhaps if the Madonna were to say it to each one of us it would seem different according to our availability. There is such an intensity of love and affection in the Madonna's words, that you can't transcribe them. Many times I have tried to describe what the Madonna is like and I look for the right words, but I have never found them, even though the behavior of the Madonna is very human. At times you can see She is a Queen, but She is also a Mother who understands, who loves, who suffers with us and gives us hope. In the world of today, the presence of the Madonna for such a long time is the most important message. As long as the Madonna is with us, there is hope.

The Children of Mary, Center for Peace

(4/99)
Mirjana's Question and Answer Session
Chicago Conference – September 13, 1998

Mirjana started the question and answer session by saying, "I'd like to say good morning to all of you, and I am prepared to hear everything that you have to ask me, and I am prepared to answer as much as I can."

Q: How will we know we will hear the secrets on TV, radio, shortwave, etc.?
A: You don't need to worry about this because that's the plan of God. And God through Fr. Petar will do the very best, and you will find out here also. You won't have to leave or move to another home or anything like that.

Q: Will Jakov choose a priest to whom he will confide the secrets at the time Our Lady decides?
A: I spoke with Jakov last night, and he received the tenth secret, and Our Lady told him that he would have apparitions once a year from now on, every Christmas. And that's all She told him till now,

but he knows that he does need to choose a priest, and he will do that, when he stops crying.

Q: Can you describe what your last daily apparition with Our Lady was like, the one on December 25, 1982? How did you feel?

A: I am laughing at Jakov now, but I know what it was like for me, and I know that it is not easy. And I understand him. That day was the worst day of my entire life. When Our Lady told me that I would no longer have daily apparitions of Her, I thought I was going to die. I thought I would go with Her, and to me, that was a beautiful idea. I can tell you, for example, that I am a mother of two children, and I would give my life for my children, but when I am with Our Lady, even my children don't exist for me. The only thing that exists for me is the desire for Her to take me with Her. And when I understand that She has to leave, and I must stay here, it is always very difficult for me, and I always have to be alone after the apparition for an hour or two to be in prayer. That's the way it is today, but you can imagine what it was like when She told me that I would no longer see Her every day.

Q: I know that Our Lady calls us to monthly confession, but I am very afraid of it and embarrassed to go. What do you suggest?

A: Nobody needs to be embarrassed before our Heavenly Father. He is the one who loves us, and He loves us with a pure love, and He is always prepared to forgive us. That's what Our Lady taught me. Because before the apparitions, I used to think that God was in Heaven and that He was just only in Heaven and that He was just looking down at me in my sins. But Our Lady taught me that's not the way it is. Last year Our Lady said to me, "I've been with you for 16 years, and through that gift, God is showing you how much He loves you." And so nobody needs to be embarrassed to kneel before God and to say what they have done. The important thing is to feel in your heart that you're sorry for what you've done and to feel that truly with your will you desire not to do those things again, and nothing else.

Q: Mirjana, do you know if Jakov, now that he will no longer see Our Lady everyday, will he see Her once a year as you and Ivanka are?

A: As I said, he will have apparitions every Christmas.

Q: Do the visionaries each have the same secrets?

A: We have never spoken among ourselves about the secrets because secrets are secrets. And so, none of us know what secrets the other one has. I can just tell you that we don't have private secrets. None of my secrets are secrets that relate only to me. The secrets are for the entire world.

Q: Please, can you give me an update on each visionary – who's married, how many children, where they are living, and also if they are working and what kind of work they are all doing?

A: And how much tax they pay annually? (Laughter) These kind of questions are very normal for us. I don't know if there are any Italians here, but Italians always ask those kinds of questions. One time an Italian woman here in America asked how much tax my husband pays! Ivanka lives in a village near Medjugorje which is called Milatina, and she has three children. She has two sons and a daughter. Marija is married to an Italian. I feel sorry for her. And she lives in Italy, and she has three sons. Jakov lives in Medjugorje, and he is also married to an Italian. And whenever he speaks to Italian groups, he always says, "I know what you guys are like. I have one at home!" He has two children, a son and a daughter. And I also live in Medjugorje, and I have two children, two daughters. Ivan is married to an American, and I also feel sorry for him! And they live part-time in Medjugorje and part-time in the United States. And they have one daughter. Vicka is not yet married. Jakov always jokes with her, and he says, "Nobody wants you yet!"

Q: How much longer do you expect Our Lady to continue to appear at Medjugorje?

A: I think She will appear every day until the rest of the visionaries receive the tenth secret, and those three that remain still are Vicka, Marija, and Ivan.

Q: How do you pray? What kind of prayers?

A: Everyday I pray the three Rosaries, the seven Our Father's, Hail Mary's, and Glory Be's, and the prayers I need to pray for nonbelievers. And one Rosary is always with the family, and that's always the Joyful Mystery because with children it is always joyful.

Q: Does the Blessed Mother look like the picture and statues we have of Her? What is Her voice like, is it soft?

A: I have never seen a picture or statue of Our Lady that I could say looks like Our Lady because I think it is impossible. Because it is not just an outer beauty we see; it is something that breathes from within Her. It is something like a mother's beauty. And when people sometimes ask me do I have anything to compare this with, perhaps the only thing I can say to compare it to is when a mother gives birth to her child, the first time that child is placed in her arms. Our Lady's expression and face most resembles that moment. I can try to describe Her. She is a little taller than me. She always has a gray dress and a white veil, except for Christmas and Easter, when She wears a gold dress. And She has long black hair, you see it here on the side of Her head and on the side by Her waist, which means She has long hair. She has blue eyes, and She is most beautiful. Because as I already said, it is impossible to describe the beauty that comes from within Her. When we were children, we asked Her children's questions. We asked Her, "How is it possible you are so beautiful?" And She smiled at us, and She said, "It's because I love," and She said, "My dear children, if you desire to be beautiful, then love." And at that time when She said this, Jakov was only ten years old. And when Our Lady left, Jakov said, "I think Our Lady is not speaking the truth here." And we asked him, "How can you say Our Lady is not speaking the truth?" He said, "Look at the six of us visionaries – we could love our entire lives and we would never be beautiful!" That's why he is having apparitions for 17 years!

Q: Mirjana, can you tell us about the beginning times of the apparitions when the villagers were with you and the other visionaries? The time I am referring to is when the visionaries got to touch the Blessed Virgin, and can you tell us more about this time?

A: Yesterday, I spoke about the beginning days of the apparitions, but I didn't mention that day when Our Lady allowed us to touch Her. That apparition took place in a hidden place in the village because that's the way it was in the beginning; we needed to hide from the very beginning. And Our Lady allowed all of those who were present to touch Her. And suddenly, we all saw that black spots were being left on Her dress, and Marija began to cry, and she said, "Don't touch Her! Don't you see that you are sinful?!" And then Our Lady left. [Translator's note: Mirjana and I have a cousin in common, and our cousin was 13 years old at the time, and this cousin said, "I washed my hands well before this time!"]

Q: Has the Virgin Mary ever talked about Heaven, Hell, or Purgatory? Where do the majority of souls go?

A: Our Lady has spoken about Heaven, Hell, and Purgatory. One day Our Lady showed Heaven, Hell, and Purgatory to Vicka and Jakov because those two were the only ones that were able to hide from the police that day. The rest of the four of us, the police took away that day. Then they told me that when Our Lady came that day, She said to them, "Now I will take you with me." They thought they were going to die. At that time, Jakov was also still ten years old. And Jakov's reply to that was, when he thought he was going to die, he said to Our Lady, "My dear Lady, Vicka has seven brothers and sisters, and I am an only child! Why don't you take her?" And Our Lady smiled at him, and She said, "No, I just want to show you that Heaven, Hell, and Purgatory do exist." And so the two of them saw this.

Q: What day do you pray with the Gospa for nonbelievers – every Tuesday, or once each month, or daily?

A: I pray specifically with Our Lady for nonbelievers on the second day of each month. Myself, individually, I pray daily for them.

Mirjana after her second of the month apparition

Q: Does Mary think the secrets will be revealed by the year 2000? Also, will this be the end of all apparitions, by 2000? Will the Triumph come by 2000, as an era of peace upon us?

A: I truly can't respond to these beautiful questions because secrets are secret. When they begin, we will see what will happen and when. I said yesterday, don't be like Fr. Petar, but you seem to be worse!

Q: Mirjana, I was in Medjugorje recently, and it had a deep impact on me. Why do you think so many get converted there? After all, Our Lord and Our Lady are also present in our churches here. P.S. What do you think of Chicago? Have you seen any of our city?

A: I'll start from the beginning. It's true that Our Lady and Our Lord are present in all the churches of the world. Our Lady says, "Open your hearts and call to me, and I'll be with you." She doesn't say that just to us visionaries; She says that to all of Her children. And now I want to tell you my personal opinion, that those who come to Medjugorje, that they are invited there by Our Lady. I'll take the Americans here, for example – who among you would leave your family and home and go on such a long way if you weren't invited to do so by Our Lady? Why would you do that if it was only because somebody told you about Medjugorje, if it was just that somebody told you about a little village somewhere in Bosnia-Herzegovina? I think it is Our Lady who places the call in our hearts to come, and many people who do go there suffer a lot, and they don't know what's waiting for them, but they're prepared to undertake everything for Our Lady. And that is why I think there are so many conversions and so many graces. Simply said, pilgrimages are necessary to recharge our batteries. I have already been to Chicago a couple times, and only last night for an hour was I able to actually see something. Thanks to Ann; she was a good tour guide.

Q: Did Our Lady say that Medjugorje is the last time She will appear on earth?

A: Our Lady never said it that way. People that want to create sensationalism say that because they pick and choose the things that they like. What Our Lady said was that, "This is the last time I will be on earth **in this way.**" She said clearly that in this way, this is the last time She will be on earth. And through my own prayer, I came to think what She meant was that this is the last time that She will be for this long of a period of time and with this many visionaries, not that She will never come to earth again.

Q: Mirjana, thank you for coming, God bless you. What can I do to best help in the conversion of my husband and others to believe in the teachings of the Catholic Church and the benefits of Mary in our lives?

A: First, thank you for the blessing and the welcome. First of all, the best thing that you can do is to give an example and to pray, and don't criticize and don't give lectures. But very simply to pray and live an example and to place the lives of those dear to us who are unbelievers into the hands of Our Lady. That is where they are most secure. I always say, "My dear Lady, I will pray, but You pray to Your Son that He does something." We can all say the same thing.

Q: Will you tell us about Heaven and Purgatory?

A: I do not want to speak about that because I didn't see it with my own eyes. Because it's different to tell what you heard from someone than to talk about what you experienced yourself. So better when you come to Medjugorje that Jakov and Vicka can tell you about it.

Q: It is widely believed that the ten secrets that you yourself have received are of such severity that Our Lady now comes to you at special times to help you cope with the immense responsibility. Other past apparent apparitions throughout the world speak of purification, warning, and chastisements, yet I have heard both you and Ivan speak against the idea of natural or supernatural impending disasters. Why the difference between your reaction to these two scenarios?

A: I don't know where it is that people are getting the idea that the ten secrets are so horrible because we never said that they're beautiful or that they're horrible. Those are private conclusions that people make. Our Lady has not come to me the second day of every month to comfort me. She has come to me to pray for Her children who have not yet experienced the love of God. But She said to me that the thing that will comfort me is the Rosary, but not that every time I need comforting that She will comfort me. And I don't know why that should be so.

Q: How has the war affected the people of different faiths living in Medjugorje? Do they still live in peace and harmony?

A: In Medjugorje, there really are not people of different faiths. We are all Catholics there, and it has always been that way. And so even now we do live in peace and harmony.

Q: I am trying to be better at the call to fast because I think God has blessed me with good health and an excellent appetite, but it's hard to resist and be faithful. Do you have any secrets for success? Please pray for me to endure.

A: I can tell you about my individual opinion because Our Lady said to me, just like She said to all of you, that on Wednesdays and Fridays we must fast on bread and water. It's not a difficult thing for me to do because I know why I am doing that. Through this act I am showing God that I love Him and that I am prepared to do something for Him, but not just ask things of Him. Because in my heart, I feel a great thankfulness for every little thing in my life. For example, this morning I was able to wake up on my own two feet and that is a gift, thanks be to God. Because we don't see these little, minute things until something horrible happens to us. And so in my heart, I desire to say a thank-you to God. I think it's not a lot that Our Lady asks us to fast on Wednesdays and Fridays on bread and water. And on Wednesdays and Fridays, I find I can pray better, maybe because I suffer more.

Q: How will we find out when the ten secrets are revealed to the priest?

A: As I said, you don't have to worry about anything, you'll know everything. As you can see, women can't keep secrets!

Q: Instead of bread and water when I fast, I fast on coffee only. It keeps me more alert, especially when driving. Would this offend Our Mother?

A: I don't understand this. I can't judge. I am not the one who can say what we need to do. I can only report that what Our Lady says. She says bread and water. She didn't mention coffee. But as I said yesterday, maybe you should take it earlier, before Our Lady wakes up!

Q: Has Our Lady given any indication that She will leave a sign or miracle at Medjugorje as She did at Fatima?

A: Yes, Our Lady will leave a sign at the Hill of Apparitions, and everybody will see that She was truly present there and that it's something from God. And the sign will be something that when you see it, it will be clear that it could not have been created by human hands. But you won't see it from America, you'll have to come there to see it. Pilgrims from the United States often ask me if we will be able to see it from home or will we have to go there to see it.

Q: Has Mary ever said anything on how we can overcome human pride?

A: Through fasting and prayer. Only in that way will we truly understand what is most important in life. Because in life we do have all the good material things of life, but if we don't have Jesus in our hearts, then we don't have anything. Because Jesus is the one who gives us peace, and if we have Jesus in our hearts, then we have peace. And in that way, we can then know how to judge what is good and what is bad and how we are to be better. Only through Jesus.

That's the last of the questions. I want to thank you for everything. Thank you for a beautiful welcome, and I want to tell you that I truly felt very good here. Thank you for this. Today I am going back to Medjugorje, and I will bring all of you back with me. I will pray to Our Lady that She may help you because I know that each one of us is carrying a cross in our lives. And I will pray to Our Lady that She not leave you alone in your crosses.

Editor's note: Thanks to Mike Sepal of Seattle, Washington, who transcribed this talk from the audiotape.

Marija (right) with her translator

(6/00)
Marija
By June Klins

On June 25, the 18th anniversary of the apparitions, Marija spoke in the new building behind the church. She looked and acted very different from her speaking appearance last year. Her curly hair-do and her constant smile seemed to look more like Vicka. She even told a few humorous stories during her talk, which was quite different from her serious demeanor last year.

Marija began her talk by speaking about her apparition the night before. She said that during this encounter, Our Lady reminded the visionaries how they felt during the first days of the apparitions. It was during these early days that the children began to pray all day. At that time Our Lady became their best friend and She helped them grow up in prayer.

Marija said that Our Lady, when She gives Her messages, uses concrete language and talks to every person. She wants our lives to become a prayer. She wants us to pray the Rosary every day, and to place the Holy Bible in a visible place in our homes and to read it every day. She wants us to form prayer groups and to have prayer meetings on a regular basis.

Marija continued that Our Lady wants us to become concrete, meaning that She wants us to be as holy outside the church as we are when we are inside the church. Marija gave an example of people ending birthday parties with the Rosary, and how lives begin to change when Her messages become the center of their lives. (Later on that evening, when our group had a party to celebrate the anniversary, we took Marija's advice by ending the party with 15 decades of the Rosary.)

Then Marija got a little more personal and talked about her own experiences. She admitted that she was very shy at first and did not like talking to the pilgrims, but through the years she learned how to witness and talk in front of people. She said that it is easier now because she and the other visionaries talk from their hearts. They consider themselves instruments in God's hands.

Marija laughed as she told a cute story about a woman who wanted to make clothes for all the visionaries so that they looked like apostles. She stressed that the visionaries are not important. She said that only Our Lady is important. According to Marija, She is our "greatest friend."

Marija concluded her brief talk by saying that God should be the top priority in our lives, and the way to do it is through prayer. Our Lady told the visionaries that man wants to place himself first, instead of placing God first. Careers and money rank before God for too many people. Pilgrims always come with problems, but when we begin to pray, our families will begin to change. Every day we can say to ourselves, "My old life is done, and my new life is beginning." When we place God first in our lives, Marija stressed, we won't have any problems, and prayer will become a joy for us.

(4/98)
Visionary Visits Seattle, Washington

Medjugorje visionary Ivan Dragicevic spoke in Seattle, Washington on October 29, 1997. The following is an excerpt from his presentation, which was tape recorded and transcribed by Linda Rogers and printed in the November 1997 Children of Mary Center for Peace newsletter:

Q: Through the years Our Lady has appeared, is She happy with the progress that people are making, or is She sad?

Ivan: When we look at the whole world, and what has happened, Our Lady is happy with the spiritual conversion, with spiritual renewal in this world, but of course, there is so much more to come, and She is asking for more.

Q: Does She speak to you at all about the other apparitions throughout the world where She is appearing?

Ivan: Our Lady has never spoken to me anything about it. Many people have asked these kinds of questions and I can't really answer in my position about them. I am not competent about this, so we must leave it to the Church and let the Church make the judgments.

Q: What can you tell us about Heaven, Hell, and Purgatory?

Ivan: I can't talk about all three because I only saw Heaven. I know that you are waiting for me to describe Heaven, but I'm not really capable of describing Heaven because the beauty is indescribable. I always like to say it like this: if we go, when we go, we will see the best what it is.

Q: When you receive all 10 secrets or when Our Lady stops appearing, will the "school of prayer" be finished?

Ivan: No. Do you know when the "school of prayer" will end? It is when we die. Our conversion ends when we die. We are in the process our whole lifetime of converting and learning how to pray, and these are gifts that we must pray for.

Q: Is it true that when Our Lady stops appearing in Medjugorje, She will no longer appear again on earth?

Ivan: In this way, no. In this kind of apparition, no.

Q: What do you know about the sign that everyone will see throughout the world? Does just Vicka know that or do you? Do you know when or does Vicka?

Ivan: Yes. Everybody will be able to see. Yes, I know when and I know what.

Q: Should we be afraid?

Ivan: I'm not afraid. Don't fear. Don't fear. This past 15 years Our Lady has been guiding us to the year 2000, to the millennium. I would suggest that together with Her we prepare ourselves, and that is why She is guiding us. We need to pray together with Her about this plan that will happen that She knows, and we need to pray with Her for that to become a reality.

Chapter Three:

Testimonies

(7/98)
Pilgrimage
By Joan Wieszczyk

I was a person who journeyed a long distance to a place I call very sacred. Holy indeed, for I believe that the Mother of God is appearing and has been appearing there for over 17 years now. Medjugorje has become my spiritual home as far as travels go. Anyone who has traveled there knows what a long journey it is. It wouldn't be as long if it weren't for those long layovers. One of the longest is Zagreb, in the former Yugoslavia. I guess our Mother gives them to us to test us in our patience. You know that patience is a virtue, virtue is a grace, and those that possess it have a smiling face. Still in all, it is a long wait.

I just came back from Medjugorje at the end of April of this year. When I came back people asked me how was my trip. The truth is that every one is different. No two are alike.

I like to peek into my previous visits (10 with the villagers). What an experience that was! They considered us a part of their family. They gave up their bedrooms so that we would have a good night's rest. (I heard the rooster crow before the sun came up.) The wife cooked us homemade meals. They spoke very little English, but we managed to communicate by using sign language, laughing and smiling a lot. I especially noticed that the man of the house was in charge, not like the United States where men and women are equal. The husband enjoyed showing off his vintage, the red and white wines. A special treat to the men in our group (not women) was their strong vodka. As a going away present, we were presented a bottle or two of their homemade wines. I still have a few bottles.

It seemed as if everyone in the village was in some way or other related to the visionaries. At least, that is what we were told. We were privileged to stay with one of Vicka's relatives.

It was on my first visit that I learned how to fast. In the beginning, I did not understand it and I did not like it. When I returned home, it sunk in. I have carried that part of the Medjugorje message in my heart ever since.

Only once have I stayed at the same place twice. Every time I go, I would try to visit with my original family. I was excited to know someone in the village. So I would bring something from home to them.

All this has changed. No longer does our group split up and live in a one-family house where you had to share a bathroom with 6 or 7 people. Now there are pansions (hotels) with a full bath (shower) and 2 beds in a room. Plenty of space for everyone. You can even request a room for yourself. That, of course, costs extra. The visionaries at times take in pilgrims, something they did not do in the earlier days.

One of the pansions in Medjugorje

I also remember visiting Medjugorje while it was under the communist regime. I remember seeing the communist helicopters flying over St. James Church. At that time, the only way we could get to Medjugorje was by JAT, a communist airline. I am so elated and thankful to God that Medjugorje is now free. That was a big change!

One of the big thrills was being in St. James Church when Our Lady would appear to the visionaries. I will never forget the time my friend and I both witnessed the flashing golden rays of magnificent light bouncing on and off the church walls during the time of the apparition. As crowded as it was, we knelt down on our knees thanking Jesus for giving us this great sign.

The seers were still single then, and at least 2 or 3 of them would be in the choir loft. Now, all but one is married and they all have families. Two of the visionaries no longer have daily apparitions. The other 4 have them, wherever they may be at the time, Our Lady appears to them.

The church is still packed for the Rosary in the late afternoon. There is a silent pause during the Sorrowful Mysteries, but the visionaries are not necessarily present. I think this is good, for I am sure that Our Lady does not want us to focus on the visionaries, but to focus our thoughts on the mysteries of the Rosary. It teaches us to pray with the heart. I love how everyone prays in their own language. It is dynamic!

The evening Croatian Mass in St. James Church (now air-conditioned and renovated) is usually overflowing with people hearing the Mass outdoors. The priests have to come outdoors to give Holy Communion to the people who could not get in the church.

Evening adoration is the same. People crowding into the church, standing room only, overflowing into the entrance. Imagine how it is in the summer. This was only last April when I was there.

Then there are the visits to the visionaries. We usually get to hear Vicka speak about what the messages of Medjugorje contain. Sometimes even Mirjana or Jakov, and even Ivan will give talks to the pilgrims. That is one of the highlights in the pilgrimage - meeting with a visionary and, if you are lucky, being present at one of the prayer meetings at night on the mountain.

Since the visionaries are older now and are traveling to other countries to deliver the messages, so are the priests. One such priest that we all wanted to see and hear is Father Jozo. (Father Jozo was pastor of St. James Church when the apparitions began in 1981.) If Father Jozo is not traveling, he welcomes all the pilgrims that come to Medjugorje. His message on Medjugorje is very powerful! A blessing, a rosary, and a portrait of Our Lady are great mementos of a visit to Father Jozo.

It is much easier to go to confession in Medjugorje now. They have the outdoor covered confessionals in which priests are hearing confessions in all different languages. It is a must to go to confession while on your pilgrimage to this holy place. It is part of Her message.

Both Mt. Krizevac (hill of the huge cross) and Mt. Podbrdo (the first place of apparitions) are still as rocky as before. It seems harder for me to climb them each time I go. Believe me, the rocks are not getting any smaller. People still go barefoot at times up these mountains. I'm sure that they are getting many blessings.

The sanitation situation (restrooms) near the church was very rough going without plumbing. Now there is a new building with full facilities that are very modern. That is a big change and a needed one.

When you are on a group pilgrimage, you are served 2 meals daily. Most likely, they are breakfast and a late supper. Lunch is on your own. Earlier, there were not many restaurants to buy lunch. Today, there are many and you have a choice.

Everyone wants to take home souvenirs. There is no trouble finding shops to shop in. They are all over. You can shop in the Franciscan store near the church and across the street, around the corner, and even on the hills. One thing I noticed was that most of the shops on the hill (Podbrdo) are closed during the Croatian evening Mass. Apparently they are in church. I would like to suggest to those pilgrims in Medjugorje that you spend more time in praying and less time shopping. That is one thing I noticed. In the earlier days, people were less distracted.

Praying…there are many places to go to be alone for personal prayer. There is the Adoration Chapel, the hills, the blue cross, the candle area and even the cemetery.

There still are some supernatural signs occurring in Medjugorje but they are not as prevalent to me as they were in my earlier visits. On my last visit, I was surprised to see so many people flocking to Medjugorje. It was as if there was never a war around that area. People came from all over. Medjugorje is alive with many pilgrims including priests and bishops. It was old home week for me. I enjoyed being with all my sisters and brothers in Christ.

All in all, I would have to say that Medjugorje has grown and it has changed, but the messages which are the most important, have

not changed. They are the same. And "Gospa" is still appearing.......
"Thank you, Jesus!"

Editor's update: All the visionaries are married now, as stated in Chapter 1.

(10/01)
A Medjugorje Surprise
By June Klins

Every Medjugorje pilgrimage is full of surprises, and my June, 2001 pilgrimage was no exception. Like thumbprints or zebra stripes, no two pilgrims' experiences are exactly alike. On this trip, some people had the awesome experience of seeing our priest's hair and face turn gold during the Corpus Christi procession. I didn't. Some people, actually most of my group, saw the sun spin. I didn't. Some people saw the cross on Mt. Krizevac disappear, and one lady saw the cross on fire. I didn't. Some people had things said to them that could not have been known by the person who said it. I didn't. These were all gifts to the people who experienced them, "a hug from the Blessed Mother," explained Sandee McAleer, our group leader. My surprise in Medjugorje was quite different from all of these, but nonetheless, just as exciting. My surprise is the story I am about to relate. And I wouldn't trade it to see the sun spin a hundred times!

My story actually began when I was in Medjugorje for the 18th anniversary. It was very crowded, so I was sitting on a curb on the side of the church for the outdoor Croatian Mass. After Mass, during the Glorious Mysteries, an adorable little boy holding a rosary walked up and looked at me, so I took out my camera and snapped a photo of him. I forgot about taking this picture until I got my photographs back from the developer. As soon as I saw that picture, I knew there was something special about it. To me, this little boy just seemed to be a "poster boy for the Rosary." Everyone I showed agreed. One lady looked at the picture and said, "Those eyes – they are the eyes of Jesus." It was if the little boy were urging, "Please pray the Rosary with me."

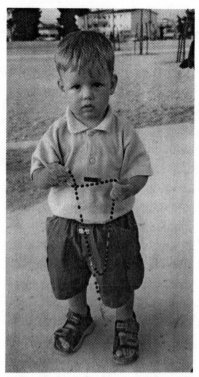

"Please pray the Rosary with me!"

A year later, I decided to have a tote bag made with my photo. Next to the picture were the words of Jesus, "Whoever does not accept the Kingdom of God like a child will not enter it." As more and more people would admire the bag, the light bulb went on in my head. Maybe I could have some more bags made and ask a suggested donation to give to an orphanage. So I gave it a whirl. The first batch went fast, so I had more made. Now I needed an orphanage to give the donations to, so I did some research on the Internet, and was overwhelmed by the number of orphanages in the world. I sent out letters and e-mails with pictures of my tote to many organizations that support orphanages. I was disappointed that I never heard from any of them.

Then, in the first week of October, I was looking at a flyer for a Medjugorje conference in Ohio and I noticed that it said that profits from the conference would benefit Hearts of the World Marian Center for Sister Janja's orphanage in Mostar, near Medjugorje. I thought it was worth a try to send them a picture of the tote, and so I did. A few weeks later, I got a phone call from a very excited woman who heads up the Hearts of the World Marian Center. She said she loved the idea of the totes, and wanted to take me up on my offer. Periodically I would send her the money I made on the totes for her to give to Sister Janja. Many people asked me who the little boy was, and wondered if he were an orphan. I said that he was not an orphan, that he was with a family when I took the photo. I had no idea where the little boy was from. There were reportedly 75,000 people in Medjugorje at the time, from many different countries.

Last spring my son and I were invited to go to Medjugorje again and we went with Hearts of the World. One of the side-trips they make is to Mostar to visit Sister Janja's orphanage. So, on Saturday, June 16, we made the 45-minute trip to the orphanage. Several of us had money to present to Sister Janja for the orphanage. When I gave Sister the latest donation I showed her my bag. Sister took one look at the tote and said, "That looks like little Boris." And then she did a double-take and said, "That is little Boris." It turns out that the child I had been calling "my poster boy for the Rosary" had actually been an orphan under Sister's care years earlier. I could not believe it. I burst into tears. What an awesome surprise, a surprise that could only have been orchestrated from Above! It became very clear to me now why none of the other orphanages had answered my letters! Sometimes when it seems that God is not cooperating with us, even when we are trying to do something good, it is because He has something BETTER in mind. He ALWAYS knows best.

This is not the end of the story though...

After I composed myself, Sister Janja proceeded to give me a little history on Boris. She said that Boris was placed in the orphanage at a young age when his mother, who was a single parent, became unable to care for him because she was disabled. Sister said that a beautiful and loving family adopted him a couple of years ago. She said that she had not heard anything about Boris in years, but recently had heard an incredible story about him that she would share with us. Sister said that about 3 weeks earlier Boris woke up one night at 1:00 A.M., jumped out of his bed and went running into his parents' room crying. When his mother asked him what was wrong, he said that he had dreamt that she had died. She hugged him and consoled him that she was just fine, and let him sleep the rest of the night between her and her husband. At 8:00 the next morning, Boris' mother got a call from a lady in the social office in central Bosnia. She called to say that Boris' biological mother passed away in the night. When Boris' mother inquired about the time of death, the woman answered, "About 1:00 A.M."

This story took the breath away from all of us who heard it. My first reaction to this story was to say, "This is a very special little boy," and Sister Janja agreed completely.

I felt so very blessed to have been gifted with the photo of this little angel. I have always felt that the best way to show appreciation for a gift is to use it. So I will continue to carry my little tote bag, which people now know as my "trademark." The bag is, after all, a very inexpensive "mobile billboard," a shrewd way to promote Our Lady's messages.

"With a little child to guide them... the earth shall be filled with knowledge of the Lord" (Is 11: 6, 9).

(6/03)
Sweet Fruit of Medjugorje
"He Was Lost and Has Been Found"
By Rev. James A. Wiley

How does one put into words the immeasurable love, mercy, forgiveness of our Heavenly Father toward His prodigal children? We can never probe the depths in this life. My purpose in writing this article is to show how His love, mercy, and forgiveness led me back to the Church and to the priesthood.

In June of 1974, I turned my back on God, the Church, and the priesthood. The decision to walk away from everything I had once valued did not come overnight. It was several years in the making, and I vowed never to return to the Church or the priesthood.

The seventeen years that followed my departure from active ministry were difficult and trying for me. But once I made up my mind, there was no turning back. A priest friend of mine once asked if I ever thought of returning. While I appreciated his concern for me, I told him it was impossible because I had stopped believing. Was God real? Was He a force in the universe? Was He a personal God? ... I wasn't sure any more. Spiritually I had hit bottom. I guess there was nowhere to go but up.

In August of 1988, a friend of mine had just returned from Medjugorje. He told me about six children who said they had seen the Blessed Virgin. She had special messages for the children and the world. In a nice way I told him I didn't believe in apparitions or miracles. We left it at that.

Several weeks later, I was watching a program called "Pittsburgh Today." The afternoon segment was devoted to the strange happenings in a little village in Yugoslavia called Medjugorje. Four individuals were going to share their experiences regarding the apparitions. One man was a journalist from KDKA T.V. in Pittsburgh, PA. There were two attorneys, husband and wife, from Pittsburgh, and a woman who claimed she had been cured of multiple sclerosis through the intercession of Our Lady of Medjugorje. For some unknown reason, I decided to tape the show for later viewing. That evening I played the tape, not once, not twice, but three times. I just couldn't get enough. I wanted to know more, and I wrote to the station asking for more information.

Slowly but surely my life began to change. Up to this point, any theology I professed was almost totally opposed to the teaching of the Church. At one point, I had denied the whole sacramental system, especially the Church's teaching on the Eucharist. What happened next was difficult to explain because it didn't happen in any sequence. I suddenly realized I believed again. There were no more doubts, no more questioning. I believed. Thank God, I believed.

I hadn't been to Confession for 18 years and I felt the need to tell it all to a priest. I sought out a Franciscan at Our Lady of the Point Church in Pittsburgh. When I walked out of the church, I was spiritually clean for the first time in many years.

The thought of returning to active ministry and priesthood had not entered my mind. I was happy and content with my new found faith – what more could I ask for? And then it happened. It was

Saturday morning, September 24, 1988, the former feast of Our Lady of Ransom. I woke up about 5:30 A.M. The first thing that came into my mind was that I should return to the priesthood. I had to be dreaming, but the thought would not go away. The thought of returning to priesthood haunted me the entire weekend.

I sought out my pastor and told him what was happening with me. He listened and then told me he would make some inquiries for me. Presuming this whole incident would all be forgotten in a few days, I told him to take his time. My job as a counselor at a mental health center was satisfying and I wanted to keep it that way. We are talking about a major job change, and I wasn't sure if I could handle that. I was anxious, to say the least.

The pastor told me it was possible to return to active ministry, but I would have to update my theology, Sacred Scripture, and Canon Law. Once this was satisfied, my case would be reviewed, and a decision would be made. So I quit my job, took up residence at a parish in Erie, and updated for the next 11 months.

One day I received a call from the bishop. He had good news. Rome had responded in my favor, and I had been returned to active ministry and priesthood. I was so overjoyed, I thought I would cry. It was like receiving the news of my ordination, April 25, 1958.

In June of 1993, I made a pilgrimage to Medjugorje to give thanks to God and Our Lady for the many blessings and graces I've received. The high point of the trip was the climb up Cross Mountain, where I got on my knees to give thanks. Concelebrating Mass each day in St. James Church was an experience I shall always remember. What happiness – what tears of joy!

November 6, 2003, will mark 13 years of active ministry. They've been among the happiest years of my life. My priorities have changed. God is now first in my life. I have a deeper appreciation of the Church and the priesthood. I attribute my return first to God, second, to Our Lady, and third, to the prayers of my mother, who prayed for seventeen years. I asked her if she ever thought I would return to the priesthood. She said she didn't know if it were possible – she just prayed. She lived to help me celebrate my "second first Mass." She died in 1995.

The parable of the Prodigal Son is my favorite, for obvious reasons. The father said to the elder son, "Now we must celebrate and rejoice because your brother was dead and has come back to life. He was lost and has been found." Amen.

Editor's note: Fr. Wiley lives in Hermitage, PA.

Brian with Bosnian woman in Medjugorje

(10/04)
My Son's Miracle- The Power of the Rosary
By June Klins

It was September 8, the day the Church celebrates Our Lady's birthday. I had no sooner arrived home from an out-of-town retreat when I received a phone call from my husband Tom requesting that I come down to the hospital right away. Upon arrival at the hospital, Tom broke the news to me that our son Brian was in surgery to repair damage he had done when he accidentally shot himself in the leg and severed a major artery. Tom was there when they brought him in, and his description of Brian was that he looked "like a casualty victim from Vietnam." Then he handed me a bank envelope and said, "Here is Brian's rosary. It is covered with mud and Brian wants to leave it that way." I went to the chapel in the hospital and knelt in front of the Tabernacle and prayed countless Rosaries until I thought it was time for Brian to come out of surgery. When it was time for us to see Brian, I could not believe my eyes. After Tom's description,

I expected the worst. Instead, I found Brian sitting up and talking and joking with the nurses. He even requested to watch the video "Young Guns!"

During the days that followed, Brian shared his experience with me. Brian told me that early on the morning of the 8th, he had a strange premonition that something was going to happen to him that day. Since it was a beautiful day, he decided to spend some time in the woods nearby. As he headed towards the woods though, he felt the urge to turn around and go back home to get the wooden rosary he had brought from Medjugorje last summer.

When Brian got to the woods he did some target shooting, and as he was putting his gun into his holster, his gun accidentally went off and hit him in the upper right thigh. Brian immediately blacked out, and when he came to, he could not hear or see anything for a time. When he realized what had happened, he yelled for help. He did not recall having seen anyone else in the woods that day though. Brian realized very quickly that he could not walk, so he tried to hop on his other leg. Each time he would try to stand up though, he would fall down again. Weakened from the loss of blood, he fell to the ground and began crawling on his belly. It was not long before he noticed he was bleeding so profusely that his jeans looked like they could be used for a Santa Claus suit in December. They weighed him down so much from the blood and the mud he was crawling in, that he eventually removed them so he could continue to move. Brian then removed his shirt and tried to make a tourniquet with it, but it was not successful because his leg had become so swollen. Soon Brian became dehydrated, so he crawled to the mud puddles and sipped the water out of them. He said that he had to stick his lips down into the puddles because of the layers of gas and oil from the ATV's that formed a film on top of the puddles. He said that by that point, even the stagnant mosquito-infested water in the mud puddles tasted good. During this time Brian's hearing began to fade in and out, and his breathing became labored. As he continued to crawl from mud puddle to mud puddle, he screamed for help, but there seemed not to be another soul in the woods that day. This went on for 2 1/2 to 3 hours.

Before Brian discarded his jeans, he took out of the pocket his wooden rosary from Medjugorje. He wrapped it around the fingers of his left hand, and crawled to the next puddle. As he lay on his back in the puddle he relaxed and began to pray the Rosary. Brian said that before he found his rosary he was very angry, but as he began to pray the Rosary he relaxed and came to terms with the idea that he might not make it out of the woods. Dragging himself from puddle to puddle, he continued to pray the Rosary. Finally he reached what looked to be the last puddle. In front of him was a big hill. He made himself as comfortable as possible, and prepared to die. He closed his eyes as he prayed in his Rosary for God to send him an angel to rescue him, or if that was not God's plan, then to let him die peacefully. "Hail Mary, full of grace..." Then he heard the noise of motors! With what little strength he had left after having crawled approximately 500 yards, he yelled for help. Two men on ATV's heard his cries and came over and asked him what was wrong. By this point, he was not bleeding anymore because he was virtually out of blood. He told them that he had been shot. Then they asked what was in his hand. Barely able to breathe, much less speak, he answered, "My rosary." The men helped him onto one of the 4-wheelers for the half-hour ride to the nearest house, where they called 911.

Brian's surgery was successful. Amazingly, the bullet had exited the leg through the back and had not done any damage to the bone, surrounding muscle or major nerve. The next day when the policeman came to the hospital, he told us how very lucky Brian was. He said that if the men on the ATV's had not picked Brian up when they did, he would not have survived. If they had gone for help and then come back, it would have been too late. He had not much more than 20 minutes left.

When the policeman gave us the names of the men on the 4-wheelers, we called them right away to thank them. Eric Swindlehurst and Christopher Firment both humbly admitted that it was God who saved Brian, that they had just been in the right place at the right time. Both men told us that they had not been planning on going 4-wheeling that day, that it was a spur of the moment decision. They also told us that they almost never go to that part of the woods, and had not been there in months. What is even more amazing is that even with their helmets on they were able to hear Brian's cries for help over their loud motors. And where they found Brian was the exact opposite direction of the way Brian had intended to go. Brian had been so disoriented, as he faded in and out of consciousness, that he headed the wrong direction in the woods he had been so familiar with since he was a child. Brian was also surprised that the men were able to see him at all, because his whole body except for his head was immersed in the deep puddle.

Several months later, as I was telling this story, a nurse asked me how much damage Brian sustained. She was surprised when I told her that he had no damage at all. She said that because of the large loss of blood over a long period of time he should have had kidney, liver, and/or brain damage. He could have lost his leg and he could have gotten a terrible infection from the stagnant water. Other medical personnel I have spoken with agreed. Brian was back at his college classes a week and a half later and began jogging again the following month. Brian even made the Dean's List that semester for the first time! Our Lady of Medjugorje said, "The Rosary alone can already work miracles in the world and in your lives" (1/25/91).

There is a footnote to this story, which is just as miraculous as the story itself. The day after Brian was rescued, my husband, who is a U.S. Army Reserve Criminal Investigator, went down into the woods to follow the path where Brian crawled, and took photographs. As he was showing the photos at the hospital, someone noticed that in the mud where Brian crawled with his rosary was an image of Mary! Mary is holding a rosary. Then we noticed another image, which we later concluded was Joseph because Baby Jesus is in the manger near Mary. Several days later as I was showing someone the photo, I happened to have it turned the opposite way, and a lady noticed an image of Jesus' Crucifixion! Coincidentally this lady's last name is "Cross" and the day she noticed it was Sept. 14, the feast of the Exaltation of the Cross!

During the weeks that followed, people began asking me for copies of the miraculous photo. When I had reprints made, I accidentally checked off "4 x 7," instead of "4 x 6," and I was surprised to find another image which we did not see at first. Above

111

the cross is a leaf that is shaped exactly like a dove. It took my breath away, as it occurred to me that in the mud we had images from the Joyful, Sorrowful, and Glorious Mysteries of the Rosary, and it was amazing that we found them in that same order. We saw the Holy Family first, then the Crucifixion, and then the Holy Spirit.

Two months later, I was sharing this story with a group of people and a man turned the photo sideways and said, "Look at the Lamb!" The Lamb is formed from the images of Mary and Baby Jesus. I could not believe we did not see this in the first place. And what does this have to do with the Rosary? Easy – the Rosary is the story of our salvation, the story of the Gospel, the story of Jesus, the Lamb of God. The Rosary connects us to Jesus and Mary, as we meditate on the life, death, and resurrection of Jesus.

As if that were not enough, a few months later, a 16 year-old student of mine noticed what he described as an "evil face" at the foot of the cross. The young man said that his interpretation was that Jesus is crushing the devil by His death on the cross. And as we pray the Rosary we are crushing the devil also.

Coincidentally, the article about Brian's rescue, and the disclosure that he was praying the Rosary when the men found him, appeared in our local paper on the morning of September 11, 2001. At Fatima Our Lady said, "Let the people continue to say the Rosary every day to obtain the end of the war." She wants us to pray the Rosary every day. In 1985, Our Lady said, "Tell everyone to pray it," (3/18/85) and "Put on the armor for battle and with the Rosary in your hands, you will conquer" (8/8/85). Brian's story is proof that miracles can, indeed, be brought about by praying the Rosary.

Editor's note: I sent this story to Pope John Paul II, and received a letter back from the Vatican on 1/2/03, saying the Pope thanked me and was sending his apostolic blessing to my family. Brian continued to make the Dean's List and graduated from college in May, 2003. He is now working in London, England, in the area of child protection. He continues to pray the Rosary.

Fr. Calloway

(4/04)
Tattooed Priest
By Denis Nolan

He took out a picture from his carry-on. "This is me before!" Rings were in his ears and nose, and his hair came down to his waist. He was holding a guitar. "My whole life was drugs, sex, and rock and roll!"

I had introduced myself to this handsome young priest three days ago in the airport as we were standing in line to receive our boarding passes. "This is my first trip to Medjugorje. But...," he said with a smile, pointing to his Roman collar, "Medjugorje is responsible for this!" Fr. Donald Calloway, M.I.C., Assistant Rector of the National Shrine of The Divine Mercy in Stockbridge, MA, (USA) told me his story:

"The picture is of me in 1992 when I was 20 years old. My life was a mess. The distress I caused my parents had driven them to become Catholics. One night that year I saw a book lying on the coffee table, *The Queen of Peace Visits Medjugorje*, by Fr. Joseph Pellitier. Picking it up, I couldn't put it down! I finished reading at 3:00 A.M. and then just waited for my mother to get up. I knew I needed to see a Catholic priest. It was hard for me to get the word 'priest' out when I asked her where to find one.... I kept forming it in my mouth but could hardly say 'priest.' I was very prideful.

"When I found a priest that morning, he told me he had to first say Mass and then we could talk. And so I sat in the back of the Church and witnessed my first Mass, and found myself telling the priest afterwards: 'That was Jesus on the altar, wasn't it?!!! That was really Him!' I received my whole formation as a Catholic in one night by reading that book on Medjugorje! It's really true. I got everything! For instance, I knew then the Pope is our father, he is 'Papa!'

"I lost all my friends when they heard I was becoming Catholic. I wrote for information right away on all the orders of priests in the Church. I chose the one that had Mary's name in it twice: 'Marians of the Immaculate Conception.' I had dropped out of high school and so they made me study for 10 years to become a priest! I was ordained three months ago!"

Fr. Calloway added: "Right now we have nine men in formation back in Stockbridge and all their vocations came from Medjugorje!" He also said something that my wife and I very much believe: "Mary has formed an incredible army of little ones throughout the world. Right now they're hidden. One day She's going to let Her army loose and on that day all the enemy's victories will be taken back from him! It will be incredible! Her army is already there – it's just lying in wait!" You can feel from this young priest a serenity – a strength – a discernable peace. With a faint smile Fr. Calloway pointed to his shoulder: "I still have the tattoos!"

Children of Medjugorje, www.childrenofmedjugorje.com

(4/98)
Statement of the Holy Father about Medjugorje to Bishop Robert Cavallero

This written testimony was sent to us October 9, 1997 by Mr. Marcello Pierucci, Via Castiglione 154, Bologna, Italy.

"During the Eucharistic Congress that was held recently in Bologna, I hosted Archbishop Msgr. Maria Rizzi, former Apostolic Nuncio in Bulgaria, and now stationed in Rome where he works on the cause for beatification of Servants of God. During a supper in the presence of my wife Anna and Msgr. Novello Pedezzini, Archbishop Rizzi narrated the following: I found myself in the private chapel of the Holy Father at morning Mass. At the end of Holy Mass, the Holy Father approached us and personally greeted all those present. Near me was Msgr. Robert Cavallero from the Shrine of Our Lady of Chiavari. When the Pope got close to us with the intention of greeting us, Msgr. Cavallero said: 'Holy Father I am just now coming from Medjugorje.'

The Pope said: 'Monsignor, do you believe?'

The Monsignor answered: 'Yes, Holy Father!'

After that Bishop Cavallero asked the Pope: 'And You, Holy Father, do You believe?'

Then after that question the Pope stopped for a moment in silence and then said at intervals: 'I believe. . .I believe. . .I believe. . .'

The next evening at my request Archbishop Rizzi repeated this testimony in the presence of Msgr. Novello Pedezzini and the bishop of Prato, Msgr. Gastone Simoni."

I confirm the authenticity of this testimony with my own signature.

Medjugorje, October 9, 1997 *Marcello Pierucci* [signature]
Information Centre "Mir" Medjugorje, www.medjugorje.hr.

Statue of Our Lady in front of St. James Church in Medjugorje

(3/04)
Star Search No More
By Kathleen McKee

I started studying astrology in 1972 and really believed in it. I went to school, studied, did astrology shows, and had lots of clients. I made a lot of money and had more than a thousand dollars worth of books on astrology. I would predict the future and tell about the past. I also went to psychics. I thought I was helping people.

When I first found out about Our Lady appearing in Medjugorje, I was so happy. I had no problem believing, and since I am Croatian, I wanted to go to Medjugorje as soon as possible. In 1990, I went to Medjugorje with my son who was a drug addict. We went to Medjugorje to ask for Our Lady's intercession in his healing. Our Lady had something else in mind, however.

While I was in Medjugorje, Our Lady spoke to me in my heart and asked me to give up the astrology. I was shocked. "But I help people," I said. I thought to myself, with all the sins I committed in my life, why this? She said, "You are taking people away from God." I heard these words in my heart and I know it was Our Lady speaking.

Then I realized more and more, people believe in astrology for an answer and were not turning to God for their answers. **We want an answer right away about our life instead of trusting in God, and realizing God is in control, not us.**

I felt terrible. The reason I did it was to help people, but little did I know that I was leading them and myself into the occult. When I got home, I gave it all up and told my clients to trust in God and that I would pray for them. I asked a priest if I could give away my thousand dollars' worth of books and he said no because I would only be spreading the occult. I threw them all out.

My whole life has changed since then. I turned all my time to prayer and to God, and have formed prayer groups. I leave everything in God's hands and I know now that He is in control, no matter what any psychic reader says. I am happy and peaceful no matter what God sends, and I pray all the time. Now when someone asks me, "What is your sign?" I proudly answer, "The sign of the Cross."

Editor's note: Kathy lives in Cupertino, CA.

(8/01)
Nun and Pilgrims Saw the Virgin Mary During Jubilee Mass in Medjugorje
By Jakob Marschner

"I am with you," said the Virgin Mary to Medjugorje visionary Marija Pavlovic-Lunetti as part of Her message from June 25th. Half an hour later She proved it by appearing in the church to a nun and to pilgrims from Bosnia and Switzerland.

Medjugorje, July 5th – A remarkable story which has been talked about for days has had its credibility considerably strengthened with the Franciscan nun Sister Marina Ivankovic confirming that she saw the Virgin Mary during Medjugorje's evening Mass on June 25th, the twentieth anniversary of the Virgin's Medjugorje apparitions.

Sister Marina, originally from Medjugorje, but now assigned to the Croatian parish of St. Cyril and St. Methodius in New York City, tells the French nun Sister Emmanuel Maillard, based in Medjugorje, that she truly got the special treat of seeing the center of events on that grace-filled June 25th. Sister Emmanuel tells the story as part of her latest report from Medjugorje, available on http://www. childrenofmedjugorje.com.

"If I am told that it is not true, I know for myself that it is true and I am ready to go on the Cross for it! Our Lady has given me a very special gift and I keep telling myself with wonder: She is alive! She is alive!" Sister Marina says in the report. The Mass had just begun, when Sister Marina, standing in the doorway between St. James Church's sacristy and choir, heard a very loud cheering coming from people in the church. She noticed Father Branko Rados trying to calm down a group of people who seemed to see something by the statue of the Virgin Mary situated to the right in the church. The pilgrims were stretching out their hands towards the statue, and out of curiosity Sister Marina went down to see what was happening.

Standing in front of the statue she saw a kind of whiteness behind it. The light was sparkling and pulsating, and Sister Marina was overwhelmed with amazement, she says. Once again the pilgrims cried out and pointed to the same spot before them. Sister Marina says that it amazed her to see how everyone reacted at the very same instant. Then a silhouette appeared in three dimensions. It was right behind the statue and wearing a blue-white veil, bordered by a distinct gold band covering the upper forehead as well, and so it was obvious to Sister Marina that this was the Blessed Virgin Mary herself. By this time the Gospel was being read in many languages, and the Franciscan nun bears witness that the Virgin was silently standing in an attitude of prayer with Her eyes looking down, listening very attentively.

Apparently this had happened four or five times, and Sister Marina had witnessed only the last time. The day after visionary Ivan Dragicevic said to Sister Marina that a pilgrim from Slavonski Brod in central Bosnia had also seen the Virgin at the same time and place. A group of pilgrims from Switzerland said they also saw Her.

"I am really very happy and I feel a great need to pray. The name of Mary has become dearer to me, and I pronounce it with intense joy. Before, of course I used to pray to Our Lady, but now prayer to Her has become dearer to me and more beautiful. I pray to Her with more reverence now," Sister Marina says in Sister Emmanuel's report.

In this immediate way the Virgin Mary confirmed Her brand-new monthly message which had been given to visionary Marija Pavlovic-Lunetti just half an hour before She appeared in the church. "I am with you," said the Virgin in Her message of June 25th, a message which says in its entirety: "Dear Children! I am with you and I bless you all with my motherly blessing. Especially today when God gives you abundant graces, pray and seek God through me. God gives you great graces. That is why, little children, make good use of this time of grace and come closer to my heart so that I can lead you to my Son Jesus. Thank you for having responded to my call."

www.spiritdaily.com

(9/03)
Veronica's Story
By Denis Nolan

Veronica and Alex have come to Medjugorje from South Africa every year since 1998 just to give thanks and praise to God. My wife, Cathy, and I had never heard Veronica's story, and so over a cup of coffee Sr. Emmanuel suggested they share it with us! For 22 years Veronica had been blind. Her retinas were damaged, and she has been unable to see. Veronica has always prayed to Jesus and Our Lady, and her faith is strong. One night in August 1998, while in pain, she began to pray. All of a sudden she saw Jesus standing before her beckoning to her with His arms outstretched. He showed her a panorama: a village, a mountain with a big cross on top, small shops and houses along the street, a large church with two steeples and inside, on the third stained-glass window, the Blessed Mother. I

119

said to Jesus, "I don't know where this place is." Jesus just looked at me and smiled and said, "Medjugorje!" In the morning she told her husband, Alex, everything she had seen and that Jesus had called the place Medjugorje. They phoned their travel agent who had helped them visit many Marian shrines, and asked him if he knew of such a place. The agent had never heard of it. They were perplexed. A few days later they were surprised to learn how to get there from a friend who had just returned from a pilgrimage! Upon arriving in the village, Alex said he knew exactly where everything was because Veronica had described it so well from her vision – the post office, the bridge, the church.... as they drove down the road every building was just as it had appeared to Veronica! They went to hear Vicka speak on the steps of the blue house. There were so many pilgrims that Alex and Veronica were squashed in the back of the group. As Vicka talked, Alex noticed that she was gazing at Veronica. Alex told her: "She is looking at you!" Then Veronica heard, "She's waving at you! She's smiling at you!" Then, when Vicka had finished speaking, Alex said, "She's coming down and walking toward you!" "She's right in front of you!" Then Vicka placed her hand over Veronica's eyes and prayed. When Vicka removed her hand, one eye was completely healed and Veronica could see! Leaping for joy and dancing in the street Veronica cried out in thanksgiving! She, who was blind, could see! To this day she's filled with such joy at the love of God that she can't resist reaching out and loving all those around her.

The next day after the healing, Veronica and Alex attended a talk by Fr. Svet in the yellow building behind the church. During his talk, to Veronica's surprise a picture of the Gospa on the front wall came alive. A silence spread over the room (everyone, it seemed, knew something was happening). Then Veronica saw that Our Lady was holding something deep blue in her hands. It was the continent of Africa! What could this mean? They prayed. Hearing Sr. Emmanuel speak the following day it became clear. They were being called to spread Our Lady's messages in Africa! As a little branch of Children of Medjugorje they have since spread thousands of audiotapes in South Africa and are spearheading an edition of Sr. Emmanuel's book, *Medjugorje, The 90's,* in Zulu!

Children of Medjugorje, www.childrenofmedjugorje.com

Painting in the yellow building that came alive for Veronica

(3/04)
A Clean Heart Create for Me, O God
By Carolanne Kilichowski

Did you ever meet someone special that you knew for a short time but stayed in your heart the rest of your life? I did. My story begins as I was ministering to patients at Hospice. Every Wednesday evening we would gather for a Communion service for those who were able to be out of bed, and to attend to others at their bedside in prayer and Communion.

One day as we prayed with this most beautiful lady, MaryAnn, my heart overflowed with warm love. There was just something in this woman's eyes that drew me to her. I found myself going back to her when the others left, since I wanted to speak with her or pray with her if she wanted. I noticed prayer books on her nightstand, so I assumed she led a prayerful life. Her sense of humor was wonderful and often I teased her just to make her laugh.

On one Sunday I went just to see how she was doing and to introduce her to my friend. She was having difficulty breathing and asked me to pray for her. I held her hand and prayed some prayers with her, finding it very hard not to cry. I could see the fear of dying in this woman's eyes. I placed her name on prayer chains and made her my priority in prayer. I wanted so much for her to live and enjoy life. She seemed much too young to be going through all this pain and agony.

Since my heart was drawing me to her I would come in early just to go and visit with her before we came in with the group. Many times I came back to her room at the end of the evening just to kiss and hug her goodnight. I was getting attached to her and I knew I would have to let go someday and let her go to God.

One evening I went to look for her in her room and she was not there. She was in another room in isolation since she now had a respiratory infection. I was not ready to give her up. I wanted to enjoy this new friendship! I begged God to give me a little more time with her. I asked her if she ever heard of Medjugorje. She told me that she did hear something one time but really did not know much. I sat down by her bed and told her the whole story. I told her all the main messages, how it started, and how I was going to Medjugorje for the fourth time in October, which was four weeks away! I told her I would pray for her on the top of Cross Mountain on her birthday! This really made her so very happy to know that. The following week, I had this overwhelming urge to take MaryAnn a medal from Medjugorje. I had a handful of them waiting to go to Hospice and to give to the patients. I kept walking out the door without them. This time, something in my heart told me I must take one especially for MaryAnn.

I went straight to her room and she was not doing so well. She asked me to pray for her, saying she needed a lot of help. I was scared because she really struggled to breathe even though she was out of isolation. I told her that I brought her a special gift and that it was a medal from Medjugorje. She asked me to put it around her neck. She cried with all of her heart. She was so deeply moved by this medal. MaryAnn then asked me to close the door since she had something to ask me. I could not imagine what it was she was going to tell me. She asked me what she should do since there were things in her life she had done and never told a priest. I told her that she should go to confession to a priest as soon as she could, and that if she said yes, I would arrange it. She said she did not know how to tell him. I told her that the priest has heard it all and that God has already forgiven her since she has such a deep sorrow for her sins. I advised her to ask the priest for a general confession and that he would ask her questions, whereby making it easier for her to say whatever was in her heart. She said, OK and she was so relieved already that a solution would resolve her troubled heart.

The next day the priest came and MaryAnn found it very easy to confess all that was bothering her. She thanked me the next day since she was like a new woman. I went to her that following day and I could not believe my eyes. She had her hair done and went to dinner with her family! She actually went out of the building. MaryAnn had about two or three weeks of a new life. I certainly enjoyed them since we told each other stories of our lives and made each other laugh. She liked to call me her "church lady" and I got a real kick out of that.

The days got closer to my trip and MaryAnn started to fail once again. This time it was much more serious. I knew she was going to God very soon. I held her hand and kissed her and loved her. The day before I left for my trip, I received a phone call from the family telling me that MaryAnn had died in peace. Since I could not attend her funeral I asked our priest to offer Mass for her on the same day she was buried at home. On her birthday I was up on Cross Mountain crying and praying for her new birth into Heaven, happy knowing that I now had a special friend in Heaven !

Editor's note: The title of this story is taken from Psalm 51, which has been described by some as the Old Testament "Act of Contrition."

(8/03)
Two Children and a Miracle
By Dawn Curazzato

Audrey Santo is a teenager who lives in Worcester, Massachusetts, and has been in a coma since falling into the family swimming pool on August 9,1987, when she was three years old. When the doctors told Audrey's mother to put the child in an institution she refused and brought her home. Given little hope by the medical profession, Linda Santo embarked on a journey of faith with Audrey and her nurse, to a place half way around the world, called Medjugorje.

Linda sought a healing for Audrey and prayed faithfully and fervently for it. God hears and answers all prayer according to His Will and Linda's prayer would be answered, but not in the way she might have imagined. Audrey, in fact, came back from Medjugorje in virtually the same state she left in. Most people's faith would be shaken; Linda's grew and her prayers intensified! St. Augustine said, "Faith is believing in what we do not see and the reward of faith is 'seeing' what we believe." Heaven was about to pay a visit to the Santo home. Shortly after returning from Medjugorje, statues and icons began weeping tears of oil and blood. The first image to weep was Our Lady of Guadalupe, Our Lady of the America's! Soon, another unusual phenomena occurred when a consecrated Host began to bleed. There are now four bleeding Hosts on the premises and it is the only place in the world where there are four consecrated bleeding Hosts! Pilgrims began coming in the spirit of faith and prayer and soon there were claims of healings and conversions. Little Audrey was looked upon as a victim soul, taking on suffering and uniting it to Christ's suffering to help heal a broken humanity. Victim souls are God's chosen ones. They have free will, but choose to do God's will. They are completely aware of their purpose and possess Divine understanding. I knew almost nothing about these suffering servants but that changed on April 2,1997.

The year before that date, my granddaughter, Katelin Amanda McQuaid, was born with severe handicaps. She was unable to breathe or eat on her own, two simple things we all take for granted. The doctors told us she would be blind by the time she was ten and she had severe hearing loss. She was a deep purple when she was born and because of a lack of oxygen, brain damage was suspected. She had many surgeries and eventually would have a trache, a feeding tube, a tube in her intestines and a tube directly into her tiny heart. Katelin was in intensive care for two months, and when she came home she was on machines and had round-the-clock nursing. She eventually had braces on her legs, and twice a year she was taken on a Mercy Flight to Boston Clinic where they could not find answers to her many problems.

I went over to my daughter Lisa's almost every day to help, and one day I found her and my son-in-law in tears. I asked what was wrong and I heard words no one should ever have to hear. My daughter said they had been to see the doctor and were told Katelin may have the trache and feeding tube for the rest of her life! Then she looked at me and said, "Mom, my little girl is never going to dance, or go to the Prom, or get married and have kids of her own! Look at her, Mom, what kind of life will she have?" Every time I tell that part of the story I am transported back to that moment and I can feel my daughter's hot tears on my cheek, and smell her hair and hear those machines; it is the hardest part for me to tell. I shook my daughter and told her not to talk like that, and then I walked out, telling her I wouldn't listen to talk like that! I left because I didn't want her to see me cry, and as I drove home I was crying so hard I pulled over on John James Parkway. It was there in my car I made a promise to the Lord. I told Him if He would heal Katelin I would make it known, and I would work for Him. I asked to be a

"Fisherman" and I would bring many people to Him in whatever "net" He provided. Next I vowed to take Katelin to Medjugorje. How God must smile at "our" plans!

Medjugorje proved to be impossible, but on Good Friday of 1997, my Dad called, telling me to come over quickly to see the EWTN tape on Little Audrey Santo. After seeing it, I knew immediately this was the place I had to go, and it did not escape me that Audrey had a Medjugorje connection. We made our plans, and on April 1st, a Nor'easter hit, closing down most travel, and our flight was cancelled. My daughter called in a panic and I told her not to worry - I would drive there! Something was calling me to go, but it is not a wise decision to drive into a blizzard, and yet that is exactly what I did. I had a child-like, expectant faith and I was going in search of the Divine Healer. I found Him at the bedside of another little girl who laid in a coma, and I will never forget what happened to us there. I dropped Lisa and Katelin off at Audrey's while I went to park my car and wait for a ride to her home. Mrs. Santo invited Lisa and Katelin into Audrey's room along with a few priests and two nuns probably because she saw how sick Katelin was. Lisa had put a trache and feeding tube in a cabbage patch doll to show what Audrey and Katelin shared in common and presented it to Audrey. Katelin crawled on the bed and hugged Audrey, and Audrey opened her eyes. The priest picked Katelin up and blessed her with the tears that were pouring forth from a statue of the Blessed Mother.

When my ride dropped me off, I walked into the little one car garage converted into a chapel and right into another world! There were about 20-25 statues weeping blood and oil and human nature got the best of me as I picked one up looking for a reasonable explanation finding none! The priests came in and said a beautiful Mass for the 50 people who were there. During the Mass, when the ciborium was brought out, the Hosts were suddenly covered with the miraculous oil and that is how we received them during Communion. After Mass the bleeding Hosts were brought out to venerate. As I approached and looked up, the Host was bleeding what appeared to be fresh blood! That was the defining moment when I said, "Oh my God, everything they tell us is true! They, being the Catholic Church and the fullness of the Real Presence, changed my heart forever.

Being like Thomas, I found myself saying his words "My Lord and my God!" What a gift but there was more to come!

Four Bleeding Hosts at Audrey's

After we got home, Katelin's trips to the hospital lessened and during the years the Pope designated to God the Father, God the Son and God the Holy Spirit she was completely healed! She sees. She hears. Gone are the tubes in her stomach, her intestines, and her heart, and off came the braces from her legs. Perhaps the greatest miracle of all is Katelin was recently tested, not only is she age appropriate – she is above, and received two awards for outstanding achievements this year! She has been in dancing school and in gymnastics! She will never be a prima ballerina or on the Olympic team. Ask me if I care! She knows the Our Father, the Hail Mary, and the Glory Be and those things will serve her far better in this life and the next! Her story has been on television, in the Catholic Paper and First Sunday, on Catholic Radio and in a book called *Memoir of a Miracle.* I am living my promise to God - writing, doing presentations and leading a prayer group known as "The Ladies of the Lord." We pray for priests, peace and personal petitions and promote Eucharistic Adoration, sacramentals, the Rosary and Divine Mercy Chaplet. I see our story this way: Katelin is the bait, I am the hook, Our Lady is the line, and Our Lord is the Fisherman! Sometimes what we end up treasuring most in life is something we may never have chosen! In a humble little house in Worcester, Massachusetts, lies a little girl in a coma who is a reminder that God exists and miracles do happen. You don't need an open mind, just an open heart!

Editor's note: Dawn's book **Memoir of a Miracle** *may be purchased by sending $15 to Memoir of a Miracle, 162 Sundown Tr., Williamsville, New York 14221*
Editor's update: Audrey went home to the Lord on April 14, 2007.

The Risen Christ statue behind St. James

(4/03)
The Risen Christ Miracle
By Sean Patrick Bloomfield

It was the summer of 2001, the dawn of my second trip to Medjugorje. My first pilgrimage only a year before had led me to a dramatic spiritual conversion. This time, however, I was toting video equipment with the intention of making a fresh documentary about the apparitions.

Minutes after my family and I arrived in the blessed village, excited people began telling me about an alleged supernatural event that was taking place: just after the 20th Anniversary of the apparitions, a local statue began seeping a watery substance, drawing curiosity seekers from all around the region.

Despite my jet lag, I grabbed my video camera and hiked into town. I could soon see an enormous crowd surrounding the "Risen Christ," a towering bronze statue located in a field between St. James Church and the cemetery.

As I drew closer I noticed that the onlookers were reaching up to touch the knee area of the statue. Others rubbed handkerchiefs, rosaries and small crosses on the knee, which struck me as peculiar until I was able to maneuver myself into the thick crowd and see for myself: water was dripping from the statue!

During my previous pilgrimage, only a year before, I had spent countless hours praying and pondering next to the Risen Christ statue, often late at night while staring at the stars. I recalled the cold, solid feel of that metal – metal which was now seeping droplets of water right before my eyes!

I stood in the crowd and recorded for nearly an hour. I placed the camera within inches of the statue's knee, hoping to capture the source of the water, but in reality there was no visible hole in the metal. In fact, the drops were forming on two areas of the statue, almost like tears, which would then fall at the same interval.

That night, I lay awake thinking about the statue. I woke my brother and convinced him to join me on a trek back to town. It was 3:30 A.M. After a long, eerie walk through the dark fields and back roads, we made it. Unlike during the day, we were now the only people present at the statue, and the water was flowing like never before. This time, I was able to film the phenomenon without being jostled by the crowd, and without them constantly wiping the water away. In fact, so much water was pouring out that it had formed a large pool on the ground.

I couldn't help but think that I was supposed to be in Medjugorje for the sole purpose of recording the water and showing it to the world. But for what reason? What, if any, was the symbolic meaning behind the weeping statue? The following day, I began interviewing witnesses to gather a range of opinions. One such observer, Father Ani Xavier, had traveled all the way from the United Arab Emirates to visit Medjugorje.

"When I seek to interpret the water that comes from the statue," Father Ani told me, "I see that Jesus does not want to see the blood of others. Water is washing away all of our sins, water is purifying the whole world. By shedding blood Jesus liberated us, and by showing us the water coming from the knee He is calling each of us to purify our life and to promote peace in the world."

My translator for the video, Maria, happened to be close friends with the visionary Vicka. After the two shared a private meeting, Maria told me that she asked Vicka about her opinion on the Risen Christ statue. "The water is coming out of the knee," Vicka reportedly said. "Isn't that a big sign for us? Like a sign that this is the time to get on your knees, to get ready."

Strangely enough, this all occurred just a few months before September 11th, 2001. The water still continues to seep from the statue on rare occasions, but never before has it flowed like it did that week.

Editor's note: Footage of the Risen Christ phenomenon can be seen on Sean Patrick Bloomfield's documentary videos, "Medjugorje in the New Millennium" and "Miracles of Medjugorje." Sean also has several other videos available. You can visit his website at www. medjugorjevideo.com, or call (toll free) 1-877-211-8018 or write to him at Sean Bloomfield Productions, P.O. Box 3035, Tequesta, FL 33469, or phone 561-748-0187.

(3/00)
Our Lady's Prayer for the Sick
By June Klins

Although I have read extensively about Medjugorje since my two pilgrimages there, it was not until recently that I was aware that Our Lady had dictated a specific prayer to be said for the sick. Our Lady said that this prayer, which She gave to the locutionist Jelena, is the most beautiful prayer that could be offered for those who are ill. I'd have to agree with Her there (not that I would ever disagree with Her anyway!).

Prayer for the Sick

My God, behold Your sick child before You. Heed his special request, that which he feels is most important to him. May You, my Lord, entrust to his heart these words: "The health of the soul, too, is vital." Lord, may Your will be done to him; if You choose his healing, may he be cured; if You choose another blessing, may he bear his cross with love. I also pray to You for all who intercede for him. Purify our hearts that we may worthily convey Your holy mercy. Protect Your child, relieve his pain, that Your will may be done in him, and that Your presence and love may be revealed through him. Grant him the grace to bear his cross with courage. Amen

After I discovered this prayer I printed a copy of it and I keep it in the notebook I use for my parish prayer line. When called to pray for someone who is sick, I say that prayer. Most of the time on the prayer line we pray for people we don't even know, many times we only know first names. But then I got the kind of call that each of us dreads, to pray for a friend who was in the hospital and not expected to live through the night. I had been planning on visiting Ann that night anyway, but after having received that call, I knew for sure I wanted to go, and to take Our Lady's prayer with me.

As I walked into Ann's hospital room, a nurse approached and asked who I was. I said I was a friend and that I had come to pray. The nurse said that would be good because Ann wasn't going to make it through the night. Because she had been so ill, she had been taken off dialysis the week before, and she was filling up with fluid. She appeared to be in a coma, and even with the ventilator, her breathing was rather labored.

I began to pray by saying the Divine Mercy Chaplet, because I knew that if someone says this powerful chaplet at the bedside of a person in their hour of death, "unfathomable mercy envelopes the soul" (from the diary of Blessed Faustina, soon to be Saint Faustina).

After the Divine Mercy chaplet, I said Our Lady's Prayer for the Sick. Then I followed that prayer with another request Our Lady has made to pray for the sick: seven Our Father's, seven Hail Mary's, seven Glory Be's, and the Creed. Finally, I touched my stone from Apparition Hill, that has the face of Jesus on it, to Ann's arm and prayed that the Father's will be done through her.

I left her room and called her husband Bob to let him know that I prayed over her. I took note of the time because of another case when I prayed the Divine Mercy over a dying man and he passed away within the hour. Before I left the hospital, I went back in to take another look at Ann, and was surprised to see that she was still alive.

The next day, when I got home from work, there was a message on the answering machine from Bob. In a very excited voice he related that when he went into the hospital that morning, Ann was sitting up, eating breakfast, and talking and joking with the medical personnel. He was especially excited that she was speaking intelligently because she had not been making much sense in the previous week. He said that her doctor was completely baffled, and could not figure out what happened and that it was a miracle that she was still alive. The doctor ordered Ann back on dialysis immediately, and recommended that she begin therapy for her leg which had been partially amputated before she had taken a turn for the worse.

As I write this story, over three weeks later, Ann is still doing well. She has been transferred to the rehabilitation unit and has been fitted for a prosthesis for her leg. After therapy with the prosthesis she will be able to go home! Bob said that he and Ann are thankful for each and every day.

When I went to visit her last week, Ann was sitting on the edge of the bed, dressed in a lovely coordinated outfit, looking the peak of health. I could not believe how wonderful she looked. Another man who was visiting at the same time could not believe it either. He remarked that he had to cancel the flowers he had ordered for her funeral that day.

I always say that the power of prayer is way underestimated in this secular world we live in. Whether it was the prayers of the people on the prayer line and all the other people who were praying for Ann, or the intercession of Our Lady, we will never know. I'd like to think it was both. Had the prayer line not called right before I was planning to leave for the hospital, I probably would not have taken that prayer with me. That's how Our Lady works! She is so awesome! Praise be to God!

Editor's note: Ann lived for another year after her recovery. The names in this story were changed for privacy.

Jim Caviezel at the Notre Dame Medjugorje Conference

(2/04)
Jim and Kerri Caviezel Return to Medjugorje

The American actor Jim Caviezel and his wife Kerri came on pilgrimage to Medjugorje from Friday, December 5, to Sunday, December 7, 2003. For Jim, this is the fourth, and for Kerry, the fifth visit to the Shrine.

During the past summer, Jim has given his testimony in front of thousands of young people gathered in Medjugorje for the 14th International Youth Festival. This time, Jim and Kerri took much time for private prayer, but they also accepted some friendly encounters with the Franciscan Youth Fraternity and with the co-workers and the children of "The Mother's Village." Privately, Jim showed to a group of friends the unfinished version of Mel Gibson's most recent movie "The Passion of the Christ," in which Jim is playing the role of Jesus.

The interview given to Fr. Mario Knezovic for Radio "Mir" Medjugorje is the first interview in which Jim and his wife Kerri publicly speak about this movie.

Fr. Mario Knezovic: *How did you hear about Medjugorje and what does Medjugorje signify for you?*

Jim Caviezel: I first heard about Medjugorje in 5th – 6th grade. They said that it was like the apparitions of Fatima, Guadalupe,

Lourdes, and they quickly said that the bishop said that it was false, so – as an obedient Catholic – I accepted what they were saying. Many years later, I met my wife, we got married, and after a few years she went to Medjugorje. While she was there, I was filming "The Count of Monte Cristo" in Ireland. She called me in Ireland, I felt that there was a change in her voice, but I wrote it off very quickly, thinking: "That's good for you, dear, who am I to take away from your spiritual experience?" She said that Ivan Dragicevic was coming to Ireland... I met with him a couple of times, and during an apparition, I felt a physical presence. Ivan told me two things that really hit me: "Jim, man always makes time for what he loves," and "The reason man does not make time for God is that he does not love God." Then, he talked to me about praying from the heart. That became like a beginning of a mission for me – to always pray from my heart.

Kerri Caviezel: I was in seventh grade and our priest showed us a film of the children during an apparition. We were told that it was true. We were from a mixed Catholic community – mostly Croatians and Italians. My grandmother is a 100% Croatian. It didn't seem hard to believe. It took me 15 years to come. When I came, I knew immediately – from what I was feeling in my heart – that it was real. I haven't seen signs or anything, but – I have been a Catholic for my whole life and I had never felt in confession as I felt when I was here. It was a tremendous healing.

Fr. Mario Knezovic: What do you expect from your stay in Medjugorje and for which intentions do you pray in Medjugorje?

Jim Caviezel: I pray for peace in the world, I pray for my family, and I pray that God may continue to make me follow Him, to make me a better Catholic and a good husband.

Kerri Caviezel: I pray that we are open to wherever Mary is leading us, and that in all the places where we go and to the people that we meet around the world, we may bring these messages.

Fr. Mario Knezovic: "The Passion of the Christ" movie, in which you are playing Jesus Christ, is almost finished. What was it like to play Jesus? How did you adjust your body and your soul to the body and the soul of Jesus? How was it to be Jesus?

Jim Caviezel: The catharsis for me to play this role was through Medjugorje, through Gospa. In preparation, I used all that Medjugorje taught me. Mel Gibson and I were going every day for Mass together. Some days I couldn't go for Mass, but I was receiving the Eucharist. Somewhere along the line, I heard that the Pope was going for confession every day, so I thought that I should go for confession as often as possible. I didn't want Lucifer to have any control over the performance. We have sins of commission, but also sins of omission. My sin of omission continuously is that I don't love enough. So, the confession was the preparation for the Eucharist. Ivan Dragicevic and his wife Laureen gave me a piece of the True Cross. I kept this on me all the time. They made a special pocket in my clothes for it. I also had relics of Padre Pio, St. Anthony of Padua, St. Maria Goretti, and St. Denisius, the Patron saint of actors. Another thing was fasting. I read many of the messages continuously. Every day everyone could see me with the rosary in my hands.

***Fr. Mario Knezovic**: Kerri, has your husband changed since he played this role?*

Kerri Caviezel: The first time I saw the cross on him, when he had all the make-up, he didn't look like my husband, he looked like Christ. They have taken a picture of the Shroud of Turin, and they used the make-up to create that, exactly that face. It was so real that people looked at him in the way that people must have reacted to Christ: some were full of reverence, some were indifferent, and some made fun of him. It struck both of us; we understand in a small way what it must have been like. It was personal in our lives; I think that he realized the weight of this role. There will never be a more important thing that he ever does.

***Fr. Mario Knezovic**: Fr. Svetozar Kraljevic, the Director of the "Mother's Village" and of "St. Francis' Garden" has organized the viewing of this film for a narrow circle of friends at the "Mother's Village."*

Fr. Svetozar Kraljevic: Jim and Kerri are here as pilgrims for a couple of days. Jim brought the 95% finished version of the "Passion-movie" that has already been seen by some at the Vatican and by some other people. He asked us to find a group of people who want to pray with us, and who are ready to see this movie. He invited us to gather together at "The Mother's Village" and to see the movie after the prayer of the Rosary. I invite everyone to pray for the success of God's plan with this movie, that God with His grace and His gifts may accompany this movie.

Fr. Mario Knezovic: How to bring Our Lady's message to today's world, how to open human hearts for God's word?

Jim Caviezel: Through one's own life. It is not what we say, but what we do. I dedicate my work to Her Son. I dedicate all that I do to Her Son. I ask Mary to guide me and my career. You can convert people only by living your life. This film is something that I believe was made by Mary, for Her Son. Because it was made by Her, it will be attacked by the enemy. In the USA, this film is under major scrutiny because of the truth that it brings. By living the truth, you will also be persecuted, the enemy will attack you, but have no fear, Our Lord will send His help and give you strength. And you will inherit Heaven.

Kerri Caviezel: To echo what Jim was saying, it has to be in how you live. When we walk on to a new movie, people on the set already have heard that we are Catholic Christians. So, they watch, they look to see how we are, in good and in difficult situations. You try to do the best as you can, and you use opportunities that arise to bring the messages and the power of love to whatever you are doing.

Information Centre "Mir" Medjugorje, www.medjugorje.hr

(9/02)
Out of the Mouths of Babes
By Shawn O' Neill

I've struggled over the last 2 years fasting. It gets better the longer you do it. Everyone should hang in there and never get discouraged. My 4 year-old son Nicholas helped me in my fast about a month ago. I was hungry on a Friday and I opened the refrigerator to make him his dinner and I paused with a hungry look at him and the food, he looked at me and said, "I love Jesus more than food." That made the days and nights and many since much easier to fast. I just remember "I love Jesus more than food" and I keep that in my mind when I'm tempted to eat.

Editor's note: Shawn lives in Purcellville, VA.

(5/00)
A Miracle!
By June Klins

As I slid into the pew of our new church on the first Friday of Lent this year, the woman in front of me spun around and exclaimed, "Jean, I have to give you a big hug." I realized who she was as soon as she wrapped her arms around me. It made no difference that she got my name wrong.

Flashback to another Friday of Lent one year ago: It was during the 8:30 A.M. Mass when it happened. During daily Mass at our church, the assembly has the opportunity to voice their petitions aloud during the Prayers of the Faithful. This particular day, a man who was a stranger to me called out, "For Paul Rosenthal, who has cancer." For some reason, which I did not understand at the time, I felt prompted to offer this man a medal of Our Lady of Medjugorje for his friend, even though I had very few medals left. So after Mass, I approached this man and his wife and asked if they thought their friend Paul would like a medal. They responded that their friend was not Catholic, but that his wife was, and that she would probably appreciate the medal. They explained that Paul was in very bad shape and that he felt very bad about leaving his wife behind because she was so dependent upon him. I said I would pray for him as we parted company. The next day when I saw them again, they said they were on their way to the hospital to give Paul the medal. I never saw them again until that first Friday in Lent this year.

Fast forward two months: It was Friday again, and I was reading the obituaries in the newspaper when a name I read struck a bell. The name was "Paul Rosenthal." It took me a minute to figure out why that name was familiar, and then it hit me. Tears filled my eyes as I realized who he was. I felt so bad because I really had hoped for a miracle for him. I decided I would send his wife Norma a sympathy card, and suggest that she keep the medal for herself to give her strength through her grief. The next day, as I reread the obituary to get her address, I noticed that Norma's maiden name was Wellington. I recognized that name, so I called my mother to ask her about it. "Don't you have relatives named Wellington?" I asked my mother. "Yes," she replied, "that's my cousin, and her husband just died." I almost dropped the phone as I burst into tears. I had given a medal to a complete stranger to give to another complete stranger, and it turned out to be my second cousin! (Now one might think that subconsciously I would have recognized the names, but that side of the family never had family reunions, and my grandfather who was the link, had passed away many years previous to this. I really had no opportunity to meet or even hear about the Rosenthals.) This is not the end of the story, though.

After I composed myself, I wrote a note in the sympathy card explaining to Norma my relationship to her. About a week later I got a thank you note from Norma which said, "Dear June, thank you for the lovely card and most of all for the medal. Paul was wearing it when he died. He had just become Catholic a month before he died. Maybe that was his miracle!!" Talk about a flood of tears.....

The funny part of it is, when I read the obituary the first time I noticed that Paul was having a funeral Mass. I was surprised at that, since I remembered that he was not Catholic. I had secretly hoped that he had converted, so when I got the note from Norma confirming it, I was thrilled. I was simply in awe of how God used me for my part in this story.

Fast forward to March, this year: As I mentioned earlier, I never knew the names of the people to whom I originally gave the medal, and I never saw them again until that first Friday of Lent this year. The woman told me her name was Therese, that she and Norma are very close, and that Norma wanted her to give me a big hug when she saw me. (It's funny that we didn't see each other for a whole year since we belong to the same parish.) Therese related to me that during the time that Paul was in the hospital dying of cancer, he kept praying to be healed, but after having received the medal he completely changed. She said that after he got the medal, his only prayers were for a peaceful death. And his prayers were answered.

This story is my very favorite of all because it involves a spiritual healing. I don't know why it took me so long to write it down since I have been telling people this story for a year now, but I guess the reason is that I needed to see Therese so that I could have the complete story.

And this is still not the end of this incredible story. As I sat down to write this I found yet another surprise in Paul's obituary, which I had saved. I could not believe my eyes when I read his date of death. It was May 13. Not only was it one of Our Lady's feast days (Our Lady of Fatima), but last year it was also the feast of the Ascension! Thank you, Mary and Jesus!

(8/03)
Rosary Class 101
By Carolanne Kilichowski

Often at lunchtime I take my rosary and walk and pray. I do not hide my rosary, but let it swing at my side as I walk. Other people are walking too and I am amazed at how much people notice that I am praying. I do not try to make it obvious, I just do not hide it.

A few weeks ago, as I was walking, I heard some teenagers yell, "Hey lady!" I turned to see who they were yelling at, and it was me they were running to see. These kids, two young girls around 12-13 and two boys a bit older maybe 15 and 16, asked me to say my prayers for their sister who is very sick in the hospital where I work. They were so very worried about her. I told them that I would rather pray WITH them. They said they did not know how to pray the Rosary and pointed to the one I was holding. It was a rosary that my daughter made for me of red, white and blue with my adopted soldier's name on it. They loved it!

They said they would pray it if they knew how. So I told them I would teach them. We all sat down on the grass on a main street and I took out my book and taught them the new Luminous Mysteries and we all prayed. They caught on very fast. I had mentioned Medjugorje and they did not know what that was. So, lo and behold, in my tote was the Special Edition, the Beginner's Guide from the "The Spirit of Medjugorje!" It really came in handy. I told them to come back the next day and I would give them each a plastic rosary from Medjugorje. They wanted to know everything. It was like a classroom on the grass. I wish I could have stayed with them all afternoon! Thank you, Blessed Mother, for sending your children to learn how to pray. They loved the Rosary so much they want the rest of the family to pray with them. They told me they will teach them. I wanted to cry, but it all hit me when I returned to my office..in fact, I had to close the door I was so very emotional.

The next day they came back so very happy. I was having a very emotional day. A three year old girl, Natalie, who just came to see me last week and was doing so well, now was terminal and in great pain. They could tell I was upset even though I was smiling to see them. I could not wait to see them and I knew it would cheer me up! They all told me that they would pray for me after giving me hugs. I cried more because these kids were so caring to someone they did not even know! Then they had asked me what was wrong. I asked them to pray for Natalie. I explained that she has cancer. They wanted to know why God could let this happen. "Oh God!" I prayed, "You gave these kids to me, so now give me the right answers since I too could ask You the same thing!" I told them in Heaven it will be perfect and that here on earth is not so easy at times. I told them that only God knows all the answers and even in bad times, He takes those predicaments and always makes good out of it.

The oldest boy told me that he has such a wonderful feeling inside when he says the Hail Mary. I told him to say the Rosary every day and he will see miracles in his life. I also reminded them to pray with their heart and not just say it to get it done. I asked them to come again to visit and we could talk more about Medjugorje. They told me they already found some websites and I cautioned them about some of the bad ones out there. I told them to follow the ones in the Special Edition guide that I gave them. They thanked me for teaching them the Rosary and told me they were practicing. They also plan on teaching all their relatives and want to have a *Rosary party!!!*

(10/03)
I'm Here Waiting For You Every Day
By Jane Monica Spurrier

In 1987, on my third trip to Medjugorje, I purchased a book about Modern Saints by Ann Ball, and therein was a story about St. Charbel. I loved him instantly and discovered, lo and behold, he was canonized on my birthday, October 9th.

I lived in New York City at the time and my church was Notre Dame on the upper west side by Columbia University. Daily Mass was said in the grotto of Our Lady of Lourdes each day at 8 A.M. One particular Saturday I woke up late, and was so hungry I ate my oatmeal.....but didn't leave myself enough time to fast before Communion. I kept praying, "Oh Jesus, what miracle could allow me to receive You" since I knew I needed one hour of fast time. This kept on, and when the Consecration occurred I did not have the required one hour to receive. During this time a rather odd looking old man entered the side door. He was dressed like a monk but didn't look like our Franciscans, and I was rather annoyed by his appearance since I thought he was some psychotic New Yorker.

After Mass ended, I stayed in the grotto to pray. I noticed to my right I could see into the sacristy and there was the priest who just said Mass changing out of his vestments and the "odd" looking monk changing into vestments. The little monk was coming out to say Mass! We never have a second daily Mass, but this visitor was going to say one and this would give me the chance to receiving Our Lord! I was overjoyed.

During the Mass the monk was praying in a language I didn't understand. It wasn't Latin, because I know Latin, but I couldn't decipher what language it was. After Mass I stayed in the grotto to praise Our Lord and thank Him some more for sending the stranger to say Mass. I was the only one there and during the Consecration the monk looked at me and his eyes said, "Do you want to receive?" I eagerly nodded back "Yes!" We both could understand each other without saying a word.

When Mass was over, I went in to thank the pastor (the first priest who said Mass and functioned as the altar server for the monk). I said, "Father, you don't know what a great miracle this was, that I got to receive Communion!" The monk smiled with a look of abundant joy, happiness and humor – the look of someone who laughs a lot and is very happy. The pastor didn't seem to get my point.

The next day I went back again. I saw the pastor and couldn't stop telling him what a great miracle it was for me. Then I said to him, "Father, by the way, who was that priest?" "I don't know," he replied, "I never saw him before." I couldn't believe my ears! What priest would allow another one to say Mass without knowing who he was?

Several months went by. I opened my book of Modern Saints again. I turned to St. Charbel and honestly, almost had a heart attack when I saw his picture. HE WAS THE MONK!!! He had appeared to say the Mass for me. Can you imagine? I later found out he has appeared numerous times since his death. I was glad I didn't know at the time who he was or I would have had a stroke. St. Charbel had a great devotion to Mass and the Blessed Sacrament.

Anyway, I haven't seen him since, but I know there is a picture of him in Charlie's store in Medjugorje. I've asked those brothers to sell me the picture, but they declined because it was a gift given to them. I thought the miracle of St. Charbel was so awesome and then today a voice inside of me said, "But I'm there waiting for you in the Eucharist everyday, to show you how much I love you. I sent Charbel so he could carry Me to you.....that's how much I wanted to receive you too."

Jesus waits for us every day in the Mass. He performed the greatest miracle on earth when He created the Eucharist. A small piece of bread, blessed, transformed into HIS presence, waiting for us. The graces we receive at Mass are incalculable. Don't miss this opportunity to meet Jesus in person...

Editor's note: Jane lives in Jersey City, NJ.

(4/98)
Testimony of Father Michael O'Carroll

Fr. Michael O'Carroll is of Irish nationality. He is a member of the Congregation of the Holy Spirit. For many years he was a professor and well known Mariologist. He is the author of several books. *Theotokos* (Mother of God) is one of his most well-known books, and the book about Medjugorje *Medjugorje, Facts, Documents and Theology. Is Medjugorje Approved?*

Last year he came again with a large group of pilgrims from Ireland. This is what he told us then about Medjugorje:

"Medjugorje is a great gift to the Church of today. It is constantly growing and spreading. It is wonderful to see the zeal for prayer and the strong faith of the people, and the multitude of penitents and confessors. Our Lady's intercession and power is evident everywhere here. The Pope also acknowledges that. When, for example, Bishop Kim of South Korea told the Pope how grateful he was to him for the liberation of Eastern Europe from communism, the Pope answered: 'No thanks to me, but rather to Our Lady of Fatima and of Medjugorje.' I personally always experience a renewal of my faith and spirit of prayer in Medjugorje." To the question as to how he as a theologian interprets so much opposition in the Church to this kind of event, he answered: "In the Church an apostasy is taking place. And I personally, like some other Mariologists also, see in Medjugorje the continuation of Fatima. With us in Ireland through Medjugorje many people have again found faith, prayer, the sacraments, especially confession and Holy Mass. Our Lady leads us to Jesus. She teaches us how to be open to the Holy Spirit. Knowing all these facts, so obvious, it is also a real mystery to me why the official Church does not see and acknowledge that. In the meantime, that should not be a problem for us. Let us continue to respond to the calls of Mary, Queen of Peace, and all the rest will take place at the time when Providence will it to be. Take care of Medjugorje. It is hope for everyone!"

Information Centre "Mir" Medjugorje, www.medjugorje.hr.

Inside the Adoration chapel in Medjugorje

(7/04)
O Come Let Us Adore Him
By Joanne Zabielski

In 1985 I heard the Blessed Virgin Mary was appearing to six children in a tiny village called Medjugorje in a communistic country, Yugoslavia, since June,1981. Immediately I felt deep in my soul that I would visit there someday. I didn't know how because there was no way I could afford it, but I felt Our Lady calling me.

A dear lady brought me back a rosary from Medjugorje that they say Our Lady blessed, with the blessing also of a priest. I lay in bed every night praying on those beads. The thought and the feeling of Our Lady being so close to me made me all the more certain I would one day visit Medjugorje.

Then in 1989, my husband and I were in an accident, and I received just enough money, to the penny, for my daughter, Alanna, and I to travel to Medjugorje!

We were off to Medjugorje with our pastor, Msgr. Richard Nugent in April of 1991. On Thursday evenings they had Adoration of the Blessed Sacrament. We were overcome with awe, not realizing that Jesus was present, but that something awesome was going on. From that day on, I became an evangelist for Jesus' True Presence in the Blessed Sacrament. Our Lord, says in John 6, "If anyone eat of this bread, he will live forever; and the bread that I will give is MY flesh for the life of the world." It is true, Jesus is present, Body, Soul and Divinity in the Blessed Sacrament. How could I have been so lost not realizing his True Presence? How much I had to be thankful for!

When I returned, one of the ladies in our prayer group asked if I would do a Holy Hour for First Fridays. Then the Holy Spirit clicked in my head - that was what we were doing in Medjugorje! We were adoring Jesus who is present in the Holy Eucharist. In Medjugorje the priest had proceeded with the consecrated Host in the monstrance throughout the Church. St. James was packed with no standing room. I was totally enrapt! Of course I will spend an hour with Jesus every month in my own parish. I told Msgr. Nugent what I had discovered. He warned me, "Joanne, I wouldn't tell people you didn't realize Jesus was present in the Blessed Sacrament. Every Catholic knows that." I replied, "Father, if I, a practicing Catholic, don't realize Jesus' True Presence, then there are many more who don't either." A study was done stating that over 70% of practicing Catholics did NOT believe in the True Presence. Wow! Do we have work to do! I remembered the church filled with people from that tiny village of Medjugorje, with fathers, sons, mothers and daughters, young and old praying together. What is wrong with us? Are we so educated that we don't need to pray I thought? Are we above it?

I heard that a neighboring parish had Perpetual Adoration. Msgr. Nugent was not in favor of Perpetual Adoration at the time. How smart he was. We needed to build. He let our prayer group begin a 24-Hour Holy Hour on First Fridays. On October 2, 1992, the Feast of the Guardian Angels, we invited families, school children to special Holy Hours, praying for families, for peace, for priests and read children's Bible stories in front of the Blessed Sacrament.

Our prayer group was still pleading for Perpetual Adoration, not realizing the intense undertaking it would require. But, still wisely cautious, Msgr. Nugent would not allow it yet. He told us if we could get enough people for Adoration Monday through Friday from 9 A.M. until 9 P.M. he would eventually consider Perpetual. I was scared now as the leader of this prayer group. How could we get people who didn't even realize Jesus' True Presence sign for Holy Hours? And, I thought, "Why ME? Because of illnesses, I barely made my First Holy Communion. I was released from Children's Hospital the day before and I fainted after receiving the Eucharist at my First Communion."

I didn't know where I was going to get my strength or knowledge to lead others to sign for Holy Hours. In my mind I was constantly pleading to God to take this burden from me. One day as I was about to receive the Eucharist, rays of light beamed from that beautiful Eucharist. My legs became weak. I could barely return to my seat. Still shaking, I knew that whatever was ahead, He would be with me. I started to rely more on Our Lord knowing it was He who was in charge. On the Feast of the Holy Rosary, October 7, 1994, we began daily Adoration with a concert by the wonderful Irish tenor, David Parkes. Then, on September 14, 1997, Msgr. Nugent allowed us to begin Perpetual Adoration. Ivan Dragecivic visited on October 10, 1997. He had his daily apparition of Our Lady in the church while 1100 people were honoring Her Son in the Blessed Sacrament.

With his encyclical released on Holy Thursday of last year, "Ecclesia de Eucharistia" (The Church of the Eucharist), the Holy Father specifically states it is the responsibility of every pastor to encourage Adoration. Believe me, great graces are there. Many miracles are there. Many blessings for both the pastor and the parish.

Some of the fruits of Perpetual Adoration in our parish: Ministries have grown in our parish; young fathers praying for their families; teenagers signing for Holy Hours; increase in Mass attendance; increase in prayer groups; priestly vocations; marriages saved from divorce; children released from drug abuse; increase in the knowledge of Jesus' True Presence; people returning to the faith.

"Today I invite you to fall in love with the Most Holy Sacrament of the Altar. Adore Him, little children, in your parishes and in this way you will be united with the entire world." (9/25/95)

Editor's note: Joanne is from Hamburg, NY.

(9/04)
Vocations through Medjugorje
By June Klins

A former 44-year-old dentist was recently named as the new parish priest of Mary Queen of Peace, Our Lady of EDSA Shrine, in the Philippines. Fr. Victor Apacible is just one of many pilgrims who have made the decision to become a priest after a visit to Medjugorje.

The Medjugorje Message, UK

When I received the above notice, I began to wonder how many priestly vocations have come through Our Lady of Medjugorje. We have written about Fr. Donald Calloway, and Fr. James Wiley (who came back to the priesthood after an absence of 17 years, thanks to Our Lady of Medjugorje). Last month we wrote that there were 8 priestly vocations that have come from the Medjugorje prayer group in Ambridge, PA. As I was thinking about this, I remembered the testimonies I heard from 2 holy Franciscan priests on my last two pilgrimages to Medjugorje.

Fr. Ljubo

In 2001, I heard Father Ljubo Kurtovic speak. Fr. Ljubo is a tall, youthful looking Franciscan priest who had been appointed to take over some of Father Slavko's duties since his untimely death. Father Ljubo's responsibilities include leading the evening Adoration, organizing seminars at the Domus Pacis house, saying Mass for the young people at the Community Cenacolo drug rehabilitation center, and writing the commentary on the monthly messages given to Marija each 25th of the month.

Father began his talk by saying, "I have to thank the Blessed Mother for becoming a priest." During the question and answer period, someone asked Father when he felt the call to the priesthood. Father gave a quick answer of "1988," and then paused before he went into detail. Father said he actually felt the seed was planted when he came to Medjugorje as a pilgrim at age seventeen. It was during that pilgrimage that he began to pray the Rosary every day. Although he had no inclination at that time to become a priest, praying the Rosary was instrumental to his vocation. After high school, he went to the university to study engineering. Then he went to work at a factory in another town. He was repairing trains, and it was difficult for him because he was too tall and it hurt his back. On his days off he would go to his uncle's and help him work in the vineyards. While in the vineyards, it gave him time to reflect, and he realized that his job did not fulfill him, that it did not bring him any joy. He used to go to the church every day and pray the Rosary. Then one day, God talked to him as he was working in the vineyards. Father acknowledged that it was not an apparition or even a human voice that he heard, but "a special inner spiritual call that is almost impossible to describe." For a while, he said he put it aside and would beg, "God, please, leave me alone." Never in peace though, it was always on his mind. Finally one day he went to his pastor about it. When he told his parents, he said they were "more than surprised." He laughed, "They thought probably I got mentally sick!" Then, at his pastor's invitation, he wrote a letter to the provincial, and went back to work while awaiting an answer. His fellow workers chided him, "You decided to become a priest because it's much easier to be a priest than to repair the train!" The temptations were back as he prayed, "God, please help my letter to get a negative response." When the positive response came 15 days later, he charged, "God, You cheated me!" He quickly added, "But today I give Him thanks because He knows what is best for us." Father is very happy to be a priest.

In 2002, our group visited St. Peter and Paul Church in the neighboring town of Kocerin. The pastor's name is Fr. Miro Sego. He was a friend of the visionaries growing up and knew about the apparitions from the very beginning. In fact, the same night as the first apparition, he had a prophetic dream. In his dream, he was in a boat and it tipped over and he was about to drown. Then a mysterious hand came out of the sky to save him. He was nagged by this dream for years, and wondered what it meant. He never told the visionaries about his dream. Years later he discerned that Our Lady of Medjugorje was the one who saved him, and that She was calling him to the priesthood!

(8/04)
I Couldn't Kneel
By Sr. Emmanuel

It's always a delight for me to meet Father Albert Shamon (from New York), who has the most mischievous sense of humor. We love to share our latest jokes together and update our collection! The quality of his theology and his deep attachment to the Church are well-known throughout the United States. One day, he decided to form his own opinion once and for all about the reported apparitions in Medjugorje. He made the best possible decision; he opted to go and see for himself! (That's being a good shepherd!)

He tells about his first day:

"A bit apprehensive, I decided to carry the Blessed Sacrament on me as a priest would on a sick call. I felt that if these apparitions were from the devil, the presence of Our Lord would raise a holy war with him!

"When I arrived, a large crowd had already gathered at the door leading to the room of the apparitions. I thought I would never be able to get in, but the Franciscan who guarded the door noticed me and beckoned. He held back the crowd and told me to enter. I attributed this privilege to the Blessed Sacrament which I was carrying.

"The room was packed to the rafters. Even though I was pushed against the wall, I was content just to be there. Marija and Jakov, escorted by Fr. Slavko, came and knelt in the doorway, and they began to pray the Rosary. They stopped at the third Sorrowful Mystery. Father Slavko came into the room and cleared a spot for the visionaries. That was fine, because everyone in front of me had been removed, and I found myself right next to Marija!

"The moment of the apparition came, and at a gesture from Father Slavko everyone knelt. Everyone except me! I tried to kneel, but somehow my knees locked. I was embarrassed that I couldn't kneel, so I bowed low in order not to attract attention. That evening, when I concelebrated Mass, my knees were fine.

"The second night, I decided to try my luck once again, and stood before the door. The same Franciscan hailed me and told me to go into the apparition room. I thanked Jesus, whom I was still carrying, for this unusual favor. I went in, and again, when Our Lady appeared, I couldn't kneel! I tried and tried again, but in vain. Once again. I had to bow low.

"Still carrying the Blessed Sacrament, I was allowed to go inside the apparition room a third time. As my knees still locked, I asked Our Lady to tell me why. She seemed to say, 'I do not want My Son to kneel before Me.'

"I left Medjugorje convinced of the authenticity of what was happening there."

*Used with permission from the book, **Medjugorje, The 90's** by Sr. Emmanuel © 1997 Children of Medjugorje*

(8/04)
The Prayer Group "Queen of Peace"
By Nedjo Brecic

The first prayer group in Medjugorje was formed on July 4, 1982, a communist holiday called "Day of the Soldier." The prayer group was formed by the invitation of Our Lady on Apparition Hill. This prayer group exists to this day. This is how it began. It happened on the balcony of Vicka's old house. There were Vicka's brothers and sisters and other young people from the village, and I was with them too. It was just before my wedding. The visionary Ivan was also there. At one stage of the night, I suggested that we go to Apparition Hill, even though the communist police had forbidden people to do so. All of us, together with Ivan, agreed to go.

Ivan was not expecting to have an apparition that night, but Our Lady appeared suddenly. We were praying the seven Our Father's on Apparition Hill. After the apparition, Ivan told us that Our Lady invited us to meet twice a week when it was suitable for us, and to not be afraid of anybody, because She would be with us. Because I was from another city, Metkovic (half an hour drive from Medjugorje), the others asked me when it would be suitable for me to attend the prayer group. I responded that Tuesday and Friday nights would be best, and they agreed.

At the next meeting, many people came, but Our Lady said that She had only invited nine of us for this prayer group. From that day, July 4, 1982, until this day, Our Lady has been leading our prayer group through the visionary Ivan, giving us Her beautiful motherly teaching and messages, of which there are so many that we could write many books.

The reason that Our Lady invited us to form this prayer group was so that we could help Her with our prayers so that Her plans could be realized. She taught us as in school, step by step, and gently, knowing our limitations and will. At the beginning, only the prayer group members were present when Mary appeared to Ivan, but later Our Lady invited others to be present as well. She would tell us the time and place of the prayer meeting and apparition. It is still like this today.

Over time, more people joined the prayer group in a special way. But some of them left the group. Our Lady often asks us to have unity, simplicity and humility, and to witness to others Her presence there, and to be a sign, light and example to others. Maybe some people expected us to be holy supernatural charismatics, who would lay hands on people and heal them, and who knows what else they expected from us. Our Lady asked from us something completely different. She asked that we grow naturally as a flower that is not watered by artificial means, but simply with water. That is how She expressed Herself for us to grow naturally. She did not ask from us more than we could offer. She came to us as to children who first start to pray the Guardian Angel's Prayer. Later, increasingly, She taught us, beginning with 5 Our Father's, then 7 Our Father's, then one mystery of the Rosary, then the whole Rosary, then Adoration of the Blessed Sacrament, which She started with our prayer group before it had begun in the parish church of St. James. She led us through personal and group meditation.

We have been tested by Our Lady. She was asking to meet us in the middle of the night, sometimes after midnight. Once it was at 3 A.M. Even when it was cold, winds and snow. Nothing stopped Her from calling us, and nothing stopped us from going. From personal experience and from others, no one ever caught a cold. We used to come back from the meetings soaking wet. On Cross Mountain, it was so windy sometimes that we could not even stand up straight. We hid behind the cross where we could. We prayed and sang for an hour before Mary arrived. The weirdest thing was that these meetings were the best. We had the strongest experiences in our hearts at these meetings, and Our Lady would be extremely joyful and She thanked us for coming rain, hail or shine. I suppose we felt that we gave something more than just words, because our body was looking for warmth, while our spirit was looking for penance.

In these 17 years we were criticized by Our Lady just once. On one occasion, we fell asleep, like the apostles at Gethsemane. That day, Our Lady invited just our group to Cross Mountain. It was really very cold. We were chilled to the bone, even though we were heavily clothed. We were shivering. Our Lady asked us to pray 3 Rosaries after the apparitions. We hid behind the cross to protect ourselves from the wind, and we started to pray. We managed to get through the first part of the Rosary. During the second part, we were nodding off to sleep, and our minds were on the warm heaters and who knows on what else. Suddenly, in the middle of the Rosary, Our Lady appeared! She thanked us for staying, but told us to go home and finish the Rosary there because our minds were far away from prayer. We walked home very sad. We found it difficult to deal with our disappointment. At the next apparition with Ivan, Our Lady was smiling and She said that we had improved since She corrected us.

The Blue Cross where Ivan's prayer group sometimes meets

We had so many beautiful meetings that could not be described in words. Since the beginning, I have been keeping a diary of these events. Sometimes, Ivan and Vicka wrote the diary entries themselves. The best meetings were at Christmas, when Our Lady would come dressed in a special way in a gold dress and the little Baby Jesus in Her arms, who was also dressed in gold. They would be surrounded by up to 5 angels dressed in gold too. I asked Ivan many times what did Jesus, Mary and the angels look like. He said he could not put it in words. During Holy Week, especially on Good Friday, Our Lady would be very sad. Sometimes She would cry, because She would remember the Passion of Her Son, and She was asking us to pray so that She would feel better, that we sympathize with Her suffering. She wanted us to experience in our hearts the Passion of Our Lord, who died for us on the cross.

Sometimes She would show Jesus on the cross to Ivan, after which he would be so shocked, describing to us Jesus with the crown of thorns, and a thorn that was pierced in His ear, and one through the forehead. He was covered in blood, sighing painfully. We were most joyful when Our Lady would arrive joyfully because Her plan

153

was being fulfilled. We never knew what Her plan was, but it must be something great because She was so joyful. She did not tell us Her plan so that we would not become haughty when we helped Her realize Her plan.

Everything is possible with prayer. If Our Lady says that war can be stopped through prayer, then it can be stopped. Would we not become haughty if we knew that one place was not bombed or one life was saved due to our prayers? In the end I want to say that as much as it is nice to have been chosen in this special way, it is also very hard to fulfill all that has been asked from us, especially when the devil is always trying to destroy love, joy and peace wherever he can. He tried to destroy our prayer group many times in devious ways from the inside, but Our Lady never let it happen. I ask you to remember us in your prayers, that we can persist to the end, not in our glory, but in the glory of God and Mary Queen of Peace.

Editor's note: Nedjo passed away on 7/4/99, the 17ᵗʰ anniversary of the prayer group. You can read more about the prayer group at Nedjo's website at: <u>*www.myhomemedjugorje.org*</u>.

(4/00)
Intercessory Prayer: The Divine Mercy Chaplet
By June Klins

When I returned from Medjugorje in the summer of 1998, I brought back over a hundred medals of Our Lady of Medjugorje. I was so grateful for the healing I had received after having been given one of these medals that I began passing them out to everyone. As time passed though, and my supply diminished, I stopped handing them out to everyone and began to let the Blessed Mother guide me as to who should receive Her medals.

I was at a graduation party in June of 1999 when my friend Pam introduced me to a couple named Rita and Walt. We talked very briefly because they were leaving to go visit someone in the hospital. At this point I only had a few medals left, but I felt prompted to offer them a medal to take to this person they were going to visit. They were deeply moved, and said that this man would be very grateful.

The following week I made a second pilgrimage to Medjugorje, and purchased more medals. When I returned, Pam asked me if Rita could have another medal. The man to whom they gave the original medal had made a remarkable recovery. He had been crippled, and the day after he received the medal, he was up and walking again. This time Rita was requesting the medal for Walt because he was very ill and in the hospital. I gave Pam a medal for Walt, and he too made an amazing recovery. In transit from the hospital though, Walt lost the medal. Rita, who is a woman of great faith, asked Pam if I could give them another one to replace the one that was lost. I, of course, granted her request.

Then in October, Pam and I were at a friend's house for a get-together, and Pam happened to mention that Walt had taken a turn for the worse and was dying. She quickly changed the subject, and it was never brought up the rest of the night. The next morning I was awakened by a strong motivation to pray the Divine Mercy chaplet over Walt. I thought it a little strange, because I really did not know Walt. I had only met him very briefly 4 months before, and I didn't even know his last name. When I called Pam to tell her about this, she was astounded. She said that she had wanted to ask me the night before if I would pray over Walt, but could not bring herself to do it because it would make her depressed when we were having such a good time. Pam and I then made plans to visit and pray over Walt that afternoon.

We arrived at Rita and Walt's around 2:00 in the afternoon. We visited with Rita for a bit first, and I was impressed by her strong faith during this trying time. She was completely accepting of Walt's impending death. Then Rita took us into a room with a large picture window overlooking a beautiful garden. Walt was lying there on a hospital bed, and a nurse was there to attend to his needs.

Walt's breathing was very labored, and he was totally non-responsive. I noticed that he was wearing the medal of Our Lady of Medjugorje on a band on his wrist. First I put Medjugorje holy water on his forehead, and gave him Mary's special blessing. Then I prayed the Divine Mercy Chaplet over him. I had read that if someone says this powerful chaplet at the bedside of a person in their hour of death, "unfathomable mercy envelopes the soul" (from the diary of

Blessed Faustina, soon to be Saint Faustina). Finally, I touched him with my stone from Medjugorje which has the face of Jesus, and asked that if it was the Lord's will, Walt be taken to Heaven soon. After I was done praying, Pam and I went into the kitchen to visit with Rita again.

A bit later, the visiting nurse came into the kitchen to tell us that Walt was gone. After Rita had a few private moments, Pam, the nurse, and I went back into the room where Walt lay. As we walked into the room, the nurse exclaimed, "Look at the butterflies." Right outside Walt's window two monarch butterflies were hovering in the garden. I cried at the sight, I felt such a sense of peace. A bit later it dawned on me that it was October 2, the feast of the Guardian Angels!

The nurse recorded Walt's time of death as 3:10. Blessed Faustina's diary describes the 3:00 hour, as "the hour of mercy." Although I never thought about the time when we made the plans to pray over Walt, I believe it was no coincidence that we were there at that exact time. I had actually been running a little late that day, and had planned on meeting Pam earlier than I did.

Although I have been saying the Divine Mercy Chaplet every day since my healing two years ago, I did not experience the real power of this prayer until I said it over Walt. When I told this story to a priest, he said, "I don't doubt that for a minute. That (the Divine Mercy Chaplet) is a very powerful prayer."

I have mulled over this story for some time now and have wondered why I was part of God's Divine plan for Walt. God could have taken Walt to Heaven without my having said the Divine Mercy Chaplet over him. In my heart, though, I believe that I was inspired that morning to pray the chaplet over Walt so that I could share this awesome story. I think God used me as an instrument to bear testimony both to Our Lady of Medjugorje, who led me to Walt in the first place, and then to His great unfathomable Divine Mercy. To Jesus through Mary.

Editor's note: St. Faustina was canonized in April, 2000. Instructions on how to pray the Divine Mercy Chaplet are in Volume I.

(2/04)
A Healing in the Confessional

Kelly, a 45 year-old American high school teacher, gives us a beautiful witness that nothing is impossible to God for those who open their hearts in prayer and truly follow the guidance of the Holy Spirit.

"A trip to Medjugorje in 1990 required my husband's approval, flying over an ocean to a communist country, money we didn't have, and a baby-sitter for the kids. But the calling was so strong, I had to go. When I broached the subject with my husband, he agreed to watch the kids. I wasn't sure what I would find once I arrived, but I thought it would be a nice break from the demands of four small children. For many years I thought that I was a terrible mother because I needed a chance to rest and catch my breath. I knew this trip would help me regain perspective on life, my family, and where we were headed.

"About the third day into the trip, I gave my typical 'grocery list' of sins to the priest and got through the 'dreaded sacrament' of confession. By the last evening, frustrated with not understanding one word of the homilies in Croatian, I brought a book of homilies to read. Immediately I opened it to a homily that spoke to my heart. I knew God was calling me back to reconciliation. I realized that there was still more I needed to deal with, something that was holding me back from a closer relationship with God.

"When we left the church not a noise could be heard, the dark sky made the weather even more cold and the empty plaza, more desolate. Strangely enough, I noticed that along the row of – what I like to call - 'outhouse confessionals' two lights were on. As I walked toward my pansion, I felt God pushing me towards the confessionals. I did not want to go, but I made a deal with myself: If one light is for English speakers, I will go. The first said, Polish. 'Whew,' I thought I was off the hook. The next one however said English. I took a deep breath and opened the door.

"As I knelt down, Father placed a crucifix in my hands. I began to speak, and then it seemed as though Father knew why I was there and a veil lifted. The issue I needed to deal with was contraception. Like so many other Catholics that I knew, my husband and I used artificial birth control throughout our marriage. We neither understood why the Church taught as it did, nor did we care. We were well-educated, responsible adults, and actually, very arrogant in our attitude. But through the power of the Holy Spirit, I understood that my husband and I were completely leaving God out of that aspect of our marriage. Our union was supposed to be based on the sacrament of marriage, yet we would give all of ourselves to each other, except the part that gives life. Our relationship was like a rope made out of three strands, each of us and God. God was the strand that held our sacrament together and when we excluded God from our union, it was incomplete and risked unraveling. My heart had completely changed, and I knew that my life would change as well. God was not saying that we had to have more children, as we already had four that were difficult for me to handle at times, but just to be open to Him in our union. When I headed for home the next morning, I felt as though I had glimpsed Heaven. I'm not sure how long I was in the confessional, but when I left, I understood that God was going to ask me to do some things that I would, before now, never have imagined myself doing.

"Once home, I had to explain to my husband about our change of plans. I was a bit apprehensive about his reaction, knowing our financial concerns at the time. When I explained everything that had happened to me and how we were being called to be open to God in our marriage – really open to God – he was in total agreement. Of course, we had so much to learn, so we did. We have been married 23 years, since 1990 we have had four more children, (there are 8 altogether now ranging in ages 21-4); and although it has been a real struggle at times, I have to say that God's plan to bless our family was greater than I could have imagined. As our friends' nests begin to empty, we still have a full house. I too crave solitude at times, but the joy that children really bring, even in the midst of noise and confusion and responsibility, are truly a gift from God. We took a chance and opened ourselves, to be generous to God, and we have found that in return, God is never outdone in generosity. Every time we have had another mouth to feed, God has provided in ways that we could never have imagined. Of course, we must be good stewards of the gifts we have been given, but we have never gone in need of anything, and have been blessed tenfold.

"I had such an intense hunger to learn when I came back and my husband joined me in that search for real food. Today I am the mother of eight wonderful children; some of whom I hope have a calling to priesthood or religious life. I teach Theology (no longer Accounting) to teens, who hunger to know God – that is my passion. I have a fire in my belly to share the Gospel with anyone who will listen. I struggle too. I am a sinner, very much in need of my Redeemer, and yet I know that I can do all things through Christ who lives in me."

Children of Medjugorje, www.childrenofmedjugorje.com

(1/04)
A Vision of Grace
By Maria Molinari

This all started last Monday. The time was around 9:30, and I was just finishing my morning prayers, when my mother came in. She told me that on Sunday, after church, we (my family and I) were going to go to Albuquerque to see Ivan, a visionary from overseas, during an apparition of the Blessed Mother, and go to Mass and pray a Rosary. I must admit that I had a few feelings about this, but I did not say them out loud. I was nervous and skeptical. Little did I know that my feelings would soon be washed clear away.

Sunday came. I was thinking how much this is going to be boring. I thought, "I don't want to be here. Why did my parents force me to come?" I was looking forward to seeing my grandmother, though. She was going to be there. That's always exciting.

When we arrived at the church, the parking lot was packed! There was no room to park and people were parking a few blocks away. My mom had a hunch that we should just look up at the front. As we did, we saw one spot not ten feet from the door! We quickly grabbed the spot and unloaded. We went up to the side door and there was a sign that said, "CHURCH FULL - GO TO PARISH HALL." We all just strolled on in anyway. Then, there were people trying to shoo us out by saying, "You can't come in here, etc.," but my family just walked past and right in to the main part of the church. We just sat down on the floor right behind Ivan. I didn't know at the time that he was Ivan, but I eventually found out. I wasn't even thinking about it. I didn't think that was odd. I didn't think it wasn't normal for my mom to walk in like that. Then, a man came and said, "I don't think you can sit here." We just looked at him. Then, he said, "I'll go ask Father." He came back and said that Father said it was fine that we sit there! I still didn't think anything of it.

As the choir was practicing in the back, a man made announcements, and then a priest came out and said we were going to start the Rosary. I was greatly blessed at the time. I felt so at peace. I felt like a child with so much innocence. I felt like I was glowing. One of the downfalls, or so I thought, was that we would do three Rosaries instead of just one. The other downfall was that I kept getting distracted and lost in the Rosary. At the last song (this was the Ave, Ave sung at the end of each decade), Ivan got up from his chair and he went over to a tan basket with ruffles, filled with petitions, and he set it in front of the altar. Then, he crossed himself and he started to glow. He started to move his mouth as if he were talking. I realized that I was in the same room as the Blessed Mother and that I was twenty feet away from Her. I was in awe and I was amazed at what I saw. Or, what I didn't see. There was such power and love in the room that I just bowed my head and prayed.

The Mass had such love and beauty done to it that I thought I was tasting a piece of Heaven. I was filled with the Holy Spirit. I had never felt this kind of love before. At the end of the Mass, Ivan gave a talk about his life and how he met the Blessed Virgin. What a blessing for him! I truly realized what he saw- a vision of grace.

Note from Maria's mother, Ginny: "Maria (who is 12 years old) is home-schooled, so I asked her to write an essay about her experience when our family went to see Ivan. I think my daughter had her own 'vision of grace.' I encourage all to bring family and friends to hear Ivan, or any other speaker on Medjugorje. Sometimes God will use another from outside our families to reach them. Don't be put off by their resistance. Just bring them, pray for them and let Our Lady reach them."

Editor's note: Maria lives in Sante Fe, NM.

(12/03)
Trip up Mt. Krizevac
By Dave Sheehan

The weather in Medjugorje had turned cold but dry near the end of our week long visit. The rain that had marked our earlier days was gone. In its place, a cold front had come in with strong cold winds from the north. The locals call this a "bura," and say that these winds come in from Siberia. We had planned on going as a group up Mt. Krizevac after Mass. This mountain overlooks the church of St. James in Medjugorje and has on its summit a concrete cross erected by the villagers in 1933 as a commemoration of Our Lord's death and resurrection and as a supplication to God to protect the village from crop-destroying hail. Since the time of its construction, the village has not suffered from hail damage. The Stations of the Cross are marked at various intervals on the pilgrims' trail that reaches to the top of the mountain. From a distance and on postcards, the mountain looks picturesque and inviting. In reality, a climb up it will drive home the point of Our Lord's difficult climb up Calvary.

Station of the Cross on Mt. Krizevac

Our noon Mass was delayed about 1/2 hour from its start as the Croatian Mass went a bit longer than usual. The villagers had a special prayer session after their Mass to honor Our Lady on the Feast of Her Immaculate Conception. By the time the English-speaking (our) Mass was over, it was about 1:30 P.M. As our small group of seven huddled outside the church, we debated on whether to climb the mountain or not, given the severity of the winds. The majority agreed to postpone it a day and see if the weather would improve.

I thought about it, and decided to give the mountain a go. I asked the Lord to accept my effort as a gift to Our Lady on Her feast day. I also asked His help to make the climb. I have climbed the mountain four times before in good weather and it has always kicked my butt. I have gone up there with a hangover. I have gone up there cold sober. It does not matter. The last time I went up there in June 2001 with one of the Gray Friars from the Bronx, Brother Gerard, I got us both lost and finally found our way back to the right trail when I spotted a "Coca-Cola" sign on an old, abandoned shack. I think Our Lord had a bit of fun with that one; I know our Croatian guide did. Unsure of whether I could make it to the top, I told our group that I was going to go up the mountain as far as I could, and that if conditions got too bad, I would turn back. My wife Peg asked me if I had a death wish. I smiled in reply, but I did not tell her that I thought God had something for me, but that it was a surprise.

So, I walked a mile or so up the road from St. James Church to the road that runs along the bottom of Mt. Krizevac. I then turned right (west) and walked another 1/2 mile until I got to the start of the trail. There are a few shops and cabs for the pilgrims, for those who have just come down from the mountain and for those who may have second thoughts like myself. Nevertheless, I began the climb with my little Croatian/English prayer book in hand. The wind that was strong and loud at Mass was still present, but seemed to be going over my head as I hugged the mountain on my way up. Around the Third Station (Jesus falls for the first time), I saw where the path split in two. Here is where I got Brother Gerard lost as I went left in the dark instead of going right. As I continued my climb, I noticed an American woman in her late fifties/early sixties climbing with a young guide. The young guide, being a local, was able to pick her way up quickly through the stones. The middle-aged American was a bit slower and more cautious. When I caught up to her, she told me that she was Helen from Wisconsin and had climbed the mountain ten years before, but that this time it was a bit more challenging. I told her that she was a great inspiration to me for her effort. The cold weather and the mountain were taking a bit out of both of us. We climbed together for a while.

At the 7th Station (Jesus falls for the 2nd time), I noticed a group of people coming down. They were Croatian and carrying a young man in a makeshift chair. At the site of the 7th Station, they lowered the chair and challenged the young man to walk. He was game to give it a go. Two women supported him, one on each shoulder and a third woman kept helping him move his feet, one after the other. In the meantime, the group was very loud, praising God for everything under the sun. They seemed to me to be charismatic in their prayers. I stood off to the side and studied the young man's face. There was joy in his eyes despite his infirmity. Whether he was going to be cured or not, I do not know. Regardless, it was obvious he was surrounded by love, LOUD LOVE, I might add!

I continued onward now alone, but on God's mountain, you are never really alone. The wind continued to roar, but seemed always several feet above my head. I likened the experience to a rock concert in my youth where the sound seems to go right through you, but physically you were untouched.

As I neared the final Station, I came to the spot where Father Slavko died on Friday, November 24th, 2000. They have placed a plaque commemorating the event with a facsimile of Father with his glasses and his grin. It is a good likeness.

I reached the top with the great concrete cross. I thank God that I have made it. During the trip up this time, I could feel His strong presence encouraging me, guiding me. There is an indescribable closeness to God now. He invited me to come up the mountain and I made it. Now on top, the wind is definitely to be felt. I huddled down near a small stone wall to drink some water and regroup. Normally, when you reach the top, you want to stay a bit, talk to God, and recollect. For me though, I feel closer to God when I am in motion but dependent upon Him for my safety and well-being. The time was about 3:40 in the afternoon. I left the church about 1:30. I had told

Peg that most likely if I succeeded in climbing Mt. Krizevac, that I would get a bite to eat in town and then get back to our lodgings about 6:00 P.M.

Peg and the group would be eating dinner at about 4:00 P.M. Under normal circumstances, there would be no way that I could climb down the way I came and get back in time for dinner. However, God began to work with me. I remember our group leader, Steve Shawl, mentioning about a back way down the mountain that is steeper but quicker. I look around and see the beginnings of a path. It seems like an invitation. I start down it, reciting the prayer of St. Patrick: "Christ with me, Christ before me, Christ behind me, Christ in me, Christ beneath me, Christ above me, Christ on my right hand, Christ on my left,...."

It is apparent that this route is taken by few. It is narrow with the thorn bushes close in, but it does descend quickly. On my way down, I slide a few times and chide my guardian angel, Sean, for pushing me so hard. Like a child in the front seat of a roller coaster, I am both scared and excited at the same time. If I fall and break something, it may take a while to find me. The sun is slowly setting in the west behind the mountains and I do not want to get caught up here in the darkness and the cold. Nevertheless, I do feel the protection of God and that is what makes it exciting. I pray for a young Irishman who lives somewhere in the area. He came over here to help the Croats fight in the Bosnian War and had the bad luck to step on a mine. He has lost both his legs. I have never met him, but I pray he receives the peace of God.

As I continue down, there are no markers to note descent. On the regular pilgrim path, you can use the number of the station to measure where you are. On this path, occasionally you get a glimpse of the town below slowly rising to meet you. There are no other markers. Then, at a certain point, the path splits. Which way to go? There is a small wooden cross there with the Roman Numeral III, the Third Station (Jesus falls the first time). If I go right, there is quite a bit of water there, and the path seems to level out. It might take me up again instead of down. I go to the left as I see the path continues to descend. I continue downward. Finally, I come out to the main road. I turn around and all that marks this entrance/exit is a little white cross. So, this is the path for the locals to use if they want to avoid the crowds of pilgrims in the summer times.

It is 4:05 P.M. I can still make it for dinner if I can catch a ride or a cab. I know that I am on the road that runs along the foot of the mountain, but I do not know how far I am from the starting point. Instinctively, I start walking east. I tried to thumb a ride as a car passes by, but no luck. Nothing looks familiar to me, but I continue to walk east, hoping for some sign. After about a mile, I see the start of the trail. It all comes into view very quickly. There is a cab there, which I gladly take. The driver is familiar with Mirjana Brecic's house and has me there in five minutes. If I had walked it, the distance would have taken me an hour. They have just started dinner. I am in luck. My wife is relieved to see me and quickly pumps hot soup, warm bread and whatever else she can, into me. I must look a sight. The next day when I look up to Mt. Krizevac, it is no longer the adversary that had kicked my butt. Somehow, the mountain and I have become friends. This was the fifth time that I climbed the mountain, but the first time that I climbed it alone. The strong wind deterred my fellow pilgrims. Perhaps, God used the strong wind so that He could speak to me alone. In the midst of that awesome sound, I felt protected and loved. God has His own way of speaking to us.

(9/02)
Sorrowful Mother
By Wednesday English- Mitchell

I was brought up Catholic and went to Catholic schools. At age twenty, I eloped and got married in a little chapel called "Doves of Happiness." By not getting married in the Catholic Church I was told by my parish priest that I was living in sin and he wouldn't be able to converse with me. I was upset with the priest and had mixed feelings about Catholicism, so I sought out other religions: Muslim, Buddha, Jehovah Witness, Latter Day Saints, Born Again Christian, and many others. They all had some good qualities and they all claim to love Jesus, but I wasn't getting the fulfillment I was seeking.

My marriage ended after 7 years, but I was blessed with two children, my son Cully, who was born October, 1978, and my daughter Nikki, born July, 1981. I came back to the Catholic Church after having my children baptized in the Catholic Church in 1981. Upon coming back to the Catholic Church I still felt that something spiritual was missing from my life. I decided to teach Confirmation classes. I taught for two years and during the two years I was at the highest level of my faith. But it faded away after my students were confirmed and as my children became of age and left home. Prayer and going to Mass then became occasional. I truly believed I was going to Heaven when I died. And why wouldn't I? I loved Jesus, I'd paid my dues, and I taught and brought up my children to love Jesus. In May, 2000, I was sitting and looking out onto the view of mountains from my backyard and dozed off for about 5 seconds. During those 5 seconds I saw a white church surrounded by green grass. This church had a steeple and a cross on top. Two days later I received a religious Mother's Day card from my son. On the cover was a church just like the church I had seen in my mind two days prior when I had dozed off. This was an unusual coincidence because my son had never given me a religious card, and Mother's Day is not a religious holiday. The following month (June), on a beautiful night and after saying some prayers, I went outside in my backyard to look at the stars with my telescope. While setting up the focus I spotted a white shining cross sitting on a mountain and nothing surrounding it. This was unusual to see a bright cross on a mountain in June. Also I was only able to see it through the telescope and I was the only person able to see it.

In September, 2000, a painting I won in July was delivered to me. I had placed a blind bid on the Internet for a painting without knowing the contents. The only knowledge I had was that it was a certified painting by the famous artist, Thomas Kinkade. I laughed out loud when I opened the package and saw that the painting was of a church centered around green grass with a steeple and a white cross on top. It resembled the picture of my Mother's Day card and of the church I had dreamed about. I then believed that I had been getting the thoughts and messages about churches because of the Thomas Kinkade painting that was en route to me.

It was the morning of October 10, 2000, and months had passed that I had not spoken to or seen my son. I was awakened that morning after having a lifelike dream. In the dream my son came to me and apologized for his behavior and the argument we had. He said, "Mom, I died from an automobile accident and I had to come back and apologize for my wrongfulness with you." The dream felt so real, and after he told me this, I went into shock while in the dream. I begged that I be awakened from this nightmare, but couldn't. Next thing I remember from the dream was kissing my son and holding his hand with a smile on my face telling him I was going to be OK. I had blocked out the middle part of the dream and only remembered the beginning and the end. When I awakened, I had a smile on my face and I was overjoyed with happiness. I had overlooked that my son had told me he had died. Because I had just awakened from a dream with a smile on my face, I thought the dream was a sign that my son was going to call me that day, and we were going to resolve our disagreement.

The phone rang 15 minutes after awakening from the dream. I was told that my son had died from an automobile accident the prior day on October 9, 2000.

On October 17, the day of my son's funeral, my eyes saw for the first time the church in which we were going to have my son's services. It was located at the cemetery and was surrounded by green grass. This was the same church that had appeared to me in many forms –in a dream, on a card, on a painting, and now it would be used for my son's funeral service.

After my son's death, I didn't want to ever pray again. I didn't want to talk to God. I said, "How dare God take my son. I was a good Christian and this is my reward?" I closed the door on everything. I felt as if I were living in Hell. God had sentenced me to Hell because I felt nothing could be worse than the loss of my child, not even Hell. I didn't go anywhere. I stayed close to home day after day. I didn't work. I did nothing but cry and go to the cemetery for the first year. I didn't want to talk to anyone, not even my daughter, who at that time, was away in college. I was alone, and that's what I wanted. I was slowing dying and that was OK.

My daughter Nikki must have felt she needed something in her life, and had a void she wanted to mend after losing her brother. Six months after my son's death, Nikki became pregnant and on December 3, 2001, she gave birth to my beautiful grandson, Caleb. Caleb was born seriously ill. It was unknown if he would live. He stayed in the hospital from birth until he was 4 months old. I feared the thought of him dying. I didn't want my daughter to experience what I was dealing with. No one should have to live with this nonstopping pain. I went to visit my grandson daily, and I'd just stare at him unable to do anything for him. I needed to do something other than stare at him, so I bought him a rosary and recited the Rosary to him daily.

In May, 2002, my grandson was released from the hospital to go home. But for me, what was next? Did I want to go back to the slow death process again? I had nobody to talk with that could possibly understand what I was going through. I was an alien to the world, and upset with God for taking my son. Then at that moment I heard and felt the presence of Our Lady. She spoke to me and said, "I understand what you are feeling and your pain. I, too, have felt the pain of losing a child. I lost my child Jesus. I saw my Son carry a cross while people laughed and spit on Him. I saw men put nails in His hands and head and saw the blood and sweat run down from His face. I saw my Son suffer and die on the same cross He carried for the life of the world. And while He was suffering I was suffering. I asked my Father to allow me to trade places. I cried. I was in pain and agony, and every day after I grieved as I thought about the memories of His death and how I missed Him. There wasn't anything I could do. It was my Father's Will. So, my child, I do feel and understand your pain. And yes, your son has died and you will miss him, but remember, because of my Son's death, my Son Jesus made it possible for your son to live again. So don't be angry with Our Lord. Love my Son as He loves Cully and you. Praise Him for the gift He gave the world."

I dropped to my knees and said, "Yes, yes, Blessed Mary, you do understand! I am so sorry for forgetting about Your pain and suffering. I was selfish when I lost my son and forgot that You too have suffered the loss of a Son, Our Lord." I couldn't stop crying or stop asking Blessed Mary for Her forgiveness. I also asked Jesus to forgive me for not trusting Him.

I knew I needed a vacation – a vacation by myself. Little did I know that I was answering the call from Our Lady. I had always loved the movie "The Song of Bernadette," so I started my travel research by searching the web for Our Lady of Lourdes. Lourdes information didn't appear, but information about Medjugorje did. I had heard about Medjugorje briefly about 10 years before, but I had no interest then. That evening I stayed up all night reading about Medjugorje and Our Lady's messages on the Medjugorje Web. The next day I made reservations and plans to travel the following month of June. On June 20th I was entering the village of Medjugorje on a bus. With tears in my eyes I was staring at a white cross, standing alone on a mountain - the same cross I had seen through my telescope in the month of June. Now it's June, 2002 – exactly two years had passed from the time I first saw the cross from my backyard.

From the moment I saw the cross and arrived at the house I would be staying at, I had made an incredible conversion. The other pilgrims in my group were unaware and would have been surprised if they knew I had lost my son 1 ½ years ago, had a serious grieving condition, that was slowly deteriorating me to my death. I had become an antisocial person and a prisoner to my house. Nobody knew about my conversion because it happened so fast. I didn't realize it myself, because I was so in tune with each moment and enjoying the closeness of God.

I was enjoying my surroundings and the people around me. I had never felt this kind of peace or love in my entire life. The peace I had been searching for, even before my son's death. I felt the presence of my son's spirit, I had a closeness with God, Jesus, the Holy Spirit and Blessed Mary. I was alive!!! I was at Medjugorje, a place that I call home on earth.

Everyday I still carry the cross with the pain of losing my son. That cross I will always carry. But the difference is I now have Blessed Mary to help me carry it.

Editor's note: When I asked Wednesday if we could print her testimony, she answered, "I hope it will comfort anyone that is experiencing grief or distress for any reason. Blessed Mary suffered and experienced the greatest pain of all, but she must have been delighted giving glory and praise when Jesus had risen and later ascended into Heaven to be seated with God the Father. When there's a storm Our Father will give us a rainbow. We might still get storms time to time, but with faith you'll know a rainbow will soon come."

Editor's update: On February 11, 2005, Wednesday took her first vows with the Sisters of the Sick Poor of Los Angeles. She is now Sr. Anne.

(7/03)
How the Gospa Taught Me to Forgive
By Phyllis Roelfs

In August of 1999, I was as far away from the Catholic Church as possible. I had just ordered books on-line which criticized the Catholic faith and debunked Catholicism. As a child, I was sexually molested by my father. I told my mother who chose to do nothing about the situation. When this happened, I lost all love, respect, and affection for my parents.

For 30 years...30 YEARS, I did not have a religion. I could not possibly join ANY faith because I simply could NOT obey the 4th Commandment.....Honor Thy Father and Thy Mother. They did not deserve my honor. I led an incredibly sinful life of lies, deceit, promiscuity, hate, anger and moral corruptness. Now I have been married to a wonderful man for 29 years, have 2 great grown children, we are successful and have everything that money can buy. Yet.........I was the most unhappy person alive.

I ended all contact with my parents 16 years ago. I simply could NOT have them in my life anymore. They didn't deserve to be in my life. Shopping had become my great love. I'd go shopping constantly thinking that buying things would make my life complete. Of course it never did, but I continued.

In August of 1999, while on a shopping spree, I walked into a bookstore in a mall to find a new book on the "New Age Spiritualism" fad that I had come to believe was the "true" religion.

Not finding a book on the shelf that looked good, I turned to leave the store and on the "religious" shelf, a book caught my eye. It was entitled *The Visions of the Children, The Apparitions of the Blessed Mother in Medjugorje.* To this day, I do NOT know why I picked up this book. I stood in line to buy it and asked myself, "Why on earth are you buying this book? You don't want to read this junk." I turned to put the book back on the shelf right as the clerk said, "May I help you?" I went ahead and bought the book.

I went back home to our summer cabin and began reading the book. I was totally engulfed in it. After reading about 40 pages, I began to experience what I believed was a heart attack. A tremendous heat started to travel very slowly down my body, starting at my head, traveling down my arms, out to my fingers, down my torso, legs and to my feet. As soon as this heat reached my feet, I ABSOLUTELY KNEW..............I KNEW WHAT I WAS READING WAS TRUE............I KNEW THE CATHOLIC CHURCH WAS THE ONE TRUE CHURCH...............I KNEW I WAS TO GET BACK INTO THE CHURCH AND I KNEW I WAS TO GO TO MEDJUGORJE IMMEDIATELY!

Now....try to explain this 180 degree turnaround to a husband and children. Then try to explain to them what happened to me and that I MUST go to Medjugorje immediately. Through the grace of God, my husband was very supportive. Within 5 weeks, I was indeed in Medjugorje! I can't go into all the miracles that happened to me before I went, while there, and after returning home. This would be too long. I will tell you this one however:

The first morning in Medjugorje, our priest guide was giving us a tour of the village. He asked us to step into the Adoration Chapel and say a quick prayer. I knelt down on that wooden floor and through tears I begged the Blessed Mother to tell me what it was She wanted of me. I said to Her, "Blessed Mother, you wanted me to come here, and I did, now please tell me what it is you want."

This is when I heard Her voice. She said to me, "IF YOU FORGIVE THEM, THEY WILL FIND THEIR WAY BACK TO MY SON." I could not believe this. I could not believe She had asked me to forgive them, so THEY would find their way back to Her Son.

I came back to Iowa and continued to attend daily Mass, say daily Rosaries, daily Divine Mercy Chaplet, daily prayers. BUT..... I was not able to forgive my parents. I knew I was disappointing the Blessed Mother, but I simply could NOT find it in my heart to forgive them such a horrendous crime against me.

Many friends were sending me many books on "forgiveness," but I knew I could not learn to "feel" forgiveness for them by simply reading a book. I flipped through one of the books one day and saw this line: "You CANNOT rid your heart of the pain and sorrow yourself. Only God can do that." I tossed the book aside, looked up to Heaven and said, "Well....what is taking you so long?"

Two days later, my husband and I were leaving our house to go to a party when suddenly I froze in my tracks. I realized at that exact moment that I had NO MORE HATE, NO MORE SORROW, NO MORE ANIMOSITY AND NO MORE DISLIKE FOR MY PARENTS. It had totally disappeared. I could not wait to see them again!

I traveled back to my hometown and arranged to see them again after 16 years. Upon seeing them, I gave them each a big hug (the first time I have ever hugged them in my life).

The Holy Spirit came to me while reading the book...the Blessed Mother led me to Medjugorje and Her Son ...and God erased the years of sorrow from my heart and reunited me with my parents. I did nothing to deserve these great graces. I lived in such sin and hate. I am still totally overwhelmed to know how much God loves me to allow these miracles.

www.medjugorjeusa.org

Editor's update: Phyllis, who lives in Waverly, IA, wrote to me recently and told me about her father's deathbed conversion, as Our Lady foretold. She wrote: " The father that sexually abused me and devastated my life for so many years found his way! He found his way through my forgiveness of him!!! Why on earth do we ever doubt?"

Chapter Four:

Living the Messages

(7/00)
A Time of Joy
By Joan Wieszczyk

Prayer for us should be a time of joy. That is what Our Lady requests it to be. Prayerful people don't have to be boring. Many people think that if you pray and live the messages of Medjugorje, you are not "with it." In other words, you are too serious, and don't fit in with the crowd. You are not allowed to laugh and have fun.

How many of us think of Jesus and Mary as humans enjoying a good laugh now and then? We must not forget that Jesus also had a human nature while on earth. He was not a boring character!

This reminds me of a painting I have of a bearded man, his teeth showing off a wide smile. It is the head and shoulders of Jesus Christ. His face is full of mirth and gaiety. The picture explodes with hope. It serves as a gentle reminder to let the burdensome matters of adulthood crowd out feelings of levity. Laughter brings unexpected gifts.

As human beings, we have a prankish nature within us. For example, on April Fools' Day, we play practical jokes on one another. Yes, laughter is good for our health. As long as the joking is non-ridiculing and enjoyable, it provides psychological, physiological and spiritual benefits. Take notice. People who laugh are usually happy people. These same people have a sense of control over events in their lives. One thing is for sure – they can pray joyfully.

Laughter also exercises the muscles of the face so that blood flow and temperature are increased, releasing endorphins which give us a sense of well being. Laughter helps us in many ways. It helps give us a sense of peace of mind. It even helps us cope during sad and tragic times.

Did you know that we are born with the gift of laughter? Children laugh about 425 times a day, while the average man laughs only 69 times a day. The average woman laughs about 55 times. Some studies show that adults average a mere 15 chuckles a day! Seems like the older we get, the more serious we get. We lose the gift of spontaneous laughter we were born with and learn to be serious.

So take a lesson from those around you who laugh easily. Learn to laugh again.

Also, take a lesson from those who pray joyfully and heartfully. Share with them and pray together. In other words, don't make prayer boring! If you learn to pray from the heart, it will be stimulating to others. It is only then when our prayers become alive. Praying with the heart also means "praying with joy." There is no spiritual life without joy.

"Today, I call you to approach prayer actively. Prayer will be your joy...if you make a start, it won't be boring to you because you will be praying out of joy." (March 20, 1986)

Be a joyful Christian. One can recognize this virtue in the visionary Vicka. She radiates the joy of Jesus and Mary within her. Her smile is the smile of love. That is what I feel when I glance at my picture of the "smiling Jesus." He wants us to be happy and full of joy, especially when we pray.

Vicka's smile

(5/02)
The Swap
By June Klins

"Keep making the swap with Our Lady. She'll take care of everything. I made the swap about my job last week. Today I got a promotion. Wahoooooooooo! It works!" After reading this note from my friend Christine, I wrote back to her and asked, "Did I miss something? What is the swap?" Christine wrote back and told me that the "swap" is giving your troubles, worries and intentions to our Heavenly Mother, while you pray for Her intentions – the conversion of unbelievers, peace in the world, priests, youth, healing of the sick, etc. Christine told me that she had 3 "swaps" taken care of in 2 days. "I can't believe how fast She handles things," Christine said. "Sister Emmanuel taught this to me. It's so easy and it works!"

Christine gave me permission to share another of the "swaps" she made with Our Lady that week. This one involved her husband, who she said had been displaying a grouchy and mean temperament at the time. She said, "Thankfully he has a spiritual life and that is what kept me from digging a hole out back and throwing him into it. I gave him to Mary and really wished Her the best of luck!" Not long after she made the swap, Christine and her husband went to a talk about Blessed Padre Pio and had the opportunity to have religious items blessed with Padre Pio's glove. Christine's husband surprised her by taking off his wedding ring and laying it on the glove. Then he asked the priest to give their marriage a special blessing. He was transformed!

I was intrigued. I wanted to know more. So I wrote to "Children of Medjugorje," the organization with which Sister Emmanuel is affiliated, and asked how I could learn more about the "swap." I was informed that I could learn more about it on one of Sister's audio tapes, "True Consecration to Mary." I immediately ordered the tape.

Sister Emmanuel reveals on the tape how the idea of the "swap" originated. She was with Ivan's prayer group on the mountain one night when Our Lady's message was, "Dear children, give me all your worries, all your problems. Then your heart will be free to pray.

And pray for My intentions." As Sister reflected on this message, she thought Our Lady was suggesting that we make a trade with Her. We give Her *our* worries and we pick up *Her* worries. A similar message was given to Mirjana in March of 1991 when Our Lady said to her, "Help me, and I will pray to my Son for you." The idea of a "swap" is hardly a new one though. Over 600 years ago, Jesus said to St. Catherine of Sienna, "You take care of My business; I'll handle yours."

Sister Emmanuel tried the swap herself and said it worked perfectly. Soon after, Sister met a man named Albert who came to Medjugorje and had a conversion. On his last day there he was very dejected and Sister asked him why. He said that he was sad because he would not be able to live the message Our Lady gave about praying in the family. His wife, at home in France, was an atheist, and had even threatened him when he left for Medjugorje. He also had hoped to return to Medjugorje but said he would have to save for many years for that. Sister Emmanuel suggested to Albert, "Let's make a deal with Our Lady." So Albert did. He said, "I give You my wife, and I wish You all the best. And I will pray for Your intentions instead of worrying about my wife." Three months later Albert was back in Medjugorje, but this time his wife was with him! He said, "She forced me to come to Medjugorje. That deal works tremendously." Albert said that now he had a new problem though – his wife prays so much that he can't keep up with her!

In a later note, Christine told me that there was also a reference to the "swap" in Sister Emmanuel's book, *Medjugorje in the '90's*, which my son had bought in Medjugorje last summer. It was easy to find the story because it was titled, "Theresa's Swap." This story was about a woman named Theresa who was worried about her daughter Vera's family. Her son-in-law, an atheist, was constantly fighting with and criticizing Vera. On the same day that Theresa left for Medjugorje, Vera made an appointment to file for divorce. In Medjugorje, Theresa heard about the "swap," and decided to try it. She went to the Blue Cross and prayed for unbelievers, young people, families, priests, those without peace in their hearts, etc. On that very night she found out that Vera canceled her meeting with the lawyer. Theresa returned each night to the Blue Cross to pray.

When she returned home she found that her son-in-law was a totally changed man. Vera and her husband have converted and with their daughter Harmony (no coincidence in that name), the family began to pray together every day.

In further explaining the "swap," Sister Emmanuel said that Mary, in the role of our Heavenly Mother, wants to help you, to make your life peaceful and joyful. She wants to take all the pressures and crosses in your life. She wants to pick up your problems, all those things that prevent you from being peaceful with God and peaceful with other people. She wants you to give the problems to Her so that She can take care of them. She knows much better than you do how to take care of your problems. After all, She has been a Mother for a very long time! So once She picks up that problem, you will be free of it. Instead of your heart being focused on a problem which will obsess you all the time, you will be able to open up your heart to the whole world. For instance, if you are praying for the conversion of one of your children, and make the "swap" with Her, then instead of your heart being focused on *your* child alone, your heart will become like Her Motherly heart, taking care of *all* the children of God. You enlarge your heart to the dimensions of God's heart! But it is not as if you have stopped praying for your own intention either, because your intention will be included in Our Lady's intentions. If you think about it, almost every intention that you pray for can be included in any one of Our Lady's intentions. Perhaps you are praying for a friend who is very ill. Our Lady's intentions include prayers for the sick. So when you pray for Her intentions of the sick, you are praying for your friend as well. Maybe you are praying for your teen-agers. Our Lady's intentions include prayers for young people. Maybe you are praying for a job situation. Chances are that the people causing you grief at your job are unbelievers, so when you pray for unbelievers, you are in essence, praying for your own job situation. The list goes on.

In my Medjugorje prayer group, when we state our intentions before we start our Rosaries, one of our members always says, "I pray for Mary's intentions, which covers every good thing." And she is right. Sister Emmanuel says that when you enlarge your heart to the dimensions of God's heart, you feel the love of God penetrate you in a new way, a deep and strong way. You become like Mother Teresa whose heart was open to the whole world. Everybody you meet becomes very dear to you because you have God's heart in your heart instead of being focused on your own problems. Not only does this freedom alleviate you of your worries, but it also frees you up for deeper prayer of adoration, contrition and thanksgiving. It frees you up to listen to what God wants to say to you too. That is an important part of prayer often overlooked.

A few months ago I decided to try a "swap." This may seem like a trivial intention, but I was having trouble with my computer. It looked like it was a lost cause, so I told Our Lady, "You get my computer fixed so I can continue to do Your work, and I will pray for Your intentions." Every time I would start to think about my problem with the computer, I would say a "Hail Mary" for Our Lady's intentions. That night, my husband worked diligently on the computer and was able to fix it. As of this writing, it is working better than it has ever worked before! Our Lady is a powerful intercessor! So you can bet I will be giving Her some more challenging projects in the future.

An added benefit of the "swap" that Sister Emmanuel did not mention is that you become more youthful looking and also healthier. Think about it. It makes sense. It is no secret that stress causes lines in your face and causes damage to your body. So if you give your problems to our Heavenly Mother, it's OK because Her glorified body can handle it. The visionaries say that She is so beautiful because She loves, and She would love to have your problem. Don't be surprised if your problem is solved in a way different than what you had planned though, because She and Her Son always know what is best.

As my friend Christine says, "Imagine if we were *all* praying for Blessed Mother's intentions instead of worrying about our own problems! Imagine what could be accomplished!" We could change the world!

(9/02)
The Divine Office and the Rosary
By Msgr. James Peterson

Historically, there is a very close relationship between the Divine Office and the recitation of the Rosary. The Office was built on the hundred and fifty psalms. For those who were unable to read, the Rosary consisted of one hundred-fifty Hail Mary's.

And as antiphons were supplied to a psalm to stress its special application for the feast day or the season, the fifteen mysteries of the Rosary were to help those who were saying the Rosary to experience the prayers in new situations with new insights.

One of the most impressive memories I have of sharing the Divine Office in a monastery is the conclusion of night prayer. The time for retirement is coming close; the basic works of the day are over; often the choir area had become dark because so many know the compline prayers by heart. Then a statue of Our Lady is lighted up, and the monastic voices are raised in tribute "Salve Regina" – Hail Holy Queen, Mother of Mercy, our life, our sweetness and our hope.

It would be miserable to go to bed hopeless. It's good to put away the worries of life and let Mary in Her motherhood and Her powerful intercession take over.

And the Rosary is ended the same way. After the final doxology, we recite Hail Holy Queen.

In monasteries, when the hymn has faded, the monks or sisters leave the choir and the abbot or prior or prioress blesses each one as they leave. With the Rosary, when the Hail Holy Queen is finished, we bless ourselves.

I love blessing and being blessed.

(3/01)
Love Letters from God
By June Klins

A little boy approached his father and proudly declared, "I know what the Bible means!" "Okay," said his father. "So what does it mean?" "That's easy, Daddy," replied the little boy. "It stands for 'Basic Instructions Before Leaving Earth!'"

In reality, the word "bible" comes from the Latin and Greek word "biblia," which translates as "book." The word comes from the city of Byblos where papyrus was produced to make scrolls which were used for writing in ancient times. Interesting, but I prefer the little boy's explanation. With its stories, prayers, prophecies and doctrines, all inspired by the Holy Spirit, the Bible is the most powerful tool we have for building a solid foundation for our everyday lives. The Bible, which I like to think of as "love letters from God," contains an immense database from which we are able to draw strength, wisdom and consolation. St. Paul tells us, "All Scripture is inspired by God and is useful for teaching, for refutation, for correction, and for training in righteousness, so that one who belongs to God may be competent, equipped for every good work" (2 Tm3: 16-17).

The reading of Sacred Scripture has been encouraged since the early years by Our Lady in Medjugorje. In 1984, Our Lady urged, "Today I ask you to read the Bible in your homes every day, and let it be in a visible place there so that it always encourages you to read and pray." More recently, in 1999, She reiterated that message, "Put Holy Scripture in a visible place in your families, read it, reflect on it and learn how God loves His people."

But how do we go about reading the Bible? About three years ago, I decided I was going to read the whole Bible from Genesis to Revelation. Not a good idea, not for me anyway. I only got as far as Exodus before I threw in the towel. Soon afterwards, I read that Father Larry Richards, a dynamic national speaker who lives in my city, was going to give a presentation entitled "How to Read the Bible." I jumped at the chance to hear his talk.

Father Larry began his talk with some fundamentals about the Bible. He described the Bible as "Jesus' diary," where Jesus tells us how He loves us. "The Bible," Father Larry said, "is the Word of God through the words of men, and is free from error in faith and morals." Father cautioned that we should always take the Bible in the context of what the Church teaches, and not read everything literally.

Father Larry said that we must make a commitment to read the Bible every day, even if it is just a sentence or two. Father quoted St. Jerome who said, "Ignorance of Scripture is ignorance of Christ." Father's own maxim is, "No Bible, no breakfast; no Bible, no bed." In other words, reading the Bible should be the first thing we do in the morning, and last thing we do at night. Then Father began to give some practical suggestions for reading the Bible. One of the suggestions he gave is playing "Bible roulette." In other words, you open the Bible at random and you read until something hits you. Before you open the Bible, though, you pray, and ask the Holy Spirit to touch your heart. You could say, for instance, "What word do You want to give me today, Lord?" Father gave a couple of examples from his life of how God spoke to him through the Scriptures. In one particular instance, in the midst of a very bad day, Father opened the Bible and came upon the verse, "Let not your heart be troubled." This method of reading the Bible could be particularly effective for those people who say that God never speaks to them. Sister Briege McKenna, in her book *Miracles Do Happen*, says, "I believe that everything that is written in the Word of God has a message for each of us...I read and reread them many times and then I try to put myself into those Scriptures to find out what they may be saying to me."

Father Larry cautioned, for those beginners who prefer to read a whole book of the Bible continuously, that it is best not to start with the Old Testament. That was the mistake I had made. Father suggested to start with the Letters of Paul, since most people enjoy receiving letters and can identify with them. Taking Father's advice, I have now finished reading the New Testament and have moved on to the Old Testament. Sister Briege suggests reading the psalms because they are full of praise. I am currently reading the Book of Psalms and have found most of them to be very uplifting.

Father Larry proposed a "five finger" method for optimum benefit in reading the Bible: listen; read; study; memorize; and meditate. To listen to the Word of God, we need only to go to Mass. Over a period of every three year cycle, we hear most of the Bible. Father Larry made a suggestion which I had also heard when I was in Medjugorje, that we should pick just one word out of the readings at Mass and let that word speak to our hearts the entire day. Another practical way to listen to the Word of God is play a tape of the Bible. You could even record yourself reading a portion of the Bible and play it back to yourself. Father Larry recommended that a good place to start would be to record the Gospel of John.

We have already discussed the second "finger," to read. Father Larry added that although some people are probably scandalized by this, it is perfectly acceptable to write in your Bible, to underline and write notes about words or verses which you want to remember. I was surprised to hear this at the time, but now, three years later, my Bible is all marked up. It definitely helps me, and I encourage the practice. Indeed, Mother Angelica of EWTN also advocates writing in your Bible. When she showed her Bible on TV, I don't know whose Bible was more marked up, hers or Father Larry's!

The third "finger" is to study. There are several ways to study the Bible. An obvious way is to join a Bible Study group, and another is to use an approved Bible Study, which can be purchased from a religious bookstore. Another way, which Father Larry did not mention, but I have found beneficial myself, is to view television programs which instruct about the Bible. Although I have not looked into this yet, I am sure that you could also study the Bible on the Internet. With all of these methods of study, we must be very careful, however, that all instruction is faithful to Church teachings.

The fourth "finger" is to memorize. Father Larry's suggestion was to choose a passage of Scripture daily and write it down to keep with you throughout the day. You can continue to repeat it to yourself until it is committed to memory.

The fifth "finger" is to meditate. This is the most difficult "finger" because it is time-consuming. Father said it takes at least a half hour to really meditate well. When you meditate, you take the Word of God from your head and put it in your heart. You can go over and over the reading and let each word echo in your heart. You can even meditate on just one word of Scripture as St. Teresa of Avila often did. For example, you could meditate on one of the words from the "Our Father," such as the word "Father," "Heaven," etc.

St. Paul described the Word of God as the "sword of the Spirit" (Eph 6:17). When in the midst of a spiritual battle, the Word of God can be used as a weapon to defend yourself. In Medjugorje,

Bible reading is listed as one of Our Lady's five weapons against Satan. Jesus Himself used Scripture when He was tempted. "One does not live by bread alone, but by every word that comes forth from the mouth of God" (Mt 4:4). Indeed, Jesus countered each of His temptations with words from Scripture. Father Larry held that the best way to deal with temptation is to follow the example of Jesus. He directed that whenever we are tempted, we should "take the Word of God and shove it down the throat of the devil!" If we spend time every day reading God's word, we will be prepared for the battle because we will be filling our minds with promises and truths that can withstand any attack. Nothing can overcome a person who is founded on the Word of God. This Lent might be a good time to heed Our Lady's call "to renew prayer in your families by reading the Sacred Scriptures," so that we can "experience joy in meeting with God who infinitely loves His creatures."

You've got mail!

Mass in the Adoration Chapel in Medjugorje

(12/98)
My Sons! Never Miss Holy Mass!
By Sister M. Veronica Murphy

The following TRUE STORY was related to Sr. M. Veronica Murphy by an elderly nun who heard it from the lips of the late Reverend Father Stanislaus, SS.CC.

One day many years ago, in a little town in Luxembourg, a captain of the Forest Guards was in deep conversation with the butcher when an elderly woman entered the shop. The butcher broke off the conversation to ask the old woman what she wanted. She had come to beg for a little meat but had no money. The captain was amused at the woman. "Only a little meat, but how much are you going to give her?" He wondered.

"I am sorry I have no money but I'll hear Mass for you," the woman told the butcher. Both the butcher and the captain were indifferent about religion, so they at once began to scoff at the old woman's idea.

"All right then," said the butcher. "You go and hear Mass for me and when you come back I'll give you as much as the Mass is worth."

The woman left the shop and returned later. She approached the counter and the butcher said, "All right then, we'll see." He took a slip of paper and wrote on it, "I heard a Mass for you." He placed the paper on the scales and a tiny bone on the other side, but nothing happened. Next he placed a piece of meat instead of the bone, but still the paper proved heavier. Both men were beginning to feel ashamed of their mockery but continued their game. A large piece of meat was placed on the balance, but still the paper held its own. The butcher, exasperated, examined the scales but found they were all right. "What do you want, my good woman? Must I give you a whole leg of mutton?" At this he placed the leg of mutton on the balance, but the paper outweighed the meat.

A larger piece of meat was put on, but again the weight remained on the side of the paper. This so impressed the butcher that he was converted and promised to give the woman her daily ration of meat.

As for the captain, he left the shop a changed man and an ardent lover of daily Mass. Two of his sons became priests, one a Jesuit and the other a Father of the Sacred Heart.

Father Stanislaus finished the story by saying, "I am from the Religious of the Sacred Heart and the captain was my father."

From the incident the captain became a daily Mass attendant and his children were trained to follow his example. Later when his sons became priests, he advised them to say Mass well every day and never miss the Sacrifice of the Holy Mass through any fault of their own.

Children of Medjugorje, www.childrenofmedjugorje.com

(1/01)
Fasting
By June Klins

"Are you nuts?" "You are going to make yourself sick." "Are you still doing that silly fasting?" These are some of the comments you are bound to hear when you make the decision to heed Our Lady's message to fast on bread and water on Wednesdays and Fridays. I know that because I have heard all of these comments and more from the few close friends and relatives who know that I fast. Of all the things Our Lady asks us to do, fasting is unquestionably the most difficult. Fasting does not fit into our self-centered, materialistic world. It doesn't fit into our social life. So why do I do it?

My decision to fast on Wednesdays and Fridays came after my first pilgrimage to Medjugorje. I was still on a "high" and thought it was the least I could do in gratitude for my healing. I didn't think I would be able to handle a bread and water fast, though, so I just gave up snacks in between meals on Wednesdays and Fridays. I did that for a few months, until I went to a Medjugorje retreat, where a man looked me straight in the eyes, as he was speaking to a group of people, and said, "Mary does not ask us to carry out *some* of Her messages. She asks us to carry out *all* of the messages." After that day I decided to fast on bread and water, which Our Lady describes as the "best fast." And I was really spurred on when, one week later, something very distressing happened in my family. I remembered the story of the healing of a boy with a demon, when Jesus told his disciples, "This kind can only come out through prayer and fasting" (Mk. 9:29). So I now had an intention along with the motivation.

The word "fasting" comes from a Hebrew word which means "to cover or shut one's mouth." Although fasting in the strictest sense involves abstaining from food, we can also fast from other things, such as alcohol, tobacco, television, or even the computer. However, in July of 1982, Our Lady told the visionaries at Medjugorje, "The best fast is on bread and water. Through fasting and prayer one can stop wars, one can suspend the laws of nature. Charity cannot replace fasting. Those who are not able to fast can sometimes replace it with prayer, works of love and confession; but everyone, except the sick, must fast."

When asked the purpose of fasting, the visionary Vicka replied, " Through fasting we purify our hearts. In order to have a pure heart, we need the grace that comes from fasting. When we pray and when we fast, Satan can do nothing to us."

Father Slavko Barbaric, the spiritual director of the visionaries, in his book entitled *Fasting*, describes fasting as the prayer of the *entire* body. He states that in prayer we *attach* ourselves to God, and by fasting we *detach* ourselves from the things that tie us to the world. He writes, "We find it easier to pray when we fast, and we fast better when we pray." Father further states that prayer will increase in quality when combined with fasting. Fasting can greatly amplify the power of prayer, even to working the miraculous. Fasting also helps us to realize our spiritual emptiness and need. We come to know and experience our dependency on God and not on the things of the world. The entire purpose of fasting is to reinforce the spirit and put it in control of the flesh. As a result, fasting along with prayer deepens our relationship with God and neighbor. It makes us more receptive to the Word of God and to the Eucharist. Good works and peace are the fruits of prayer and fasting.

The call to fasting is as old as the Old Testament. A study of the Old Testament shows that prayer and fasting could bring about reprieve even in the most precarious conditions. And, of course, we know that Jesus fasted. (Lk 4:1-4) It was through His fasting that Jesus found the strength to overcome temptation.

The Wednesday / Friday fast actually has its origins in the early Church. The call to fasting at Medjugorje is only a reiteration of what Jesus had already said and done Himself, and what the early Church had put into practice. Fasting is one of the fundamental principles of Christian life. More recently, Pope John Paul II, in his encyclical, "The Gospel of Life," encouraged the practice of fasting, saying that with prayer and fasting evil can be recognized and fought more easily.

But why bread and water? Bread is a basic food and is also a symbol of LIFE. Water is a sign of spiritual purification. Together the bread and water message tells us to come back to life, to come out of our impurities to be pure. Bread is also the food of the poor. The willingness to live on bread and water for the day demonstrates a willingness to be poor before God and disposed towards His will. It also helps us to be more empathetic to the needs of the poor in our world, and thus to be more benevolent in our care for them.

Health professionals acknowledge that fasting is actually good for the body, contrary to popular belief. Fasting cleans the toxins out of our bodies. So the claim that it is not healthy to fast is erroneous. I personally know a number of people who have been fasting on bread and water for more than ten years, one woman in particular for fourteen years. Not only are these people healthy, but they are also very joyful and loving people, which attests to the fact that fasting is good for the body and spirit equally. Father Slavko explains that by strengthening the spirit, we become more resistant to psychological and physical illnesses. So we can actually lengthen our lives by fasting! Furthermore, the Blessed Mother, as any good mother, would never ask us to do something that is unhealthy or detrimental to us.

The fact that God encourages us in our endeavors to fast can be illustrated through a story related to me recently by a friend. One day my friend was fasting for an intention, but was with a group of people who wanted to go out to eat after a meeting. It was 10:30 at night when she arrived at the restaurant. Her car was the first to arrive of the large group, and thus, the first to order. She really did not want anyone to know she was fasting, as Jesus advises us (Mt. 6:18), so she went ahead and ordered. She ended up being one of the last people served, even though she was the first to arrive. When she finally got her food, it turned out that the order was wrong, and she had to send it back. By the time she finally got her food, it was just past midnight! So during the hour and a half that she waited for her food, she was able to complete her fast! "God has a sense of humor," she laughed.

We have the ability to change the world by fasting. I know it works because the near-impossible intention I fasted with the first year was granted. If you are looking for ideas for a New Year's resolution, consider fasting. Start out slow, though, lest you get discouraged. Start with one day a week, perhaps skipping dessert, for example. Gradually you can work up to a bread and water fast one day a week, and finally move to a fast two days a week. Vicka cautions, "The first time is always the most difficult. When we try to fast, Satan tries hard to distract us. We have to pray hard the first time, really hard. The second time will be easier and the third time even easier. Then it will become natural."

As Our Lady has asked us to "pray with the heart," She has also asked us to "fast with the heart." By that She means to accept fasting as a means of growing closer to God and to others. If we feel apprehensive about fasting, we can always ask Her for the special graces to fast well, and we can be sure that She will answer this prayer, for She urgently needs our help. In 1985 She said, "Heed the call to fasting because by fasting you will ensure that the total plan of God here in Medjugorje will be fulfilled." Although fasting may seem difficult, the rewards far outweigh the inconveniences. Fasting takes patience, practice and perseverance, but the results are, literally, out of this world!

Below is an abbreviated version of a beautiful prayer written by Father Slavko, to be said on fast days.

Prayer for Fasting

Loving Father, today I have decided to fast. I can remember that your prophets of old fasted, that Jesus Our Lord fasted, as did His disciples. The Blessed Virgin also fasted and has called me as well. Eternal Father, I offer this day of fasting to You. May it draw me closer to You, teach me Your ways, and open my eyes to see Your many gifts. May love for You and for my neighbor fill my heart to overflowing.

Lord, may this fast help me to grow in understanding the hungry, the deprived, the poor. Let me see my possessions as gifts for the journey meant to be shared. Grant also to me the grace of humility and the strength to do Your will.

Lord, may this fast cleanse me of bad habits, calm my passions, and increase Your virtues within me. And may You, Mother Mary, obtain for me the grace of a joyful fast, that my heart may sing with You a song of thanksgiving. I place my decision to fast firmly in Your hands. Teach me through fasting to be more and more like Your Son, Jesus Christ, through the Holy Spirit. Amen.

Editor's note: I did not put my name on the original article since we should not let people know we are fasting. However, since I am now editor of "The Spirit of Medjugorje" everyone knows I fast anyway, since Our Lady has told us not to tell others to live the messages if we don't live them ourselves!

(8/02)
What Wounds God the Most?
By Sr. Emmanuel

Father Xavier P., a young priest visiting Medjugorje, witnesses:

"The other day I came to truly understand the Sacrament of Reconciliation. The point is not so much to confess one's sins, but first to confess the Mercy of God and to welcome it. In fact, I went to see my spiritual director to take stock with him and I told him, 'I'd be very happy to go to confession, but I have already been yesterday during a weekend retreat. I therefore have no sins to confess, and I fear that to go to confession once again would be spiritual gluttony.' My spiritual director, guessing my wrong perception of this sacrament, told me something which I will remember all my life: 'One doesn't need to have something to say, since confession is above all to put oneself at the foot of the Cross of Jesus in order to receive the Mercy which flows from His Heart.'

"So I dared to ask him to hear my confession even though I didn't know what to say. 'If you feel the need, why not?' he said to me. I was happy to be able to do this without having prepared a whole list of sins, and kneeling down, I felt that I was about to experience something very powerful. I said, 'Lord I am coming to the foot of Your Cross, I ask forgiveness for all my sins, I am open to receive Your Mercy!' I was then overwhelmed by the love of God to the very depths of my being and heard myself say something which I had never thought of before, 'I ask forgiveness for my lack of trust in You.' In saying this, I really understood what had wounded the Heart of God the most in my life. Usually, I would carefully line up my sins one after the other, but here, since I had the right not to say anything, suddenly it came to my heart what pierced the Heart of God. And here is what it was – I did not truly trust Him! As for the rest, He did not care!

"That day I experienced what contrition is, that is to say, the fact of suffering from having wounded the Heart of God. I discovered my deepest sin. For this, Jesus had invited me close to His Cross, right there where my sin had pierced Him, from there His pardon flows!"

(3/99)
Be Not Afraid
By Fr. Slavko Barbaric

It is sad that many who are involved in Marian movements are also wounded by fear. Many Catholics today spread an apocalyptic atmosphere, and in doing so, spread only more fear. Here in Medjugorje we have never heard anything in the messages of which are meant to be afraid, but exactly the opposite, that we need *not* be afraid, because in the end, God is Lord and Ruler, and He will turn everything to the good. That is why I want all of us, and especially those who live in fear, to hear these words very clearly... BE NOT AFRAID.

Statue of Fr. Slavko at Mother's Village in Medjugorje

Editor's note: Fr. Slavko died on Cross Mountain on 11/24/00. The next day Our Lady said in Her monthly message that Fr. Slavko was in Heaven.

(6/04)
Write a Love Letter to Your Mother
By Romilly Fenlon

Recently I was listening to one of Sr. Emmanuel's CD's called "Portraits of Mary" in which she tells the story of a man who lived in Medjugorje and who loved Our Lady very, very much. He loved Her so much that for years he wrote Her love letters every day and hid them in a special place. Then one day he thought, "Who do I think I am that Our Blessed Lady would take any notice of my letters?" so he stopped writing. After a week he just had to write Her another love letter and he put it in the same place. He then went to Marija's for her evening apparition.

Afterwards Marija looked for him because Our Lady had asked her to find him and say to him, "How happy I am for his letter today, because for one week I have missed his letters so badly." Sr. Emmanuel says that Our Mother loves to have letters from us and wherever we put them She will read them.......... Imagine that?

I do hope that many of you will begin corresponding with your Heavenly Mother in this way, and remember, She also asks us to write to our Guardian Angels because this brings us closer to them.

There are many other incidents and miracles on this tape all showing just how much Our Blessed Mother loves us.

The Welsh Medjugorje Apostolate

First Communion in Medjugorje

(7/03)
Prayer After Holy Communion
By Brother Craig Driscoll

This time I want to refer to a very special type of prayer – making a thanksgiving after Holy Communion. It is a very special time to pray. I came to learn its value when I was a student in Rome. I would attend Mass in the evening at the church of Our Lady of Light. And then I would, as we say, make my thanksgiving. I found that I prayed with greater recollection and stillness just having received Jesus. And I prayed to Jesus within me. After Holy Mass it is good, if possible, to remain in church and pray for fifteen minutes. Or go somewhere, even in your car, and pray for fifteen minutes. I believe if you do this, it will enrich your prayer and spiritual life. This time period is important. (The Presence of Jesus remains within a person for about fifteen minutes until what is just the form of bread dissolves.) So for fifteen minutes you are a tabernacle! Jesus is with you – Body, Blood, Soul and Divinity. This time after Holy Communion is a very precious time for prayer. Do not lose it to do other activities. Cherish and protect this time, your thanksgiving each time you receive Holy Communion.

Editor's note: Brother Craig, the founder of The Monks of Adoration, can be contacted at his website www.monksofadoration.org.

(11/02)
Grace Comes in a Hurry When We Thank God and Stop Complaining
By Michael H. Brown

Want to surprise yourself with happiness? Want to feel a sudden infusion of grace? There's one way to do that, and it's simple: stop complaining. You'll be astonished at how much closer God is when you're grateful than when you're in a state of dissatisfaction.

To complain means to grumble, to be annoyed, to express resentment. It's one thing to speak out when there are injustices or to report a serious situation. It's another to complain. When we complain – when we act like our lot in life is never good enough, when we are always declaring ourselves mistreated – we only give energy to whatever it is that is irritating us. Check this out. Next time someone bothers or even insults you, suffer silence. Don't mention it. Zip it. Offer the silence up. You'll be amazed: though it may cause a niggling aggravation for a short period of time, the "sting" will leave much sooner than if you complain about it! Jesus never complained on the way to the Cross nor during the Crucifixion, and His reward was Resurrection. His reward was rising to the right Hand of the Father. So it is with us. The Lord told us to take up our crosses each day and often this cross is when something irritates us and we're tempted to voice anger.

While our psychologists tell us we need to "vent" our emotions (and while there are times we do need to express certain problems), for the most part "venting" makes a problem worse. It makes an insult last that much longer. It fans the flames. Worst of all is when we complain about something we have prayed for! Think about that. We pray for a job – and then when we get it, we're full of complaints about it! We pray to get married and then complain about our husbands and wives! We pray for kids – and then complain when we have to get up in the middle of the night!

This is ingratitude, and it's the opposite of thankfulness. It's a manifestation of pride. When we're resentful we believe we deserve better (indeed, that we deserve Heaven on earth), and are indignant of anything less. That's a good way of falling out of God's favor. It never works. It compounds a bad situation. It's counterproductive in the extreme. Did Mary complain in the manger? Did She complain about how little She was given? Did She complain that here She was having a Child in the most inconvenient of circumstances? Instead of complaining we should be thanking God – and praising Him in all circumstances. Easier said than done? Yes. Much. We're all in this struggle called life. It's one big test! There are constant aggravations. But when we pass the little quizzes along the way – when we make it over one of the countless obstacles, and when we offer up our silence – there is often an outpouring of grace. This is especially true when we are silent in the face of unfairness.

When we can do that – when we can shake off even something unfair – then grace is not only powerful and not only long-lasting but often arrives in an instant.

www.spiritdaily.com

(6/02)
Unbelievers
By June Klins

"My angel, pray for unbelievers. People will tear their hair, brothers will plead with brothers, they will curse their past lives which were lived without God. They will repent, but it will be too late. Now is the time for conversion." What a compelling message Our Lady of Medjugorje gave in August of 1985. But what did She mean by "unbelievers?" Polls confirm that only a small percentage of people do not believe in the existence of God. Even the terrorists attest to the fact that they believe in God. Indeed, Satan and his cohorts also believe in God. So to whom is She referring?

On my first pilgrimage to Medjugorje, I was captivated when I listened to Mirjana speak about unbelievers. Mirjana explained that although she does not get daily apparitions any more, Our Lady appears to her every year on her birthday, March 18, and every 2nd of the month to pray together for unbelievers. Mirjana clarified that unbelievers are not necessarily people who do not believe in God. She described unbelievers as those people who have not yet accepted God's love in their lives. Mirjana testified that when we pray for unbelievers we are really praying for ourselves, and ultimately the whole world, since it is because of the unbelievers that we have violence, hatred, wars, abortions, and other ills in our world. For, if people were true believers, they would not commit these atrocities. In other words, when we pray for unbelievers, we are really praying for a peaceful world and an end to all evils. That made perfect sense and Mirjana certainly had me convinced.

Desiring to know more about what Our Lady said regarding unbelievers, I was directed to an interview that author Janice T. Connell had with Mirjana. The complete interview can be found in her book, *The Visions of the Children*. Mirjana said, "The Blessed

Mother says from time to time even Her most faithful children are unbelievers. We all have our moments during the day, during each day of our life, where even the most faithful among us do not believe. So the Blessed Mother prays for each one of us too... She recognizes sadly that many of Her children throughout the world go to church or places of worship just because it is tradition, but they are unbelievers because they do not really know and love God. They only go to places of worship as a social custom. The Blessed Mother says they need much prayer so that they, too, can believe." Mirjana told Janice that sometimes even the best of us are unconscious unbelievers. "From time to time, all of us lack belief in God – in God's love – and we lack trust in God's love for us. Every day we need to pray for faith, for hope, for love, so that we can be a believer – a total believer." Our prayer should be, like the man in the Gospel, "I do believe, help my unbelief" (Mk 9:14-27).

Upon my return home from Medjugorje, I had the insatiable urge to pray for unbelievers. I was "on fire" and wanted to help save the world. In my zeal to spread the messages to the unbelievers, I think in the process, I may have inadvertently turned some people away. Then I read the words of St. Francis of Assisi, "Preach the Gospel at all times. If necessary, use words," and I realized that is precisely what Our Lady had said to Mirjana when She said, "Do not impose your faith on unbelievers. Show it to them by your example, and pray for them" (2/2/90). So now, although the mission has not changed, my "game plan" has – to simply live the messages of Medjugorje the best that I possibly can, particularly fasting (which is very powerful), and to pray, pray, pray. I remembered hearing somewhere that faith is "caught, not taught," so I silently say a prayer for those who reject Our Lady's messages.

At a retreat I attended recently, Father John Corapi contended that we do not have any idea of how powerful our intercessory prayers really are in the salvation of souls. He said that we could talk until we are "blue in the face" to a person who is in serious sin (i.e. an unbeliever) and he still will not "get it." Jesus had the same problem, so if they treated Jesus that way, of course, they will treat us that way too. An unbeliever cannot begin to understand, Father explained, until he repents. And in order for an unbeliever to repent, he needs grace. How does he get that grace? From our prayers, fasting and sacrifices. To offer Masses for unbelievers is especially powerful. A great Doctor of the Church, St. Anselm, declared that a single Mass offered for someone during their lifetime may be worth more than a thousand celebrated for them after death. Father Corapi said that by our prayers we could be saving the soul of someone we do not even know who lives in another part of the world, perhaps even as far away as China. Isn't that an awesome thought! Then Father related a true story of intercessory prayer, repentance and conversion.

Father Corapi works sometimes with drug addicts, having been one himself before his extraordinary conversion. One day he told the congregation at his retreat to pray for a special intention of his, which happened to be a young woman who was a drug addict. After Mass, a woman who had cancer approached Father and told him that she would offer all her prayers and suffering for his intention. Later, Father found out that at the same time that the congregation was praying for this young drug addict, she was on her deathbed. An angel appeared to her and told her that it was not her time yet. Her life was saved, and ultimately she cleaned up her act, and eventually became a daily Communicant. The power of intercessory prayer for unbelievers is dreadfully under-rated! "How very large are the numbers of unbelievers! That will change only if you help me with your prayers," Our Lady said in 1984.

Father Zlatko Sudac (the Croatian priest with the stigmata) suggested that we use analogies when speaking about God. So to understand the way that the intercessory prayers work to help save an unbeliever, the following simplistic image occurred to me. God, Who is all Love is continually raining down His rays of grace upon us like the rays of the sun shining upon the earth. Some, by virtue of their birthright, have been absorbing these rays since Baptism. These are believers. Blessed are they, but, as Jesus reminds us, "To whom more is given, more is expected." Then there are those who have put up an umbrella at some point to shield themselves. They live in constant darkness. These are the unbelievers. The grace of God cannot penetrate the umbrella. For God will never force Himself on anyone. But when someone intercedes by prayer and fasting for one of these unbelievers, the result is similar to the effect of sun rays shining through a magnifying glass. A little hole gets burned into the umbrella. Sometimes that is all it takes. In her diary, St. Faustina said, "One thing alone is necessary: that the sinner set ajar the door of his heart, be it ever so little, to let in a ray of God's merciful grace, and then God will do the rest." The unbeliever feels the warmth and the light coming through that little hole, and the umbrella comes down. He becomes a believer. "For you were once darkness, but now you are light in the Lord. Live as children of light, for the light produces every kind of goodness and righteousness and truth" (Eph. 5:8-9).

For some people though, it takes a lot more prayer. God gave us free will. St. Faustina continued in her diary, "But poor is the soul who has shut the door on God's mercy, even at the last hour. It was just such souls who plunged Jesus into deadly sorrow in the Garden of Olives." So we continue to pray and fast and sacrifice until that hole becomes bigger and bigger. Or if many people are praying the umbrella begins to serve as a sieve. Sometimes there are people who just don't want to take down the umbrella though, but we continue to pray and pray so that the whole umbrella ends up in shreds – which could even happen at the moment of the unbeliever's death. A case in point would be Timothy McVeigh. Once a believer who had even received his Confirmation, at some point in his life Timothy put up the umbrella and became an unbeliever. Timothy kept that umbrella up, and lived in darkness as he continued to refuse to see a priest before his death sentence was carried out. Although we will never know what transpired in those final moments, it was reported that Timothy finally did give in and asked to see a priest before his execution. It seemed that his umbrella had become shredded from all the prayers, particularly the Divine Mercy Chaplet – that were said for him during those final days. (Remember that as Christians we are to hate the sin, but love the sinner. Christian believers should never wish that anyone be condemned for eternity.) We follow the example of Jesus, who said, "Father, forgive them, they know not what they do" (Lk 23:34).

"Dear children! Wake up from the sleep of unbelief and sin, because this is a time of grace which God gives you... Pray in a special way for those who have not come to know God's love, and witness with your life so that they also can come to know God and His immeasurable love" (2/25/00).

May we all join our Heavenly Mother and say, "My soul magnifies the Lord."

(6/02)
Children and Prayer

Tips for teaching children the value of prayer:

(1.) Example: Let children see you in prayer, both in time of need and in time of thanks.

(2.) Location: A special place of prayer is good. Make that place holy with a Bible or crucifix or candle.

(3.) Time: A regular prayer time helps, early morning or after school or before bed.

(4.) Attitude: Cultivate a sense of God's presence, a loving and caring presence embracing our every moment.

(5.) Reflect: Let the events of the day be content for prayer; prayer is talking things over with the Lord.

(6.) Scripture: Bible prayers and stories lead to family discussion of who God is and how He works in our lives.

(7.) Silence: Good to have quiet time; communicating with God is speaking but also listening.

(8.) Amen: End in some regular way – the "Our Father" or a little song or blowing out a candle.

Church Bulletin

Children praying in Medjugorje

(4/01)
Surrender
By Msgr. James Peterson

The willingness to share the plan of Mary for peace in the world involves the willingness to share in Her surrender. For Her, for Jesus, the basic mental frame they bring to God's call is "Here I am, Lord; I come to do Your will."

For us to enter into that attitude we need to accept the difficulties of life without seeing them as rejections by God or as a reason for self-pity and complaint.

I like the parable about a man who was always angry at the crosses he had to bear. Other people had such easy lives even when they were indifferent to God and to others. Self-pity and complaint became a way of life for him.

In his depression, he asked God for a different cross. So God sent him to pick out whatever he wanted. There was a hall filled with all kinds of crosses – big, little, heavy, light, harsh, varying in size. He went past all of them and picked out the littlest, most comfortable looking of all. Then he turned to God and said, " This is the one I want."

And God said, "Really, this is the one you had all along. I put it in the hall there when I let you lay it down."

The message of the parable is, "If you want to help bring peace to the world, stop complaining."

So stop complaining.

(2/04)
Distractions in Prayer
By Tom Hubbard

Several years ago a very holy priest shared this with me concerning distractions in prayer. He said to imagine yourself in a garden with Our Lady, but become distracted from Her because you've seen a beautiful flower. So you walk over to the flower that distracted you, pick it and then bring it to Our Lady.

His point was for us to understand that distractions are going to happen. When they do, just acknowledge the distraction, remove it from thought and bring it to the Blessed Mother. Offer it to Her, and then proceed on with your prayer. Our Lord wants our will to pray, but sometimes our emotions are in turmoil and He understands this. But, if we just give Him our will, He can do so much. And don't forget your very powerful intercessor, the Blessed Mother, who can take our sometimes humble and weak efforts in prayer and make them a beautiful bouquet before Her Son. Just ask!!

Editor's note: Tom lives in Fairdale, KY.

(10/00)
Spiritual Prozac
By June Klins

It was one of those days when I couldn't seem to stop the tears from flowing. I had plans to visit someone whom I did not want to see me in this state, so I reached for some pain medication I used to take for the severe pain I had before the Blessed Mother had interceded for my healing. I knew that this medication, in addition to alleviating my pain, always elevated my moods. I opened the prescription bottle and took out a pill. "This is wrong," I thought to myself. I was not in any physical pain, and had no business taking that pill. So I put the pill back in the bottle.

Still crying, I got into the car. I picked up the crocheted rosary from Medjugorje that I keep there, and decided to say a Rosary for myself. I say at least 15 decades of the Rosary every day, but I always pray these Rosaries for the intentions of others, *never* for myself. Today, I thought, I am going to pray for myself. Part way through the Sorrowful Mysteries, I realized that I was not crying any more, and by the time I got to the last decade, I felt exceptionally good. I felt an inner strength that I didn't know I had. It was an incredible feeling, a "spiritual high." The people I went to see had no idea that

I had been crying just twenty minutes before, and when I left, they even thanked me for brightening their day!

In the days that followed, as I reflected upon the peace and tranquility that the Rosary had given me, it occurred to me that the Rosary was a kind of "spiritual Prozac." But this "spiritual Prozac" works instantly, not over a period of a month, and has no harmful side effects!

A week or so later, one of my friends had asked me to pray for her sister who was depressed about a situation in her family. I wanted to tell her how the Rosary had helped me, but then the Holy Spirit moved me to a more creative solution. I took an old prescription bottle, and ripped off the label. I inserted a Rosary and made a new label for the bottle, and placed these words in just the same places as a prescription: "Prescription #101; Take 3 times a day; Refills – indefinite; Expiration date –none."

When I gave it to my friend she was delighted. The following week my friend told me that her sister was just thrilled with her new "prescription." A few months later, my friend told me her sister was doing better and wanted to know where she could buy a Rosary ring, so she could have the Rosary with her at all times!

It is not surprising that recitation of the Rosary can help lift our spirits. After all, Our Lady said at Medjugorje, "Even one Rosary alone can work miracles in the world and in your lives," and " Prayer renews your body, soul, and heart." She also said, "I urge you to ask everyone to pray the Rosary. With the Rosary you will overcome all the troubles which Satan is trying to inflict." (Satan loves for us to be depressed, because if we are depressed, we are not able to love God and others as we should.) And in 1990, Our Lady told the visionaries, "Prayer is the best medicine these days."

When I shared the idea of the prescription Rosary with others, they were enthusiastic. Perhaps you know someone who could use a prescription Rosary. Be creative! Let the Holy Spirit direct you.

Editor's note: Over the years I have given out hundreds of these prescription bottles with rosaries in them. However, I changed the prescription number to MT 6:24-34, which represents the Bible passage Our Lady asks us to read every Thursday. I also changed the

number of times to "3 or 4" to reflect the addition of the Luminous Mysteries which were instituted in 2002. And I also added a line about side effects: "May cause illumination to eyes and face." Finally, I added a doctor's name: "Dr. Simon Mir."
(Simon helped Jesus as the Rosary helps us, and "Mir" means "peace" in Croatian.)

Confessional in Medjugorje

(3/04)
Sins That Need To Be Confessed
By Fr. Larry Richards and Fr. Ed Lohse

Abortion.....Adultery.....All use of illegal drugs.....Any dealing with the occult (Ouija boards) .....

Artificial birth control.....Blasphemy- disrespect toward God or toward His Holy Name.....Breaking promises deliberately..... Bringing dishonor to family, school, community or the Church..... Calumny- telling lies about another...Despair - to believe that God will refuse to forgive you.....Destruction of other people's property..... Detraction – telling an unkind truth about another.....Disobedience toward parents/teachers.....Drunkenness including any drinking under the legal age.....Excessive materialism.....Gluttony - eating or drinking to excess.....Gossip - talking about others.....Hatred.....

Homosexual actions…..Improper thoughts…..Indifference to good or evil…..Ingratitude…..Intentional violations of school rules…. Jealousy…..Laziness…..Lying…..Malice- the deliberate choice of evil…..Masturbation - impure actions with yourself…..Missing Mass on any Sunday or Holyday…..Murder…..NOT PRAYING EVERY DAY…..Premarital sex, including oral sex, intercourse, impure touching of another…..Presumption – sinning and saying God MUST forgive me…..Reckless driving that endangers you, passengers or others…..Rudeness…..Selfishness…..Stealing….. Superstition…..Unjustified anger…..Using others for your own personal gain…..Watching or looking at pornographic material

Editor's note: To read and hear more of Father Larry's teachings you can visit his website, www.thereasonforourhope.org.

(1/04)
Coffee. Tea, or……..Water ???
by Carolanne Kilichowski

When I was a little girl in the 1950's I heard a phrase that seems to be obsolete in today's world: "Offer it up!" I heard these words from the nuns in school, from my mother when I did not want to eat my supper, and from the priest in his homilies. Does anyone do penance anymore and offer it up to God in reparation for the sins of the world?

In Fatima, Portugal, in 1917, the Blessed Mother repeated three times the words, "Penance, Penance, Penance!" In Lourdes, Our Lady told St. Bernadette to do penance and to pray and to relay to the world to do the same. Today and for the past 22 years, in Medjugorje, the words of Our Most Holy Mother are the same as She pleads for sacrifices and asks us to live a life of penance and prayer.

In pondering these thoughts one day, it occurred to me that I needed a plan of action to bring me to a life of penance as Our Lady requested. Knowing my nature, I needed someone else to give me a penance for the day since I knew it would work best for me. I wanted to do the proper thing and not look for an easy way out. I have a prayer partner who helps me to grow spiritually and helps me to follow through on living the messages of prayer, fasting, reading the Bible, confessing once a month, and making the Eucharist the center of my life. I asked my prayer partner to give me penance when I would start to slack off on reading the Bible daily. (Penance that would be spiritual and would be related to the act of omission or wrong act committed.) So then I would have to spend extra time with my nose in the Bible to make up for the lost time. If it was cheating on a fast day then an extra fast day was in order.

As time went on I saw this plan of action worked really well for me. It helped me to truly live the messages of Medjugorje that I love to relay to others. You cannot stand up and tell others to do something that you are not doing! It was essential that I "live the message" that I encourage others to do. I found that knowing I would be asked about my actions helped me to do that Bible reading even though I did not feel like it that day or gave me that push to go to confession in a new month because I wanted to please Our Lady and certainly if I was asked I wanted to be able to say, "Yes! I am doing it !"

The plan worked out so well that I was inspired to make daily penances. Each month my friend and I make up penances. For example, we would add things that feel like penance to us. I love my hot peppermint tea so if I cannot have it for a day it is a real penance. So, when "No tea today!" is picked for a day......it is a true penance for me. We have extra prayers such as litanies of the Holy Name of Jesus, or to a saint, go out of your way to compliment someone today in an honest way, pray for someone who has hurt you. We have made a penance box and add these new penances once a month. We even made it fun and have added a free day of no penance. My prayer partner says three Hail Mary's so that Our Lady will guide her into choosing the correct penance for the next day and then she takes one for me from the box and one for herself. We are so very happy that we are doing our best to make Our Lady and Our Lord happy. Won't you do the same? We challenge others to try the penance box with a partner and watch the blessings flow into your lives. Our prayer is that you will be inspired to have the desire to live a life of penance and prayer. The blessings that you will receive will be abundant! God Bless you all and thank you for responding to Her call!

Editor's note: Carolanne has started a "penance group" to do penance for Our Lady's intentions. She sends out the penance every day by email to the group. If you would like to join, you can e-mail Carolanne at ckilichowski@msn.com

Sr. Emmanuel

(11/03)
Every Day Should Be Thanksgiving Day
By Sr. Emmanuel

One day a large crowd had gathered in Marija's courtyard. Her friend and translator, Kath, could barely find enough space next to her. As Kath's eyes swept through the crowd, she was struck by a face which stood out sharply from the others. This face was so bright that it radiated like the sun piercing the mist. What joy! Kath was fascinated. As soon as Marija had finished, Kath headed straight towards the "sun" that was shining next to the wall. He was actually very small, a tiny little priest, and so old that he could have belonged to another century!

"Please excuse me, Father, if I'm being nosy, but I would really love to know what makes you so radiant with joy. You must have a secret..." Kath asked.

The priest was Italian. She looked at the expression in his eyes. Despite his advanced years, he had the innocence of a little child.

"I'll tell you, Ma'am," he answered. "I am 95 now. But at the age of 5, I discovered with great sadness that people were always complaining. They would complain for trifles, and find 100 good reasons to feel frustrated, and this shocked me as a child. I also felt that Jesus was saddened by this. I wanted very badly to console Him, so I decided to make a contract with Him. I promised Him that during the first 100 years of my life, I wouldn't complain once. On the contrary, I would bless Him and thank Him for everything, for the good and the not-so-good, but above all, I would always celebrate the gift of life. And you know, Ma'am, I must say that I've kept my promise! During all these years that I've spent celebrating life, no evil could ever touch me; I've avoided all demons!"

"Incredible! But since you are now 95, your contract will come to an end soon!" Kath exclaimed, smiling.

"Well, yes, I've thought about that, too. But it's okay; I told Jesus the other day that I was ready to renew the contract for the next 100 years of my life!"

This wonderful priest became a "blesser" at the age of 5. As Our Lady said, "Bless and seek the wisdom of the Holy Spirit." His life of blessing God for everything, the good and the not-so-good, gave him a special connection with the Holy Spirit. He lived a joyful, consecrated life as a holy priest, in the power of the Holy Spirit. We can learn so much from this story. May we learn to bless God, and in turn all creation. We will then find ourselves open to the will of God in our own lives, which will in turn serve Our Lady's plan for the Triumph.

Children of Medjugorje, www.childrenofmedjugorje.com

(10/99)
Prayer Groups
By Joan Wieszczyk

One who prays the Rosary alone receives the graces and merits of only one Rosary. When you pray with others, you multiply the amount of graces and merits by the number of people you are praying with.

If, for example, you are praying with a group of eight, you gain eight times the amount of graces and merits. If you pray with more, you get more. The prayer of the Rosary is very powerful, especially when prayed in a large group. That's the reason for prayer groups. **We need many Rosaries! We need many prayer groups!**

Prayer is part of the message of Medjugorje. We are asked to spend time in prayer. Why not start a family prayer group? Pray the Rosary together. That's what Our Lady is asking us to do. She needs our prayers of the Rosary to fulfill Her plans. We are all included in that plan. Your family Rosary might be the one holding it up. Don't let that happen. Start now in the month of the Rosary.

Bring the family together in prayer. Remember, we are all Her family. Let us respond to Her by answering the call of prayer, especially the prayer of the Rosary.

Station of the Cross behind St. James Church in Medjugorje

(7/04)
Christmas in July
By Susan Tassone

Alongside the Mass and Holy Rosary, The Way of the Cross is a most powerful and at the same time easily available means of helping the Poor Souls in Purgatory and acquiring merit for ourselves. Nothing is more pleasing to Our Lord than devout meditation on His bitter sufferings. Many teachers of the spiritual life assure us that more benefit is derived through loving meditation on the sufferings of Our Lord than by the practice of rigorous penances and the recitation of long prayers. Moreover, contemplating Our Lord in His bitter sufferings is the best means to fill us with contrition for sin and invite us to the practice of penance and mortification. The atoning merit which we thus acquire may be applied to the Holy Souls and will, without doubt, afford them great relief in their pain.

In the life of the Venerable Mary of Antiqua, a nun of her convent appeared to her after death and complained, "Why is it you do not perform for me and for other suffering souls the Devotion of the Stations of the Cross?" The Servant of God stood speechless at these words. Then she heard Jesus say to her, "The Devotion of the Stations of the Cross is so profitable to the souls in Purgatory that this soul has come to demand it of you in the name of all. It is a most efficacious suffrage for the souls in Purgatory who on their part, will be praying for you and defending your cause before My Justice."

Our Lady of Medjugorje tells us, "Most souls are released on Christmas Day, not All Souls Day." So we invite you to give the Holy Souls "Christmas in July!" The summer is a time to relax, vacation, and travel. Unfortunately, for the Holy Souls languishing in Purgatory, they never have time off. They suffer day and night - 24 hours a day, 7 days a week! We tend to forget our Holy Heroes when they need us most desperately. What an ideal time to help them and ourselves.

An efficacious means of obtaining favors from Heaven is to assist at Holy Mass and pray the Stations of the Cross for the Holy Souls in Purgatory for 33 consecutive days for the Holy Souls in honor of

Our Lord's 33 years He spent on earth. What a marvelous summer devotion in July for the Holy Souls. You can easily do these at home if you are unable to attend Mass. Many favors have been obtained by this means that were not received through the intercession of the saints.

The month of July is dedicated to the Precious Blood. The Souls long for the Precious Blood of Jesus. St. Thomas Aquinas tells us that "as the dew refreshes and raises up the withering plants and flowers, so does the Blood of Christ revive and comfort and bring renewed hope to the Poor Souls in Purgatory." The 33-Day Devotions for the Holy Souls offer a powerful method of praying for departed family and friends. It will surely elevate your soul as well! And remember, ingratitude has never entered Heaven! The Holy Souls will intercede for you all the days of your life until you are safely home in Heaven! What a summer bargain!

Editor's note: Susan Tassone is author of the besting selling books for the Holy Souls: **The Way of the Cross for the Holy Souls in Purgatory; Praying in the Presence of Our Lord for the Holy Souls; The Rosary for the Holy Souls in Purgatory; 30 Day Devotions for the Holy Souls; Prayers for Eternal Life and Prayers of Intercession for the Holy Souls** *on CD/Cassette. (The Way of the Cross for the Holy Souls is recited by Fr. Benedict Groeschel and the novices along with The Rosary recited by Fr. John Grigus of Marytown, Benediction and the Litany of the Holy Souls.)*

(9/02)
Conversational Prayer
By Brother Craig Driscoll

One form of prayer that I like to do and recommend is conversational prayer. First, you need to realize that you need not only talk to God only about religious subjects. Talk to God about your everyday, ordinary activities. He is interested in these. Second, ignore the thought that what you tell God in prayer He already knows. God wants to hear about them in your own words.

Talk to God about: - What you've been doing lately - Your plans or hopes for the future - Your interests. These could be knitting, woodworking, cooking, etc. Tell about them in detail. Tell God about that P.T.A. meeting, something that happened at work or about that new recipe you tried. Your plan and hopes for the future. Talk to God about "small" plans like going to the library, or that trip to Mexico. If you do conversational prayer often you'll become very good at it.

Editor's note: Brother Craig, the founder of The Monks of Adoration, can be contacted at his website www.monksofadoration.org.

(1/03)
Praying for Priests
By June Klins

"If only you could see the tears that Blessed Mary has on Her face," Mirjana said after Our Lady appeared to her last October 2. Although Mirjana said Our Lady was crying because of all the unbelievers, I would bet that more than a few of those tears were for Her beloved priests. In a talk given last fall in Medjugorje, Mirjana said that if there are any privileged souls to Our Lady they are the priests. Our Lady says, "They are representing My Son."

Mirjana talked about the difference between the way the people in Medjugorje treat their priests and the way other Europeans and Americans do. In Medjugorje, if a priest enters a home, no one will sit down until the priest sits down, and no one will start speaking until the priest speaks. Mirjana said, "We know with this priest Jesus is entering our home, but it is not up to us to judge whether he is really and truly representing Jesus or not. God is going to do that." Mirjana continued, "But God is also going to judge *us*, what our way of treating our priest was. Our Lady says that the priests do not need your criticism or your judgment. They need your love and your prayers."

In a conversation with Sister Emmanuel, Vicka reaffirmed Mirjana's words: "If I hear that a bishop has been charged with this or that, who am I to judge his conscience? No! I'm not going to judge, but I must examine my own conscience and ask myself: 'For so many years, the Gospa has been calling us to pray for priests, bishops and the Holy Father. What have I done to help them? Have I prayed for them with all my heart?' That is the question! And the rest is for God to know. As for me, I must help and do my part the best way I can and not waste my time commenting on everyone else. Far too many words are spoken and not enough prayers!"

Priests concelebrating Mass in Medjugorje

In a talk given in August at his parish of Siroki Brieg, Fr. Jozo said: "A priest cannot be compared with any vocation. A priest is a sacrament chosen from God, anointed, consecrated, and returned back to the Church. The Church is responsible to protect its priests." He continued, "You cannot see a priest as someone who earns a wage, who is like another profession, a doctor or lawyer." Father talked about how important it is to support our priests with love and prayers. "There is no Sacrament of Confession without the priest. Without the priest, there is no Eucharist." He said it is especially important to support our priests when it is difficult for them, because they are only human. "He grows tired, he falls, but he must be helped to be raised again," Father said.

"How scandalous stories have shaken the entire world of our time," Father bewailed. "It all comes from the enemy, from the dragon, from those who want to destroy the Church. We need the priests because we need forgiveness, we need love, we need grace and salvation." Father pleaded, "Pray for your priests. Love your priests. May an evil or negative thought never be born in your heart, in your soul, against a priest. May you never doubt in the priesthood. Pray that every priest may persevere, that we may persevere on the way of holiness, that we may be an example to you, that we may extend to you a path trodden by our good works and holy lives." He emphatically implored, "Love your priests, protect your priests, support your priests."

In his talk, Father Jozo gave a practical example of how the people in his area pray for their priests. He said that for 16 years they have had an apostolate called "Margarita," named after a flower with seven petals. Each of the petals signifies one of the days of the week. In the heart of the flower they write the name of the priest, and on each petal signifying one day of the week, the parishioners fill in the names of who will be praying for the priest on that particular day. Father said, "And then for the priest's birthday, name day, Easter, Christmas or special days, we can bring the sign of our love to our priest to say to him, 'Do not be afraid. We are protecting you upon our knees. While you rush to proclaim the Word of God, we kneel for you, that you may be able to walk erect. Our hands are raised in supplication while you pray and bless and preach, while you give out grace. You remain in our prayers.'"

In a very similar endeavor here in the U.S.A., a lady told me recently that her prayer group called all of the parishioners and asked them if they would pray one day a week for a year for the bishop, local priests and deacon. Then they presented them with a pretty wreath, with all the names on hearts.

At my parish, in a very simple gesture, we pray for the priest before he begins the Mass. He asks us to raise our hands and we ask God's blessing on him. Perhaps you could suggest that to your priest.

People in my Internet prayer group have what they call an "Honor Roll for Priests." Anyone can send them the name of a cardinal, bishop, priest, deacon, seminarian, religious brother or sister. In their post once a month they state: "God knows their special needs so we will just list names. This way we can print it off and take it with us to Adoration or have it in our Bible or prayer book. Our Blessed Mother needs our help – in Her messages She asks us to pray for priests and for Her Pope and his health. Our priests and our Church NEED OUR PRAYERS!! In the Gospel of Matthew 9:32-38 Jesus said to His disciples: 'The harvest is good but laborers are scarce. Beg the harvest master to send out laborers to gather His harvest.' Please let us also remember to pray for vocations. Mother Theresa once said that the reason we don't have very many vocations is because we are not praying for them. There needs to be prayers for graces for vocations. So please pray for our beloved priests and pray for vocations to the priesthood."

Another way to pray for priests is to "adopt" a priest. There is an order of sisters in New Mexico, the Handmaids of the Precious Blood, who administer what they call "The Lay Associates of the Priesthood," an association of Catholic laity dedicated to supporting the Priesthood through prayer. Each member receives the first name of a bishop or a priest for whom they "pray in secret," never revealing his name. There are no dues for this membership. The only requirement to "adopt" a priest is to pray daily for that priest. If you are interested in joining this association you can send your name and address to:

Rev. Mother Prioress
Handmaids of the Precious Blood
Cor Jesu Monastery – P.O. Box 90
Jamez Springs, NM 87025

Within a few weeks you will receive the name of your priest. You will also receive an enrollment form that you can make copies of to distribute to encourage your friends and acquaintances to join as well.

"I ask you to pray in a special way for Pope John Paul II and for priests," Our Lady pleaded in July of 1992. St. Teresa of Jesus knew the importance of praying for priests and that is why she made prayers for the priesthood the first duty of her Carmelite family.

Let us pray for priests and seminarians every day and encourage others to as well. It's a matter of Life or death. No priests – no Bread of Life. Just do it!

(6/00)
The Sacraments and Medjugorje
By Msgr. James Peterson

Any visit to Medjugorje makes clear the importance of the sacramental life in Mary's plan for peace. The village itself has its center in St. James Church. And the church, besides the evening Rosary and Marian visits, has a constant schedule of Masses and a constant stream of pilgrims using the sacrament of Reconciliation.

The visionaries have said often that the Mass is the most important part of the day. Mary has told them if they ever have to choose between a Mass and a visit from Her, the Mass should come first.

The message is not only for the people of Medjugorje and those who visit there, but it is for the whole world. Those who visit are to carry the message.

That means we need to bring alive again the importance of regular Confession. Mirjana said in a recent interview that there is not a person on earth who doesn't need Confession at least once a month.

And that means further, if we believe the validity of Mary's message, that we ought to review our response to Mary's request. That's self-discipline and fasting; that's daily Rosary; that's a deepening life of inner prayer; that's respect for the sacraments; that's using the sacraments knowing that every one of them is a visit with Jesus, the Christ.

That's not an option. It is the use of a great gift for which we will answer God someday.

(2/00)
Fr. Jozo Speaks
By June Klins

On June 27, we traveled by bus to Siroki Brijeg to listen to Father Jozo Zovko speak and to get his healing blessing. Father Jozo was the pastor of St. James Church when the apparitions began. He was imprisoned for supporting the apparitions and subsequently removed

215

from any future position at St. James as a condition of his release. We were fortunate that the group was small enough that he could speak in a room behind the church. Last year he spoke inside the church and there was such an echo that we could not hear his talk at all.

Father Jozo was the last of the speakers that we would hear on our Medjugorje pilgrimage, and he seemed to underscore many of the themes that we had already heard in the talks by the visionaries and the other priests. The theme of Father's talk was that we are called to be witnesses. Jesus told us all to be witnesses, to tell what we have seen or heard. "A witness," he said, "is a spiritual athlete." To witness, is to sacrifice, because we must renounce the way we see things and accept the way God sees things. But we cannot be a witness or have peace or joy without prayer.

Fr. Jozo

Father admitted that he at first did not believe the children back in 1981, until June 29, the feast of St. Peter and Paul. It was on that day that the children were apprehended by the police, and at 2:00 A.M., he heard very joyful singing. Vicka said to him, "Are we not prepared to suffer anything for Our Lady?" From that instant on, Father Jozo never questioned the authenticity of the apparitions again. He then went on to talk about Vicka. Years ago, she was given the choice of health or illness. Vicka chose health and her apparitions would cease for 10 days. At the hospital, there was no sign of illness, but then Vicka changed her mind because she did not want the apparitions to cease. Vicka asked for forgiveness and then she got sick again, but as the sickness intensified, so did her joy intensify.

When pilgrims come to Medjugorje, Father continued, we are trying to choose what is right. We come asking for forgiveness and help to do what is right. If we do not change, though, we are a "false witness." It is not important how many pilgrims come to Medjugorje, he said, but how many are living the messages. "A person who does not live the messages denies God," he proclaimed. Our Lady, through the power of the Holy Spirit, helps to make each of us a new person. As a witness, we must bear witness to our families, something that is lacking in today's families.

Father used the stories of Abraham and Sarah, and Mary and the angel Gabriel as examples of strong faith. He said that there is no faith without sacrifice. So many people ask why they have to suffer, but even Job and Tobit never asked that through their trials. When trials come, Father comforted, faith grows and there is evidence of how God loves His people.

Father requested that during the time we are in Medjugorje that we do not waste the time sleeping. He said that we must completely surrender ourselves so that God will lead us to become joyful witnesses. He continued that Jesus does not want us to preach, but to be a witness. "The speech of the heart is visible," he said. Everything about us speaks and is a witness. We must start over again and return to the ways of the faith. Our Lady is looking for new disciples.

Father then told the story of a Buddhist man who, in 1983, heard an inner voice tell him three times to come to Medjugorje. He brought his video camera, but the police put him in jail and confiscated his camera and tape. They wanted to use it for propaganda, but whenever they played the tape it would be blank and one time they just heard birds chirping! While he was in Medjugorje this man received a rosary from Father Jozo. When he went back to China that year he started a prayer group to pray the Rosary, and now there are over 100 prayer groups in China started by this man. It has not been easy for him, however. He has been imprisoned five times in China for spreading propaganda.

Father began distributing rosaries to us as at the conclusion of his story. He said that a witness must be willing to suffer and be persecuted for the faith, like the Buddhist man, but that it is an honor to be a witness. The rosary he was giving to us, he insisted, is NOT a souvenir. It is a mission, and we need to pray it every day. Without prayer and conversion there is no joy. He appealed to us to pray together with our families and our neighbors. It is not easy, he said, but it is possible and necessary.

Father suggested that when we return home we make an altar in our homes and on it place a crucifix, a statue of Mary, a family Bible, a family rosary, and holy water. We should bless our homes once a week.

Father's reference to fasting was very brief. He smiled in jest as he said that fasting is the easiest message to fulfill. But seriously, he said, fasting is very important and that if you are not able to fast for health reasons, you can fast in other ways such as giving up smoking or something else.

Father concluded his talk by telling us that Our Lady asks us to pray for priests. We need to pray for them because a priest is a sign of God's presence among us and that God loves us. Without our priests there is no Eucharist or Confession, which is what the enemy wants.

(11/04)
A Thanksgiving Message

The following is an excerpt from the last homily of Fr. Slavko Barbaric, O.F.M., given on the morning of his last day on earth, November 24, 2000, at 9:00 A.M. Mass in St. James Church, Medjugorje:

The unity of the Holy Spirit be with you all. Almost every message of Our Lady ends with the sentence, "Thank you for having responded to my call." I have often asked myself, whom does Our Lady give thanks to, who is so important that She comes down from Heaven to say "Thank you" to that person? She does not expect a lot from us, but She sees everything good we have done already and that is why She thanks us...

Gratitude is the best guideline in education. When you want to educate someone, you must first look at the good inside that person; however insignificantly small it may be. Then you must try and visualize how the individual could be and work on that together with the person. If we are blind to these things we only see the negative aspects; things that are imperfect; things alien to our momentary fancy and so we can get cracking with our criticism; we condemn and reject.

Mary, on the other hand, only sees the good things in this world. She also sees what could be better, and right there She begins with Her teaching. Read the messages! They are positive and they give hope, they are encouraging. In the same way, Mary has awakened the positive power within us and that is why we thank Her.

The one who follows Mary has no time to criticize. Mary gives us courage to do something even where we might believe it might disturb, or not be good, or be too much for us. Only in this way can Mary, together with Her Son Jesus, enter the third Millennium. Therefore, thank all the people in the world who follow Mary, who visit us untiringly, who organize pilgrimages without ever getting tired.

Let, as Mary says, a new dawn arise, a new springtime. It is not springtime in a calendar sense, but it is springtime of a new decision. Let the New World begin, where we believe it is outdated, contaminated and destroyed. When you decide to love God and our neighbor as yourself and when many besides you do likewise, then the new time has arrived.

(9/02)
The Mercy/ Blessing Prayer
By June Klins

"Sticks and stones will break my bones, but names will never hurt me." Who in the world ever made that one up? Have you ever been hurt by something someone said about you? If not, what planet are you from?

Not too long ago someone I care about hurt me deeply by saying some unkind things about me. After I heard this I could hardly look this person in the face again. It was eating me alive because it was impossible to avoid this person. I confided in my friend Pat about this, and she gave me some good advice.

Pat said that Father Larry Richards once taught her a prayer to say when she was deeply hurt and angered by some people. He told her to say this prayer every time she thought of them (which she says was constant at first): **"Father, have mercy on me and bless them."** Pat explained, "If you're like me, you think the words are mixed up, but they're not. You're asking God to forgive YOU and bless THEM! When I started saying it I was so angry that I said the words but couldn't mean them. All these thoughts raced through my mind (i.e., I don't need forgiven. I didn't do anything wrong, it was them! They don't deserve to be blessed. It should be ME! I'm a victim.) After a day of 'praying' like that I sat down on my sofa in the middle of the night, exhausted from the day of wrestling with that prayer and my thoughts of those people. I realized I had actually been wrestling with God. I started crying uncontrollably, telling God I was really sorry and He knew what was best for me and those people. And for once, I said the prayer 'Father have mercy on me and bless them' and **really** meant it from my heart. I was flooded with peace about the whole situation and it never left me. Within days, God removed those people from my life (they unexpectedly relocated)! I still sometimes pray for them and have no animosity toward them, although I had previously felt I'd never be able to forgive them for putting my family and me through that nightmare."

I took Pat's advice and said the prayer, from the heart as Our Lady tells us, every time I thought of the person who hurt me. I was soon able to face them and felt perfectly comfortable. I felt like a new woman!

A few weeks later, a lady on my Internet prayer line wrote to me for advice on how to handle the pain her brother-in-law and sister-in-law had inflicted on her. I told her about this short but powerful prayer that I have named "The Mercy/Blessing Prayer." A month later I wrote to her to see how she was doing and she replied, "I am feeling wonderful, in fact I no longer have any anger in my heart at all. Yes, I'm still blessing her and I thank you so much for your good advice and prayer. I feel like a heavy weight has been lifted from both my shoulders and my heart."

This prayer can even be used in situations where someone is not necessarily hurting you, but is irritating or annoying you in some way. For instance, one morning I arrived at church a half hour before Mass was to begin so that I could pray a Rosary first. Two women were there conversing (and to make matters worse, gossiping) with such loud voices they could have woken the dead. As much as I tried to block them out, I could not. So I prayed, "Father, have mercy on me and bless those two women." I prayed it several times, and then all of the sudden, they stopped talking, and one of the ladies went to another pew. It worked.

A few days ago, my son was very upset because the tenants would not move out of the house he had leased weeks earlier. He became even more upset when he found out that by law they could possibly be there another 90 days while they waited for the loan on their house to be approved. So I told him about the Mercy/Blessing Prayer, and said I was planning to write an article about it. I suggested that he say the prayer faithfully, and told him that if the people moved out I would write about it. He said he would consider it. The next day, I asked him if he was saying the prayer and he replied, "Oh, yea." Tonight the landlord called to say that the tenants were gone!

Our Lady of Medjugorje said, "Pray for your enemies and call the Divine blessing upon them" (6/16/83). Maybe we could change the world with this simple prayer. Repeat after me, "Father, have mercy on us, and bless the terrorists."

(8/02)
The Jesus Rosary
By June Klins

This special Rosary is popular in Medjugorje. It has a Crucifix, and one bead on the tail, and continues with a circular formation of seven "decades" of beads, each containing five beads. Although I have been to Medjugorje 3 times, I had not been familiar with this devotion. My friend and I sat at the Blue Cross and used Father Slavko's wonderful book, *Pray with the Heart!* for the meditations for this Rosary. This ancient chaplet renews a form of prayer from centuries ago. It is rapidly spreading around the world, particularly in prayer groups and communities. The Rosary is said in remembrance of the 33 years of Jesus' life on earth. It consists of the Apostles Creed, 33 Our Father's, and 7 Glory Be's. It is divided into 7 mysteries, each inviting the individual or group to meditate on an aspect of Jesus' life.

The Jesus Rosary (As Gospa taught Jelena)

After the first six intentions, pray 5 Our Father's, and then pray, "O Jesus, be strength and protection for us." (The 7th mystery has only 3 Our Father's.)

Pray the Apostles Creed

1. Mystery:
Contemplate - the birth of Jesus
Intention: Pray for peace.
2. Mystery:
Contemplate - Jesus helped and gave all to the poor.
Intention: Pray for the Holy Father and for the Bishops.
3. Mystery:
Contemplate - Jesus trusted in His Father completely and carried out His Will.
Intention: Pray for priests and for all those who serve God in a particular way.
4. Mystery:
Contemplate - Jesus knew He had to give up His life for us and He did so without regrets because He loved us.
Intention: Pray for families.
5. Mystery:
Contemplate - Jesus made His life into a sacrifice for us.
Intention: Pray so that we, too, may be capable of offering our life for our neighbor.
6. Mystery:
Contemplate - The victory of Jesus over Satan. He is risen.
Intention: Pray that all sins may be eliminated so that Jesus may live in our hearts.
7. Mystery:

Contemplate - The Ascension of Jesus into Heaven
Intention: Pray that the Will of God may triumph, so that His Will may be done.

After this, contemplate how Jesus sent us the Holy Spirit.
Intention: Pray so that the Holy Spirit may descend upon us.
7 Glory Be's

(3/03)
Medjugorje Fasting Bread

1 Pkg. dry yeast
1 1/2 cups warmed milk
3 Tablespoons softened butter
1 1/2 teaspoon salt
1 Tablespoon sugar
3 cups all purpose flour

Put yeast into the warm milk and butter in large mixing bowl, let this dissolve for 1 minute.

Add salt, sugar, flour and beat or mix for about 1 minute.

Pour batter into greased loaf pan. Slash the top, cover and let rise for about 35 minutes.

Bake at 375 for about 45 minutes.

Take out of pan and let cool.

Editor's note: This bread is so delicious it won't even feel like you're fasting!

(6/03)
Safe Tanning
By June Klins

The large church parking lot was jammed, and I could hardly find a parking place. I thought to myself, "Wow, Jesus is going to be so pleased at all the people who showed up for this month's Adoration." My excitement quickly turned to disappointment, though, when I walked into the church and could count on two hands how many people were there, and have a few fingers left over. I found out afterwards that all the cars were there because of a cheerleading competition in the school gym. I felt blessed to have been one of Jesus' cheerleaders. People just don't know what they are missing.

Bishop Fulton Sheen never missed a day of prayer in the presence of the Blessed Sacrament in his 54 years of priesthood. He was living the messages of Medjugorje before Our Lady even began appearing there. In 1985 Our Lady said, "Unceasingly adore the Most Blessed Sacrament of the altar. I am always present when the faithful are adoring. Special graces are then received by them." Bishop Sheen said that when you pray in front of the Blessed Sacrament daily, your major problem in life will be solved. You become like a magnet for graces from Heaven. Wow!

Adoration Chapel in Medjugorje

There are so many fruits, the first being that you develop a personal relationship with Jesus. You will be able to hear the word of God in your life and God will speak to you. You get what I've heard a number of priests refer to as a "Son tan." This tanning is safe though. Instead of getting skin cancer, this kind of tanning actually burns away cancer – the cancer in our souls caused by sin. Bishop Sheen made that comparison decades ago, when he compared it to a "cobalt treatment." Today we would call it "chemo," with no nasty side effects! Either way, Jesus is the "Divine Radiologist." In your encounter with the Son of God, the rays of His Love make your soul more beautiful to the Father. When we spend time with Jesus we will become more like Him, since people usually become like the people with whom they associate.

Another fruit is that vocations increase in parishes that have Adoration. What's more, abortion clinics have even been known to close their doors when there is an Adoration chapel nearby.

The most compelling fruit of making a holy hour every day though, according to Bishop Sheen, is that you will be given 'power over souls,' that is, the grace to influence the lives of other people by what you say or what you do. Just think, you would be able to inspire your grouchy, controlling boss to change his life just by spending time with Jesus!

Probably one of the reasons that there are so few people at Adoration is that, sadly, many people do not believe in the Real Presence of Jesus in the Eucharist. There are many stories of Eucharistic miracles, but the following story is one if my favorites.

In October of 1995, Pope John Paul II was scheduled to visit St. Mary's Seminary in Baltimore. His plan was to first make a visit to the Blessed Sacrament. Security personnel made a sweep of the building, and highly trained dogs were used to detect any persons who might be present. These intelligent canines went through the halls, offices, and classrooms, and then were sent to the chapel. They went up and down the aisles and finally into the side chapel where the Blessed Sacrament was reserved. Upon reaching the tabernacle, the dogs sniffed and whined and pointed, refusing to leave. They remained there, their attention riveted on the tabernacle, until called out by their handlers. They found a real living Person in the chapel. Even animals know He is there.

Standing in line at the grocery store one day I noticed a magazine called "Sun Signs." The magazine misguides readers into thinking that signs in the sun can change your life. The Father invites you instead to visit Jesus in the Blessed Sacrament as often as possible to experience how this Son can indeed change your life. And you will never get burned!

"Dear Children! Today I invite you to fall in love with the Most Holy Sacrament of the Altar. Adore Him, little children, in your Parishes and in this way you will be united with the entire world. Jesus will become your friend and you will not talk of Him like someone whom you barely know. Unity with Him will be a joy for you and you will become witnesses to the love of Jesus that He has for every creature. Little children, when you adore Jesus you are also close to me"(9/25/95).

(2/03)
Praying with the Heart
By Fr. Jozo Zovko, O.F.M.

In the first days of the apparitions, we really competed with each other, seeing who could pray more Rosaries each day. That was unhealthy competition. Although Our Lady was exhorting us to pray not that way, but with our hearts, we did not understand what it meant to pray with the heart. That night She said to us, "This evening, before you start praying, you should all forgive one another." We thought, "That's something simple, we do that in every Holy Mass!" But by no means was it easy; it was quite an effort. It meant that everyone who had built up hostilities within his heart had to give them to God immediately with love and joy. I explained what Our Lady's request meant and asked all the faithful if they understood. Everyone said yes, but no one did anything. We felt as if we were in a desert, and we were even a little afraid. Moreover, Our Lady would not allow us to pray until we had personally reconciled with each other - until we had forgiven each other from our hearts. A silence came over us; it seemed to last forever. We suffered a desert-like anguish, and it grew later and later.

Everyone felt very depressed. A fight was raging within us. Finally I suggested, "Let's pray the Rosary, that we may become able to forgive." So we began praying what we call "the Psalter," all three groups of the mysteries of the Rosary. After about half an hour, a voice announced in the church, "Lord, I have forgiven. Please forgive me!" Everyone began crying and sobbing loudly. This prayer touched our hearts, and floodgates of tears were opened. We all had the desire to say, "We have forgiven. Please forgive us, too!" And everyone looked for a hand, any hand, to hold. With relieved hearts, we continued our prayer. After the prayer there was a true celebration of reconciliation throughout the whole village.

The morning that followed will go down in the history of Medjugorje. Overnight the people had torn down all the walls in their hearts, walls which had been separating them from one another. The next morning, everywhere in the village, people went to houses in which they had never set foot before because of one incident or another; many had even stopped greeting one another. Farmers can be petty, too. Hate and estrangement often had developed. But now, in their neighbor, they recognized their brother. In their neighbor they recognized Jesus. It occurred to them sadly why, for such a long time before, they had been unable to have such joy and beauty. And so I no longer have to ask anymore, "Do you want to forgive? Do you believe in God the Father?" We now carry out our baptismal promises day by day, everyone making an effort, even if only mentally: "I reject Satan... I believe in God..."

It was then that people saw the Croatian word "MIR," meaning "PEACE," in capital letters in the sky. I, too, witnessed this event. The letters moved as if animated, streaming towards us like a car's headlights. It felt like we were experiencing the end of the world. I cannot imagine anyone ever forgetting such a thing - not the letters, but the interior experience, I mean. It is engraved within our hearts, into our lives, and into our entire being, the meaning of "Medjugorje" - engraved within the new man, within children of God who love and forgive.

(8/00)
Spiritual Warfare
By June Klins

"Your Mama wears combat boots." Not an image most of us have ever had of the Blessed Virgin Mary, but this is the way Father John Corapi described Her, not once, but three times during three different talks at the Medjugorje Conference at Notre Dame University in May. Maybe this is why She appears on a cloud, so that her feet are not visible!

We should not be too surprised at this portrayal, however. St. Paul refers to this type of garb a number of times in his letters, most notoriously in the 6th chapter of his letter to the Ephesians : "Put on the armor of God so that you may be able to stand firm against the tactics of the devil. Therefore, put on the armor of God that you may be able to resist on the evil day, and having done everything, to hold your ground. So stand fast with your loins girded in truth, clothed with righteousness as a breastplate, and your feet shod in readiness for the gospel of peace."(Note that Our Lady's principal message is a gospel of peace.) St. Paul continues, "In all circumstances, hold faith as a shield, to quench all the flaming arrows of the evil one. And take the helmet of salvation and the sword of the Spirit, which is the word of God."

Between the Notre Dame Conference and another Medjugorje retreat I attended the following weekend, the theme underscored by the dozen or so speakers was the same - We are at war! As Father Corapi put it so clearly, "The devil has been given a lot of rope." In one of the earlier messages to the visionaries at Medjugorje, Our Lady proclaimed, "The hour has come when the demon is authorized to act with all his force and power. The present hour is the hour of Satan."

One need not look far to see the evidence that it is indeed Satan's hour. Not only was the 20th century the bloodiest century in history, but the relentless attacks on families, the increase in violent crime, drugs, the AIDS epidemic, etc. all have his brand on them. According to Our Lady, "All disorder comes from Satan."

Over the years, Our Lady has warned us of Satan's attacks, not just on society, but on individuals. In Her messages She has alerted, "Satan lies in wait for each one of you. Every day he tries to plant doubt in you. Satan plans to work ever more fiercely to take away your joy. Satan is trying to find emptiness in you, so he can enter and destroy you." Satan's ultimate goal is simply destruction. Our Lady's emphasis on the reality of Satan is NOT meant to frighten us, but, on the contrary, to protect us. As in any war, we need to know what the enemy is planning. To be forewarned is to be forearmed.

God in His infinite mercy wills ALL men to be saved, and so He sent Jesus to us through Mary. Now She brings us to Her Son. That is Her mission, to bring each one of us to Jesus. As Father Corapi so simply stated, "There is a battle that goes on in every soul for Heaven or for Hell." And that is why Our Lady must wear combat boots! "Our Lady is a sign of hope in a world that is losing hope," Father Corapi continued. Our "armor" is the gospel and Her messages of conversion, faith, peace, fasting, and prayer, especially the Rosary. In June of 1985, Our Lady said, "I urge you to ask everyone to pray the Rosary. With the Rosary you will overcome all the troubles which

Satan is trying to inflict." Then in July of 1988, She pleaded, "Do not surrender! I will pray with you. Do not pray just with your lips, but pray with the heart. In this way prayer will obtain victory." And in 1985, She decreed, "Through prayer, you can completely disarm him and ensure your happiness." Our Lady's message echoes the gospel of Mark when Jesus' disciples asked Him, "Why could we not drive it (the demon) out?" and He replied, "This kind can only come out through prayer and fasting" (Mk. 9:28-29).

No doubt all of us want that happiness of which Our Lady speaks, so let us all put on our armor, join Her army and ensure victory by using the five powerful weapons She tells us to use: prayer from the heart, especially the Rosary; daily Eucharist; daily Bible reading; monthly confession; and fasting on bread and water on Wednesdays and Fridays. Then She can take Her combat boots off, and give Her feet some much needed rest!

(6/01)
Change
By Msgr. James Peterson

When I was younger and heard about Mary's appearances to Juan Diego and to Bernadette and to Jacinta , Francisco and Lucia, it always awakened in me amazement. Elizabeth asked, "How have I merited that the Mother of my Lord should come to me?"

As I got to know something of the history of those visionaries, it was clear that their lives were never the same afterward. They were different. Their world was different. Their perception was different.

And now we are at the twentieth anniversary of Our Lady coming to Medjugorje. To me it is very gratifying to be part of this monthly publication.

By Her coming, Our Lady is calling us all to be different, to help make the world different, to see things differently. Time and again, our articles help to explain how the town of Medjugorje is different, how the congregation of St. James parish is different, how many lives are touched miraculously in simple ways, on the marvels of conversion.

Today, I'll ask you to spend a little time in self-examination: "How have I merited to be part of this? Am I changing? Am I helping the world change?"

"Am I close to being like Mary in the way I perceive things, and in the way I respond? My soul magnifies the Lord."

Chapter Five:

Other Bits and "Peaces"

(5/03)
The Rosary Has a Spell On Me
By Michael Serafin

The Rosary has a spell on me
A good one in a way
It sings to me
It talks to me
It makes me want to pray.
I cannot explain to you
What the Rosary does to me
But in a way it seems to say
"Mary, help me on my way."

Editor's note: Michael is from Johnstown, PA. This poem was written when he was in the third grade.

Icon of the "Resurrection"

(8/99)
Icon of the "Resurrection"

This icon is found in the chapel of the Community Cenacolo in Medjugorje. It was painted by three young men in the Community. It portrays the "Anastasis" - the Resurrection. Like all icons, the background of gold is symbolic of eternity. At the center of the icon is Jesus Christ Risen, dressed in a shining white tunic. The white color is a symbol of purity and of the glory of the Resurrection. The golden stole on His arm is the sign that Jesus is the first and the last true priest. The three Greek letters in the halo of Christ signify that Jesus is the Alpha and the Omega, the First and the Last, the Beginning and the End. The eyes of Jesus are painted in such a way that whoever contemplates the icon from any direction has the impression that they are turned toward him or her. The celestial circles at the shoulders of Jesus and the green field are symbols of the Reign of Heaven. The two rocky mountains at the skies are the sign of the Holy Spirit that embraces the universe. At the right of Christ stand King David, King Solomon and the prophet Elijah. At the left stand the just, who number only three in the original icon. We have added a fourth personage who represents all the young men of the Community already in the Heavenly Reign. Jesus grasps Adam and Eve by the arm, as they are the symbols of all humanity destroyed by sin, and pulls them out from the tomb of the dead. Eve has the left hand covered because it is the hand of the original sin. The black color is the sign of darkness, of death, and of evil. The keys, the lock, and the chains represent the slavery of sin. The three nails are those of the Passion of Christ who has broken the chains of evil, freeing us from sin to give us salvation.

Information Center "Mir" Medjugorje, www.medjugorje.hr

(10/02)
Pope John Paul II Thanks Fr. Jozo for Medjugorje
By Denis and Cathy Nolan

An unexpected event for Fr. Jozo Zovko broke out in the Croatian media! We want to share with you what was reported last Saturday evening, August 24, 2002, in the Zagreb daily newspaper, "The Vercernji List." The headline states, "A surprising gesture from the Vatican. The Pope thanks Father Jozo for Medjugorje!"

The cover photo was taken when the Holy Father welcomed Fr. Jozo in 1992 , in the midst of the Bosnian war. At that time the Pope told him: "I am with you, protect Medjugorje! Protect Our Lady's messages!"

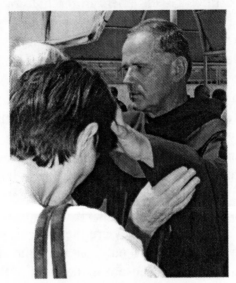

Fr. Jozo blessing pilgrim

The article in the paper shows also Fr. Jozo at his desk, reading the Pope's letter, with a caption to the left of the picture: "The Pope has signed a thank you note to Fr. Jozo Zovko." A translation of the article from the Croatian reads:

Siroki Brijeg - The world renowned Franciscan, Fr. Jozo Zovko, was more than surprised when yesterday Polish pilgrims came to thank him for twenty-one years of testifying to the Medjugorje apparitions, and especially when they handed him a thank you note personally signed by the shaky hand of their best known compatriot, John Paul II. Actually, after coming back from Poland the Pope wrote from the Vatican to personally thank and send his apostolic blessing to Fr. Jozo Zovko.

' Our Poland is grateful for your every word, for ever thing that you have done for us,' said the Pope's collaborator, Krystyna Gregorezyk, who personally handed the thank you note to Fr. Jozo in the Siroki Brijeg church. 'So far I have received hundreds of gifts and thank you notes but none can compare with this one. I am

most pleasantly surprised,' a visibly shakened Fr. Jozo said for our paper.

Fr. Jozo Zovko is a member of the Hercegovinian Franciscan Province. As a witness to the Medjugorje apparitions, he has become one of the best known priests in the world. Many tribes have made him their chief and he is connected with many miraculous healings. According to a poll conducted by "The Daily Catholic," Fr. Jozo has been elected among twenty-nine Catholics of the century." (J.P.)

The English translation of the Pope's letter reads:

"I grant from the heart a particular blessing to Father Jozo Zovko, o.f.m. and I invoke a new outpouring of graces and heavenly favors, and the continuous protection of the Blessed Virgin Mary."

Then, his handwritten signature: Joannes Paulus II.

Now, according to what Krystyna Gregorezyk reported when she presented the message, the letter was written this month (August) in Rome right after the Pope's return from Poland. Krystyna, who works as a collaborator of the Holy Father in the Vatican, had breakfast with him and several other Polish people before they left for Medjugorje. The Pope signed the letter in front of Mrs. Gregorezyk.

It seems therefore that the words reported in the newspaper, "Vercernji List," are real. In a verbal message to Fr. Jozo, conveyed by Krystyna, the Pope also said that he is thankful for his apostolate for Medjugorje, for what Fr. Jozo is doing and has done so far. The Pope said he was happy to give him a sign of support.

Krystyna said that the Pope was very joyful during this breakfast and asked many questions about Medjugorje. He was also happy to hear the testimonies about Medjugorje that the Polish pilgrims reported to him.

This is the first written personal word of encouragement, from the Pope, made public by the media, to a witness of Medjugorje. This simple letter stands as a tangible and visible document in support of the Holy Father's heartfelt thanks and encouragement that he sent to Fr. Jozo through Krystyna. All are encouraged to spread this news - that the Holy Father has sent such a heartfelt blessing to this champion for Medjugorje and Our Lady's apparitions!

Children of Medjugorje, www.childrenofmedjugorje.com

(1/98)
What is A Pilgrimage?

As we are well into the pilgrimage season for many shrines, it is well to remind ourselves of what a pilgrimage should be, and these words of Padre Pio may help to focus our minds on the spiritual task ahead.

It is no longer time to sleep, but to watch in order that humanity might be saved. But how?

If you have a fire between your shoulders, ready to devour you, would you not seek every means of putting it out? When you are ill, do you not seek every possible remedy, going from here to there to find the most expert doctors? On the other hand, when unfeeling and asleep in unrepented sins, do you not think of the tragedy awaiting you on the part of God's justice?

Blind and unfeeling, help yourselves as much as you can with the arms of faith, with the arms of penance, with the arms of shame, with the arms of prayer! Act now to implore pardon and mercy for all the brutalities of the world!

Let Marian groups of pious souls, in a spirit of reparation, organize pilgrimages to the sanctuaries of the Madonna, praying the Rosary together for God's Mercy and Pity. The Most Blessed Virgin, compassionate Mother, who sheds tears of blood over today's world, calls all Her children to penance and prayer.

Let these pilgrimages be made in a spirit of penance and let the clothing of women be modest and simple, without vanity.

In former times, such pilgrimages were made barefoot, heads sprinkled with ashes and with rigorous fasting. Thus on certain sad occasions the justice of God was appeased.

If a plague were imminent, if an atomic bomb were about to explode – in such cases, Oh! how we would pray with tears, how quickly we would hasten to the nearest sanctuaries, how quickly we would put aside the frivolities of life!

The time now is the hour of darkness. Therefore, increase Marian pilgrimages to counteract the works of Satan and to prepare for the Triumph of the Immaculate Heart of Mary.

In some parishes, recreational trips are organized. Why not think to organize Sacred Pilgrimages in a spirit of penance? Let us fear the chastisements of God. Let us give up some licit pleasures. Let us be like a family which, seeing one of its members dying, thinks only of prayers to save it.

I speak to you thus not to make you fear, but so that each one may regulate his own conduct to make the world better. If you do NOT listen, yours is the responsibility.

The Medjugorje Herald

(5/03)
In Largely Unknown Comments Mother Teresa Endorsed Medjugorje
By Michael H. Brown

She was the most recognizable Christian after the Pope. Many considered her a saint when she was still alive. And her devotion to the Virgin Mary appeared to be total. Her name was Mother Teresa of Calcutta and in looking back at her life we note that she had all but directly endorsed the apparitions of Mary at Medjugorje in Bosnia-Hercegovina.

"I am grateful to Our Lady of Medjugorje," she once told a magazine called "Mir Monthly." "I know that many people go there and are converted. I thank God for leading us during these times this way."

That's a lot coming from a woman who was herself a miracle-worker. We recall a documentary that showed her visiting Beirut, Lebanon, during the unending civil war. When told she wouldn't be able to go across town on her endless business of helping the poor, she said that she had prayed to the Mother of God and there would be no problem. The next day, for the first time in weeks, there was no sound of gunfire.

She told another periodical, "Medjugorje Messenger," that Mary was "my mother. She is the Mother of Jesus. She is the source of our joy, especially in the communities of the Order. She is there to help. She is there to protect." When asked about Medjugorje's central messages of confession, prayer, penance, fasting, and peace, she described these as "precisely the requirements for the present day."

Prayer and fasting, she said, leads to a clean heart. And as for peace: "The world has never needed peace so much as now," she said, commenting on a site where the Virgin comes as Queen of Peace. "There is also so much evil, so much destruction, especially of life itself."

The "living saint" -- who died in 1997, but is already up for beatification -- had an interesting request. "Tell everyone who comes to Medjugorje: 'pray to Our Lady of Medjugorje for a drug to cure AIDS!'"

That doesn't sound like she had much doubt about what was occurring. Indeed, the apparitions had started in 1981 -- not far from her native Albania -- and she had obviously heard constant reports about them. According to a booklet called "Medjugorje: What Does the Church Say?" Mother Teresa wrote a revealing letter to Denis Nolan, coordinator of the annual Marian conferences at Notre Dame and now director of Children of Medjugorje, on April 8, 1992. In that handwritten note this soon-to-be saint indicated not only a belief in Medjugorje, but an incipient practice of devotion. "We are all praying our Hail Mary before Holy Mass to Our Lady of Medjugorje," she wrote, "asking Her to give us the medicine for AIDS patients."

According to "Medjugorje Messenger" she specially recommended this prayer: "Mary, Mother of Jesus, give us Your heart, so beautiful, so pure, so immaculate, so full of love and humility, that we may become worthy to receive Jesus in the Bread of Life, to love Him as You loved Him, and to serve Him in the poorest of the poor."

www.spiritdaily.com

(8/01)
Feed My Poor
By Joan Wieszczyk

In the village of Medjugorje, there is a nun named Sister Muriel Geisler. She belongs to the congregation of Our Lady of the Cenacle. For 20 years, she worked with the youth. Her main work was in spiritual directions, such as retreats. Now she works with the poor.

She came to Medjugorje in 1992 for 6 months while the war was going on. Then she left for Florida to study, then on to Jerusalem for more study. The last 3 months there, she lived in a hermitage. She was in charge of keeping it cleaned. One day, while she was picking up rocks and raking, she found a holy card. It was of Our Lady, Queen of Peace - Medjugorje. Previous to this, she was praying and praying, asking God what He wanted her to do. Now she said to herself, "That's the place." So in 1993, she went to Medjugorje.

Sr. Muriel

An important part of Sr. Muriel's life is delivering food. She feels this is her calling from God. Back in 1993, when she was in Medjugorje, she did not have any transportation to get around to deliver food. Through the generosity of some Irish people, she was given 2 vehicles. Now she could go about her mission feeding the poor. She is another Mother Theresa.

Sister delivers to 50 villages, serving about 400 people. The greatest need is to the poor and the elderly, women 65 years and older, some as old as 90-95 years of age. They are women who do not have pensions and do not have any means of sleeping at night. They live in stone houses, with dirt floors, no heat, no running water, no toilets (they use the fields). You wonder how people could live like that today. It is hard, but they have always done this. Therefore, Sister would like to give them a little bit of comfort before they leave. Many have died, but there are always new ones coming in. Some of them are refugees, some are displaced persons and some are people who lived there all their lives. Sister finds them very ill, very poor, and dying with no food and no beds. "They are just a mess."

One day, while she was working with the refugees, they came and asked her for sugar. They wanted to make Christmas cookies, but she had no money. When she got home, there was an envelope for her. With that gift of money, she felt God wanted that money spent on sugar, so she bought 100 pounds of sugar, enough for everyone in that village. Sister has a helper living with her. The two of them go around delivering food, picking up people and taking them where it is necessary. Four days a week is just distributing food, which means they have to stay up nights to fill the bags. They usually make up and give two big shopping bags. Since they don't have powdered milk, they have to carry liters, full liters. It is the kind of milk that stays on the shelf for a year. It can be kept but once it is opened, it has to be refrigerated. They like powdered milk because you can dilute it with water, but it is hard to find. Most of the food they buy and distribute are the basics - barley, corn meal, jam, cheese, sugar, salt and margarine. Once in a while they get frozen chicken, but they do not distribute meat. They don't eat cereals. They eat a lot of bread and cabbage soup. That is their main diet especially in the wintertime.

Sister Muriel's biggest wish is to one day be able to build an assisted living home, just one floor. Something very plain and simple, nothing with anything extraordinary. They just want a clean place for these people to live, to be taken care of and have nursing care. A place enough for 25-50 patients, giving them therapy, good food, clean atmosphere, etc. She would take in the old people without pensions (and there are plenty of them), the poor whether they be Muslims or Serbs, but they must be destitute. Until that time comes, she is continually distributing food. This is her main mission.

Prayer is an important part of the life of Sister Muriel. She prays 3 hours a day to find out what God wants of her. She believes and trusts in the powerful prayer of the Rosary and of the Divine Mercy. With prayer she can fulfill her mission.

This article on Sister Muriel Geisler was made possible with the help of John Zamary of Youngstown, Ohio. John is associated with "Gospa Florida," an organization led by Barbara Stephens of Palm Coast, Florida. She takes pilgrims to Medjugorje. He is also a dear friend and promoter of Sister Muriel's work for the poor.

Editor's update: Sister Muriel's dream has become a reality with the assisted living home which has now been built in Medjugorje. To read more about Sr. Muriel's work or to make a donation, go to www. saintjosephtheworker.org.

(7/03)
Don Gabriele Amorth (Famous Exorcist & Author) Visits Medjugorje

Don Gabriele Amorth is an exorcist in the diocese of Rome and the president of honor of the Association of Exorcists that he founded in1990, and of which he was president until the year 2000. During his stay at Medjugorje in July, 2002, he gave an interview to Fr. Dario Dodig.

INT: In Her messages in Medjugorje, Our Lady says often that Satan is strong and She invites us to pray, to fast and to be converted.

DGA: Yes, this is true. In an Italian magazine, I had the occasion to comment on Our Lady's messages where She speaks about Satan. She often spoke about this. She underlined that Satan is powerful and that he wants to destroy Her plans. She invited us to pray, to pray, to pray.

INT: In Her messages, Our Lady spoke about the Rosary, about the Adoration of the Blessed Sacrament, about prayer before the Cross, and She said even that through prayer wars may be stopped.

DGA: Yes. Through prayer, we can even stop wars. I always understood Medjugorje as a continuation of Fatima. According to Our Lady's words in Fatima, if we had prayed and fasted, there would not have been World War II. We have not listened to Her and therefore there was a war. Also here in Medjugorje, Our Lady often calls to prayer for peace. In Her apparitions, Our Lady always presents Herself under another name to show the goal of Her apparitions. At Lourdes, She presented Herself as the Immaculate Conception, in Fatima as the Queen of the Holy Rosary. Here in Medjugorje, Our Lady presented Herself as the Queen of Peace. We all remember the words "Mir, Mir, Mir" (peace, peace, peace) that were written in the sky at the very beginning of the apparitions. We see clearly that humanity is running the risk of war, and Our Lady insists on prayer and on Christian life to attain peace.

INT: In Her messages, the Queen of Peace also underlines fasting, which is a bit forgotten in the Church. She speaks about fasting according to what is written in the Gospels - that through fasting and prayer we can eliminate all influence of Satan.

DGA: This is true. First in Fatima and now here in Medjugorje, Our Lady speaks often about prayer and fasting. I think that this is very important, because contemporary men are following the spirit of consumerism. Humanity searches how to avoid any kind of sacrifice and so it exposes itself to sin. For Christian life, except prayer, we need a certain austerity of life. If there is no austerity of life, there is no perseverance in Christian life. I will give you an example - today, families fall so easily apart. They celebrate the wedding, but the couples divorce quickly. It happens because we are not used to sacrifice any more. In order to live together, we have to be able to also accept the deficiencies of others. The lack of spirit of sacrifice leads to the fact that we do not live Christian life in fullness. We see with what facility abortion is being committed, because of the lack of readiness to make a sacrifice to educate children. This is how the first reason of marriage is being destroyed. This is because there is no practice of making sacrifice. Only if we are used to sacrifice ourselves, we will be able to live Christian life.

INT: The fruits of Medjugorje are numerous. Conversions are numerous. A theologian says that here, Heaven came down on earth. Our Lady invites us to abandon ourselves totally to Her so that She may lead us to Jesus. Isn't this the essential for Christian life?

DGA: No doubt! Medjugorje is really a place where one learns to pray, but also to sacrifice oneself, where people are converted and change their lives. The influence of Medjugorje is worldwide. It is enough to think about how many prayer groups came about thanks to the inspiration of Medjugorje. I also lead a prayer group, which was founded in 1984. This group is already 18 years old. We live one afternoon as it is lived in Medjugorje. There are always 700 or 750 people. We always meditate on Our Lady's message of the 25th of the month and I always read this message in relation to a sentence from the Gospel, because Our Lady does not say anything new. She invites us to do what Jesus taught us to do. Groups like mine exist all over the world.

INT: Is it true that Medjugorje is a "big mouthful" for Satan?
DGA: Surely. Medjugorje is a fortress against Satan. Satan hates Medjugorje because it is a place of conversion, of prayer, of transformation of life.

INT: Would you give us your advice?
DGA: The "testament" of Mary, Her last words written in the Gospel, are "Do whatever he tells you." Here in Medjugorje, Our Lady insists again that the laws of the Gospel are respected. The Eucharist is at the center of all Medjugorje groups, because Our Lady always leads to Jesus. This is Her main concern: to make us live the words of Jesus. This is what I wish to everyone. May the Immaculate intercede for you, so that the blessing of God may descend on all of you in the name of the Father, and of the Son, and of the Holy Spirit. Amen!
Information Center "Mir" Medjugorje, www.medjugorje.hr

(1/01)
In Memory of Father Slavko Barbaric, O.F.M.
By Denis Nolan

It is with tears but also with joy that I write you today within the week of our dear Fr. Slavko Barbaric's return to his Father's home. The circumstances of his death are amazing and most beautiful! We are in awe of the way God called His faithful servant, whom he found keeping watch and praying at the hour of his Master's return. The name Slavko comes from the Croatian word "slava" which means glory, and it is at the glorious panel of the Resurrection, just below the top of Krizevac, that the Risen One came to draw His servant and took him into His everlasting embrace. On November 24, Fr. Slavko was leading the Way of the Cross for the parish as he does every Friday. On that day, exceptionally, he did not finish the prayers at the foot of the big Cross of Krizevac, but instead at the panel of the Resurrection, a few yards after the 14th and last station, "Jesus Is Buried In The Tomb." A few astonishing things to note: 1) Fr. Slavko had just finished praying the Way of the Cross and the Church offers a plenary indulgence to those who fervently make the Way of the Cross. 2) This is the Year of the Great Jubilee, and he died on a Friday at the time of Divine Mercy! 3) This happened on the 24th of the month, the day of the first apparition in Medjugorje. Fr. Slavko's last words on earth to those who had climbed up with him, were: "May The Gospa pray for us at the time of death." His last gesture was to bless the group. As he began his descent he had to sit down. (He did not slide as I mistakenly wrote on that day. Sorry for that.) Then, without a word, he smoothly lay down on his side and while his close friends were attending him, he stopped breathing, in great peace, without trauma or suffering. The clouds which had brought some rain on the way up divided and let the sun shine through momentarily just on that spot of the mountain. The group then saw a rainbow appear over the valley, the arch of which seemed to rise up from St. James of Medjugorje. A doctor in the group certified the death. Accompanied by fervent and sorrowful prayers, the body of Fr. Slavko was carried down the hill by his friends. Fr. Svetozar who had been sent for, as he ran uphill saw him at a distance and said to himself: "He looks like a king! What majesty!" He also shared with me: "I had an inner conviction that Fra. Slavko was already glorified. The whole thing was so solemn and supernatural! The people who were carrying him down were being given a great grace!" Fr. Svet said the prayers for the dying and anointed him with holy oil.

Later the same day, when Our Lady appeared to Marija, we were hoping that she would refer to Fr. Slavko's death and maybe tell us if he was with Her. She did not, but rather gave us a directive which sounded very much like Fr. Slavko: "Nastavite dalje!" (Keep on going!)

Fr. Slavko's grave in Medjugorje

Up until the funeral, Fr. Slavko's body was exposed in the Adoration Chapel, the coffin open according to the custom in this region. We were able to stay by his side in prayer, a number of us receiving great graces. I remember how I marveled at his face, which seemed jubilant. In the simple and beautiful Croatian way, his family kept covering him with kisses, caresses and tears. Fr. Svet, who came to lead the evening Rosary, blended his meditation with their sobs. We were between Heaven and Earth (and actually, even after a few days, we still are).

Our bishop Msgr. Peric came to celebrate the funeral on Sunday, the 26th, the Feast of Christ the King, in the presence of a huge crowd of thousands standing around the rotunda. Overwhelming testimonies, which will be reported later, were given after the Mass. An endless procession wound its way through the streets of Medjugorje to escort the coffin of their priest and apostle and pay him homage. By special permission, Fr. Slavko was buried in Kovacica graveyard behind the church. In the name of all the visionaries, Jakov thanked him for having been with them for all these years, in the best moments as well as in the worst (Fr. Slavko arrived in Medjugorje in 1982). He rests next to Fr. Krizan Galic (a pastor of Medjugorje assassinated by the Communists). That day was a real mourning day for the entire village. All bars, restaurants and shops were closed.

The eve of the funeral was the day of the message, the 25th. I will never forget the moment when, in the little team of translators, we read the message received by Marija before being spread around the world. Marija, whose eyes were red with tears, was laughing as she repeated: "Slavko u nebo! Slavko u nebo!" (Slavko in Heaven!) Except for the Holy Father, the Gospa had never named anyone in Her official messages, but She did it for Her son Slavko! Fr. Slavko was untiring in proclaiming the messages of the Gospa to the world; in return, She, the Mother of God, proclaimed him before the world in a message. Did not Jesus say: "He who acknowledges me before men, the Son of Man also will acknowledge before the angels of God?" (Luke 12, 8-9) What deceased has enjoyed such a birth-into-Heaven announcement from Mary herself, broadcast to millions of friends in just a few hours!!?

Children of Medjugorje, <u>www.childrenofmedjugorje.com</u>

(11/02)
What Happens to the Petitions?
By June Klins

Many people sent in petitions for me to take to the visionaries on my recent Medjugorje pilgrimage. A question frequently asked was, "What happens to the petitions?" Petitions can be dropped in the basket in the Information Office near the rectory, where they are then delivered to Vicka, who would present them to Our Lady in Her Apparition that day. Then the petitions are burned. In prior years I had been blessed to have been able to hand the petitions directly to Vicka. This year, however, Vicka is not speaking with the pilgrims because she is not feeling well during her pregnancy.

Since our priest knows Vicka's mother, we delivered our petitions to her at her home near Apparition Hill on October 10. She said she would then give them to Vicka later that day.

When we took the petitions, some of the people in our group also gave Vicka's mother presents for the baby. One young woman, Rachel Young, crocheted Vicka a baby blanket. We ask you to keep Vicka, her husband and their unborn baby in your prayers.

Editor's note: You can send your petitions directly to Medjugorje by email. All petitions will be presented to Our Lady by Vicka or Ivan during one of their apparitions. Your petitions will not be read by anyone. Only Our Lady will know their content. Email your petition to: molitvene.nakane@medjugorje.hr and write "petition" in the subject line.

(6/03)
Statue Where Vision Occurred Has Hidden Links to Major Apparitions
By Michael H. Brown

It was on the 20th anniversary of Medjugorje, at the jubilee Mass in St. James Church, that it occurred. The Mass had just begun when a nun originally from Medjugorje (now assigned to a parish in New York) witnessed an extraordinary silhouette of the Virgin in a kind of whiteness behind a statue situated at the right of the church. Others noted phenomena on at least five occasions.

Through the years we've heard similar reports. This statue is one of the hidden treasures of Medjugorje, the apparition site in Bosnia-Hercegovina that lately has generated remarkable news. The statue is not to be confused with the more famous one of Mary in Tihaljina. The one in the church is not as well-known but in some ways is more fascinating -- and may hold clues as to the nature of the apparitions. The reason: it incorporates the aspects of several major Church-approved apparitions. Overall the statue looks like the Immaculate Conception pose from Lourdes, with the blue sash confirming that general similarity.

Lourdes is the closest association, but the statue also bears resemblances to images from Fatima, where three peasant children saw Mary on a similarly stony hillside in 1917. This is especially true with the face. Its shape and chiseled features are very similar to a statue from Fatima that is molded according to the specifications of seer Sister Lucia dos Santos. Simply put, the face of the Medjugorje Madonna looks like the face of the Fatima Madonna.

Statue in St. James Church in Medjugorje

In addition to Lourdes and Fatima, the statue brings to mind the famous Mexican site of Guadalupe. How does it remind us of Guadalupe? In the serious mouth, in the way Mary looks nearly down and to Her right, in the prayerful hands, and especially in the starlike pattern on the blue sash, stars that are virtually identical to the stars on Her robe at Guadalupe (with Guadalupe in turn bearing further similarities to yet older images like Our Lady of Czestochowa!). The fleur-de-lis at Guadalupe is a flower-like pattern that is also to be found on the famous Black Madonna of Our Lady of Czestochowa in Poland.

Then there's the matter of Her crown. At Medjugorje Her crown is portrayed on the statue as 12 stars hovering over Her head. This is interesting because it directly connects with the Miraculous Medal apparitions in 1830 to St. Catherine Laboure in Paris. St. Catherine had 12 stars put on the back of the Miraculous Medal.

Thus we see that the statue inside St. James takes us from the beginning of the Age of Mary, which many consider to have begun in 1830, right through the major apparitions of Fatima and Lourdes and to our own time, in which matters seem to be coming full circle.

As the statue portrays Mary praying, so must we pray. As Mary implores God's mercy, so must we beseech mercy. Prayer--it's the message of Fatima; it's the message of Medjugorje; and it's the message of this remarkable statue.

www.spiritdaily.com

(1/03)
"I Bless You All with My Motherly Blessing"

What does this really mean? This includes all Her activities as a Mother for us. So it is not only a saying like "God bless you", which is also important, but it is Her presence, Her prayers for us, Her prayers with us, Her intercession for us, Her bringing us before Her Son Jesus; She is our mediator, She is our consoler, She is the one who intercedes for us and who makes this pilgrimage with us. All this is Mary's Motherly Blessing, Her whole behavior toward us. In the past, She has also said that She takes us in Her Motherly lap or protects us under Her Motherly cape; we also remember that She once said that we can give Her Motherly Blessing to others and we must become absolutely aware that we can and should carry this blessing in our families and to all people, but not only as a saying but with our totally new behavior toward the others and toward God.

The word 'blessing' comes from the Latin word 'benedicere,' which means 'to speak well, to defend, not to judge, to be there for mankind' and that is the blessing. At this moment I hope it is appropriate to say that we should be careful when we carry blessed objects that we don't slip into some sort of magical behavior or mentality. Magic means to have a formula by which a person can get God under his power; black magic is when a person has the formula to put evil spirits under his power and white magic is when a person thinks that through a certain prayer or a blessed object he can put God under his power. The blessed objects, Mary's Blessing and blessings in general are certainly a protection for us but even more, they are an invitation to become aware how we are really behaving. The blessing should call us to do good, to fight against evil and to change our life. The danger is that someone will search for the formula of the blessing or the blessed objects in order to protect himself to be able to continue to do bad things and to continue to behave in a negative manner and so through the blessing keeps the space to remain in sin. Mary's Motherly Blessing is a great protection but an even greater invitation to really behave in a manner befitting Her children.

Fr. Slavko Barbaric, Medjugorje, June 29, 1998

(10/99)
Mary
By St. Bernard

When you follow Her, you will not go astray;
When you pray to Her, you will not despair;
When you think of Her, you will not err;
When She holds you up, you will not fail;
When She protects you, you will not fear;
When She leads you, you will not be fatigued;
When She favors you, you will arrive safely.
She keeps the devil from hurting us;
She keeps our virtues from escaping us;
She keeps our merits from being destroyed;
She keeps our graces from being lost.

Mother

Appendix: The messages
January 1998- December 2004

January 25, 1998

"Dear children! Today again I call all of you to prayer. Only with prayer, dear children, will your heart change, become better, and be more sensitive to the Word of God. Little children, do not permit Satan to pull you apart and to do with you what he wants. I call you to be responsible and determined and to consecrate each day to God in prayer. May Holy Mass, little children, not be a habit for you, but life. By living Holy Mass each day, you will feel the need for holiness and you will grow in holiness. I am close to you and intercede before God for each of you, so that He may give you strength to change your heart. Thank you for having responded to my call."

February 25, 1998

"Dear children! Also today I am with you and I, again, call all of you to come closer to me through your prayers. In a special way, I call you to renunciation in this time of grace. Little children, meditate on and live, through your little sacrifices, the passion and death of Jesus for each of you. Only if you come closer to Jesus will you comprehend the immeasurable love He has for each of you. Through prayer and your renunciation you will become more open to the gift of faith and love towards the Church and the people who are around you. I love you and bless you. Thank you for having responded to my call."

March 25, 1998

"Dear children! Also today I call you to fasting and renunciation. Little children, renounce that which hinders you from being closer to Jesus. In a special way I call you: Pray, because only through prayer will you be able to overcome your will and discover the will of God even in the smallest things. By your daily life, little children, you will become an example and witness that you live for Jesus or against Him and His will. Little children, I desire that you become apostles of love. By loving, little children, it will be recognized that you are mine. Thank you for having responded to my call."

April 25, 1998

"Dear children! Today I call you, through prayer, to open yourselves to God as a flower opens itself to the rays of the morning sun. Little children, do not be afraid. I am with you and I intercede before God for each of you so that your heart receives the gift of conversion. Only in this way, little children, will you comprehend the importance of grace in these times and God will become nearer to you. Thank you for having responded to my call."

May 25, 1998

"Dear children! Today I call you, through prayer and sacrifice, to prepare yourselves for the coming of the Holy Spirit. Little children, this is a time of grace and so, again, I call you to decide for God the Creator. Allow Him to transform and change you. May your heart be prepared to listen to, and live, everything which the Holy Spirit has in His plan for each of you. Little children, allow the Holy Spirit to lead you on the way of truth and salvation towards eternal life. Thank you for having responded to my call."

June 25, 1998

"Dear children! Today I desire to thank you for living my messages. I bless you all with my motherly blessing and I bring you all before my Son Jesus. Thank you for having responded to my call."

July 25, 1998

"Dear children! Today, little children, I invite you, through prayer, to be with Jesus, so that through a personal experience of prayer you may be able to discover the beauty of God's creatures. You cannot speak or witness about prayer, if you do not pray. That is why, little children, in the silence of the heart, remain with Jesus, so that He may change and transform you with His love. This, little children, is a time of grace for you. Make good use of it for your personal conversion, because when you have God, you have everything. Thank you for having responded to my call."

August 25, 1998

"Dear children! Today I invite you to come still closer to me through prayer. Little children, I am your Mother, I love you and I desire that each of you be saved and thus be with me in Heaven. That is why, little children, pray, pray, pray until your life becomes prayer. Thank you for having responded to my call."

September 25, 1998

"Dear children! Today, I call you to become my witnesses by living the faith of your fathers. Little children, you seek signs and messages and do not see that, with every morning sunrise, God calls you to convert and to return to the way of truth and salvation. You speak much, little children, but you work little on your conversion. That is why, convert and start to live my messages, not with your words but with your life. In this way, little children, you will have the strength to decide for the true conversion of the heart. Thank you for having responded to my call."

October 25, 1998

"Dear children! Today I call you to come closer to my Immaculate Heart. I call you to renew in your families the fervor of the first days when I called you to fasting, prayer and conversion. Little children, you accepted my messages with open hearts, although you did not know what prayer was. Today, I call you to open yourselves completely to me so that I may transform you and lead you to the heart of my Son Jesus, so that He can fill you with His love. Only in this way, little children, will you find true peace - the peace that only God gives you. Thank you for having responded to my call."

November 25, 1998

"Dear children! Today I call you to prepare yourselves for the coming of Jesus. In a special way, prepare your hearts. May holy Confession be the first act of conversion for you and then, dear children, decide for holiness. May your conversion and decision for holiness begin today and not tomorrow. Little children, I call you all to the way of salvation and I desire to show you the way to Heaven. That is why, little children, be mine and decide with me for holiness. Little children, accept prayer with seriousness and pray, pray, pray. Thank you for having responded to my call."

December 25, 1998

"Dear children! In this Christmas joy I desire to bless you with my blessing. In a special way, little children, I give you the blessing of little Jesus. May He fill you with His peace. Today, little children, you do not have peace and yet you yearn for it. That is why, with my Son Jesus, on this day I call you to pray, pray, pray, because without prayer you do not have joy or peace or a future. Yearn for peace and seek it, for God is true peace. Thank you for having responded to my call."

January 25, 1999

"Dear children! I again invite you to prayer. You have no excuse to work more because nature still lies in deep sleep. Open yourselves in prayer. Renew prayer in your families. Put Holy Scripture in a visible place in your families, read it, reflect on it and learn how God loves His people. His love shows itself also in present times because

258

He sends me to call you upon the path of salvation. Thank you for having responded to my call."

February 25, 1999

"Dear children! Also today I am with you in a special way contemplating and living the Passion of Jesus in my heart. Little children, open your hearts and give me everything that is in them: joys, sorrows and each, even the smallest, pain, that I may offer them to Jesus; so that with His immeasurable love, He may burn and transform your sorrows into the joy of His resurrection. That is why, I now call you in a special way, little children, for your hearts to open to prayer, so that through prayer you may become friends of Jesus. Thank you for having responded to my call."

March 25, 1999

"Dear children! I call you to prayer with the heart. In a special way, little children, I call you to pray for conversion of sinners, for those who pierce my heart and the heart of my Son Jesus with the sword of hatred and daily blasphemies. Let us pray, little children, for all those who do not desire to come to know the love of God, even though they are in the Church. Let us pray that they convert, so that the Church may resurrect in love. Only with love and prayer, little children, can you live this time which is given to you for conversion. Place God in the first place, then the risen Jesus will become your friend. Thank you for having responded to my call."

April 25, 1999

"Dear children! Also today I call you to prayer. Little children, be joyful carriers of peace and love in this peaceless world. By fasting and prayer, witness that you are mine and that you live my messages. Pray and seek! I am praying and interceding for you before God that you convert; that your life and behavior always be Christian. Thank you for having responded to my call."

May 25, 1999

"Dear children! Also today I call you to convert and to more firmly believe in God. Children, you seek peace and pray in different ways, but you have not yet given your hearts to God for Him to fill them with His love. So, I am with you to teach you and to bring you closer to the love of God. If you love God above all else, it will be easy for you to pray and to open your hearts to Him. Thank you for having responded to my call."

June 25, 1999

"Dear children! Today I thank you for living and witnessing my messages with your life. Little children, be strong and pray so that prayer may give you strength and joy. Only in this way will each of you be mine and I will lead you on the way of salvation. Little children, pray and with your life witness my presence here. May each day be a joyful witness for you of God's love. Thank you for having responded to my call."

July 25, 1999

"Dear children! Also today I rejoice with you and I call you all to prayer with the heart. I call all of you, little children, to give thanks to God here with me for the graces which He gives to you through me. I desire for you to comprehend that I want to realize here, not only a place of prayer but also a meeting of hearts. I desire for my, Jesus' and your heart to become one heart of love and peace. That is why, little children, pray and rejoice over everything that God does here, despite that Satan provokes quarrels and unrest. I am with you and I lead you all on the way of love. Thank you for having responded to my call."

August 25, 1999

"Dear children! Also today I call you to give glory to God the Creator in the colors of nature. He speaks to you also through the smallest flower about His beauty and the depth of love with which He has created you. Little children, may prayer flow from your hearts like fresh water from a spring. May the wheat fields speak to you about the mercy of God towards every creature. That is why, renew prayer of thanksgiving for everything He gives you. Thank you for having responded to my call."

September 25, 1999

"Dear children! Today again I call you to become carriers of my peace. In a special way, now when it is being said that God is far away, He has truly never been nearer to you. I call you to renew prayer in your families by reading the Sacred Scripture and to experience joy in meeting with God who infinitely loves His creatures. Thank you for having responded to my call."

October 25, 1999

"Dear children! Do not forget: this is a time of grace; that is why, pray, pray, pray! Thank you for having responded to my call."

November 25, 1999

"Dear children! Also today I call you to prayer. In this time of grace, may the cross be a sign-post of love and unity for you through which true peace comes. That is why, little children, pray especially at this time that little Jesus, the Creator of peace, may be born in your hearts. Only through prayer will you become my apostles of peace in this world without peace. That is why, pray until prayer becomes a joy for you. Thank you for having responded to my call."

December 25, 1999

"Dear children! This is the time of grace. Little children, today in a special way with little Jesus, whom I hold in my embrace, I am giving you the possibility to decide for peace. Through your 'yes' for peace and your decision for God, a new possibility for peace is opened. Only in this way, little children, this century will be for you a time of peace and well-being. Therefore, put little newborn Jesus in the first place in your life and He will lead you on the way of salvation. Thank you for having responded to my call."

January 25, 2000

"Dear children! I call you, little children, to pray without ceasing. If you pray, you are closer to God and He will lead you on the way of peace and salvation. That is why I call you today to give peace to others. Only in God is there true peace. Open your hearts and become those who give a gift of peace and others will discover peace in you and through you and in this way you will witness God's peace and love which He gives you. Thank you for having responded to my call."

February 25, 2000

"Dear children! Wake up from the sleep of unbelief and sin, because this is a time of grace which God gives you. Use this time and seek the grace of healing of your heart from God, so that you may see God and man with the heart. Pray in a special way for those who have not come to know God's love, and witness with your life so that they also can come to know God and His immeasurable love. Thank you for having responded to my call."

March 25, 2000

"Dear children! Pray and make good use of this time, because this is a time of grace. I am with you and I intercede for each one of you before God, for your heart to open to God and to God's love. Little children, pray without ceasing, until prayer becomes a joy for you. Thank you for having responded to my call."

April 25, 2000

"Dear children! Also today I call you to conversion. You are concerned too much about material things and little about spiritual ones. Open your hearts and start again to work more on your personal conversion. Decide everyday to dedicate time to God and to prayer until prayer becomes a joyful meeting with God for you. Only in this way will your life have meaning and with joy you will contemplate eternal life. Thank you for having responded to my call."

May 25, 2000

"Dear children! I rejoice with you and in this time of grace I call you to spiritual renewal. Pray, little children, that the Holy Spirit may come to dwell in you in fullness, so that you may be able to witness in joy to all those who are far from faith. Especially, little children, pray for the gifts of the Holy Spirit so that in the spirit of love, every day and in each situation, you may be closer to your fellow man; and that in wisdom and love you may overcome every difficulty. I am with you and I intercede for each of you before Jesus. Thank you for having responded to my call."

June 25, 2000

"Dear children! Today I call you to prayer. The one who prays is not afraid of the future. Little children do not forget, I am with you and I love you all. Thank you for having responded to my call."

July 25, 2000

"Dear children! Do not forget that you are here on earth on the way to eternity and that your home is in Heaven. That is why, little children, be open to God's love and leave egoism and sin. May your joy be only in discovering God in daily prayer. That is why, make good use of this time and pray, pray, pray; and God is near to you in prayer and through prayer. Thank you for having responded to my call."

August 25, 2000

"Dear children! I desire to share my joy with you. In my Immaculate Heart I feel that there are many of those who have drawn closer to me and are, in a special way, carrying the victory of my Immaculate Heart in their hearts by praying and converting. I desire to thank you and to inspire you to work even more for God and His kingdom with love and the power of the Holy Spirit. I am with you and I bless you with my motherly blessing. Thank you for having responded to my call."

September 25, 2000

"Dear children! Today I call you to open yourselves to prayer. May prayer become joy for you. Renew prayer in your families and form prayer groups. In this way, you will experience joy in prayer and togetherness. All those who pray and are members of prayer groups are open to God's will in their hearts and joyfully witness God's love. I am with you, I carry all of you in my heart and I bless you with my motherly blessing. Thank you for having responded to my call."

October 25, 2000

"Dear children! Today I desire to open my motherly heart to you and to call you all to pray for my intentions. I desire to renew prayer with you and to call you to fast which I desire to offer to my Son Jesus for the coming of a new time – a time of spring. In this Jubilee year many hearts have opened to me and the Church is being renewed in the Spirit. I rejoice with you and I thank God for this gift; and you, little children, I call to pray, pray, pray – until prayer becomes a joy for you. Thank you for having responded to my call."

November 25, 2000

"Dear children! Today when Heaven is near to you in a special way, I call you to prayer so that through prayer you place God in the first place. Little children, today I am near you and I bless each of you with my motherly blessing so that you have the strength and love for all the people you meet in your earthly life and that you can give God's love. I rejoice with you and I desire to tell you that your brother Slavko has been born into Heaven and intercedes for you. Thank you for having responded to my call."

December 25, 2000

"Dear children! Today when God granted to me that I can be with you, with little Jesus in my arms, I rejoice with you and I give thanks to God for everything He has done in this Jubilee year. I thank God especially for all the vocations of those who said 'yes' to God completely. I bless you all with my blessing and the blessing of the newborn Jesus. I pray for all of you for joy to be born in your hearts so that in joy you too carry the joy I have today. In this Child I bring to you the Savior of your hearts and the One who calls you to the holiness of life. Thank you for having responded to my call."

January 25, 2001

"Dear children! Today I call you to renew prayer and fasting with even greater enthusiasm until prayer becomes a joy for you. Little children, the one who prays is not afraid of the future and the one who fasts is not afraid of evil. Once again, I repeat to you: only through prayer and fasting also wars can be stopped – wars of your unbelief and fear for the future. I am with you and am teaching you, little children: your peace and hope are in God. That is why draw closer to God and put Him in the first place in your life. Thank you for having responded to my call."

February 25, 2001

"Dear children! This is a time of grace. That is why pray, pray, pray until you comprehend God's love for each of you. Thank you for having responded to my call."

March 25, 2001

"Dear children! Also today I call you to open yourselves to prayer. Little children, you live in a time in which God gives great graces, but you do not know how to make good use of them. You are concerned about everything else, but the least for the soul and spiritual life. Awaken from the tired sleep of your soul and say yes to God with all your strength. Decide for conversion and holiness. I am with you, little children, and I call you to perfection of your soul and of everything you do. Thank you for having responded to my call."

April 25, 2001

"Dear children! Also today, I call you to prayer. Little children, prayer works miracles. When you are tired and sick and you do not know the meaning of your life, take the Rosary and pray; pray until prayer becomes for you a joyful meeting with your Savior. I am with you, little children, and I intercede and pray for you. Thank you for having responded to my call."

May 25, 2001

"Dear children! At this time of grace, I call you to prayer. Little children, you work much but without God's blessing. Bless and seek the wisdom of the Holy Spirit to lead you at this time so that you may comprehend and live in the grace of this time. Convert, little children, and kneel in the silence of your hearts. Put God in the center of your being so that, in that way, you can witness in joy the beauty that God continually gives in your life. Thank you for having responded to my call."

June 25, 2001

"Dear children! I am with you and I bless you all with my motherly blessing. Especially today when God gives you abundant graces, pray and seek God through me. God gives you great graces, that is why, little children, make good use of this time of grace and come closer to my heart so that I can lead you to my Son Jesus. Thank you for having responded to my call."

July 25, 2001

"Dear children! In this time of grace, I call you to come even closer to God through your personal prayer. Make good use of the time of rest and give your soul and your eyes rest in God. Find peace in nature and you will discover God the Creator, Whom you will be able to give thanks to for all creatures; then you will find joy in your heart. Thank you for having responded to my call."

August 25, 2001

"Dear children! Today I call all of you to decide for holiness. May for you, little children, always in your thoughts and in each situation, holiness be in the first place, in work and in speech. In this way, you will also put it into practice; little by little, step by step, prayer and a decision for holiness will enter into your family. Be real with yourselves and do not bind yourselves to material things, but to God. And do not forget, little children, that your life is as passing as a flower. Thank you for having responded to my call."

September 25, 2001

"Dear children! Also today I call you to prayer, especially today when Satan wants war and hatred. I call you anew, little children: pray and fast that God may give you peace. Witness peace to every heart and be carriers of peace in this world without peace. I am with you and intercede before God for each of you. And you do not be afraid because the one who prays is not afraid of evil and has no hatred in the heart. Thank you for having responded to my call."

October 25, 2001

"Dear children! Also today I call you to pray from your whole heart and to love each other. Little children, you are chosen to witness peace and joy. If there is no peace, pray and you will receive it. Through you and your prayer, little children, peace will begin to flow through the world. That is why, little children, pray, pray, pray, because prayer works miracles in human hearts and in the world. I am with you and I thank God for each of you who has accepted and lives prayer with seriousness. Thank you for having responded to my call."

November 25, 2001

"Dear children! In this time of grace, I call you anew to prayer. Little children, pray and prepare your hearts for the coming of the King of Peace, that with His blessing He may give peace to the whole world. Peacelessness has begun to reign in hearts and hatred reigns in the world. That is why, you who live my messages be the light and extended hands to this faithless world that all may come to know the God of Love. Do not forget, little children, I am with you and bless you all. Thank you for having responded to my call."

December 25, 2001

"Dear children! I call you today and encourage you to pray for peace. Especially today I call you, carrying the newborn Jesus in my arms for you, to unite with Him through prayer and to become a sign to this peaceless world. Encourage each other, little children, to prayer and love. May your faith be an encouragement to others to believe and to love more. I bless you all and call you to be closer to my heart and to the heart of little Jesus. Thank you for having responded to my call."

January 25, 2002

"Dear children! At this time while you are still looking back to the past year I call you, little children, to look deeply into your heart and to decide to be closer to God and to prayer. Little children, you are still attached to earthly things and little to spiritual life. May my call today also be an encouragement to you to decide for God and for daily conversion. You cannot be converted, little children, if you do not abandon sins and do not decide for love towards God and neighbor. Thank you for having responded to my call."

February 25, 2002

"Dear children! In this time of grace, I call you to become friends of Jesus. Pray for peace in your hearts and work for your personal conversion. Little children, only in this way will you be able to become witnesses of peace and of the love of Jesus in the world. Open yourselves to prayer so that prayer becomes a need for you. Be converted, little children, and work so that as many souls as possible may come to know Jesus and His Love. I am close to you and I bless you all. Thank you for having responded to my call."

March 25, 2002

"Dear children! Today I call you to unite with Jesus in prayer. Open your heart to Him and give Him everything that is in it: joys, sorrows and illnesses. May this be a time of grace for you. Pray, little children, and may every moment belong to Jesus. I am with you and I intercede for you. Thank you for having responded to my call."

April 25, 2002

"Dear children! Rejoice with me in this time of spring when all nature is awakening and your hearts long for change. Open yourselves, little children, and pray. Do not forget that I am with you and I desire to take you all to my Son that He may give you the gift of sincere love towards God and everything that is from Him. Open yourselves to prayer and seek a conversion of your hearts from God; everything else He sees and provides. Thank you for having responded to my call."

May 25, 2002

"Dear children! Today I call you to put prayer in the first place in your life. Pray and may prayer, little children, be a joy for you. I am with you and intercede for all of you, and you, little children, be joyful carriers of my messages. May your life with me be joy. Thank you for having responded to my call."

June 25, 2002

"Dear children! Today I pray for you and with you that the Holy Spirit may help you and increase your faith, so that you may accept even more the messages that I am giving you here in this holy place. Little children, comprehend that this is a time of grace for each of you; and with me, little children, you are secure. I desire to lead you all on the way of holiness. Live my messages and put into life every word that I am giving you. May they be precious to you because they come from Heaven. Thank you for having responded to my call."

July 25, 2002

"Dear children! Today I rejoice with your patron saint and call you to be open to God's will, so that in you and through you, faith may grow in the people you meet in your everyday life. Little children, pray until prayer becomes joy for you. Ask your holy protectors to help you grow in love towards God. Thank you for having responded to my call."

August 25, 2002

"Dear children! Also today I am with you in prayer so that God gives you an even stronger faith. Little children, your faith is small and you are not even aware how much, despite this, you are not ready to seek the gift of faith from God. That is why I am with you, little children, to help you comprehend my messages and put them into life. Pray, pray, pray and only in faith and through prayer your soul will find peace and the world will find joy to be with God. Thank you for having responded to my call."

September 25, 2002

"Dear children! Also in this peaceless time, I call you to prayer. Little children, pray for peace so that in the world every person would feel love towards peace. Only when the soul finds peace in God, it feels content and love will begin to flow in the world. And in a special way, little children, you are called to live and witness peace – peace in your hearts and families – and, through you, peace will also begin to flow in the world. Thank you for having responded to my call."

October 25, 2002

"Dear children! Also today I call you to prayer. Little children, believe that by simple prayer miracles can be worked. Through your prayer you open your heart to God and He works miracles in your life. By looking at the fruits, your heart fills with joy and gratitude to God for everything He does in your life and, through you, also to others. Pray and believe little children, God gives you graces and you do not see them. Pray and you will see them. May your day be filled with prayer and thanksgiving for everything that God gives you. Thank you for having responded to my call."

November 25, 2002

"Dear children! I call you also today to conversion. Open your heart to God, little children, through Holy Confession and prepare your soul so that little Jesus can be born anew in your heart. Permit Him to transform you and lead you on the way of peace and joy. Little children, decide for prayer. Especially now, in this time of grace, may your heart yearn for prayer. I am close to you and intercede before God for all of you. Thank you for having responded to my call."

December 25, 2002

"Dear children! This is a time of great graces, but also a time of great trials for all those who desire to follow the way of peace. Because of that, little children, again I call you to pray, pray, pray, not with words but with the heart. Live my messages and be converted. Be conscious of this gift that God has permitted me to be with you, especially today when in my arms I have little Jesus - the King of Peace. I desire to give you peace, and that you carry it in your hearts and give it to others until God's Peace begins to rule the world. Thank you for having responded to my call."

January 25, 2003

"Dear children! With this message I call you anew to pray for peace. Particularly now when peace is in crisis, you be those who pray and bear witness to peace. Little children, be peace in this peaceless world. Thank you for having responded to my call."

February 25, 2003

"Dear children! Also today I call you to pray and fast for peace. As I have already said and now repeat to you, little children, only with prayer and fasting can wars also be stopped. Peace is a precious gift from God. Seek, pray and you will receive it. Speak about peace and carry peace in your hearts. Nurture it like a flower which is in need of water, tenderness and light. Be those who carry peace to others. I am with you and intercede for all of you. Thank you for having responded to my call."

March 25, 2003

"Dear children! Also today I call you to pray for peace. Pray with the heart, little children, and do not lose hope because God loves His creatures. He desires to save you, one by one, through my coming here. I call you to the way of holiness. Pray, and in prayer you are open to God's Will; in this way, in everything you do, you realize God's plan in you and through you. Thank you for having responded to my call."

April 25, 2003

"Dear children! I call you also today to open yourselves to prayer. In the foregone time of Lent you have realized how small you are and how small your faith is. Little children, decide also today for God, that in you and through you He may change the hearts of people, and also your hearts. Be joyful carriers of the Risen Jesus in this peaceless world, which yearns for God and for everything that is from God. I am with you, little children, and I love you with a special love. Thank you for having responded to my call."

May 25, 2003

"Dear children! Also today I call you to prayer. Renew your personal prayer, and in a special way pray to the Holy Spirit to help you pray with the heart. I intercede for all of you, little children, and call all of you to conversion. If you convert, all those around you will also be renewed and prayer will be a joy for them. Thank you for having responded to my call."

June 25, 2003

"Dear children! Also today, I call you with great joy to live my messages. I am with you and I thank you for putting into life what I am saying to you. I call you to renew my messages even more, with new enthusiasm and joy. May prayer be your daily practice. Thank you for having responded to my call."

July 25, 2003

"Dear children! Also today I call you to prayer. Little children, pray until prayer becomes a joy for you. Only in this way each of you will discover peace in the heart and your soul will be content. You will feel the need to witness to others the love that you feel in your heart and life. I am with you and intercede before God for all of you. Thank you for having responded to my call."

August 25, 2003

"Dear children! Also today I call you to give thanks to God in your heart for all the graces which He gives you, also through the signs and colors that are in nature. God wants to draw you closer to Himself and moves you to give Him glory and thanks. Therefore, little children, I call you anew to pray, pray, pray and do not forget that I am with you. I intercede before God for each of you until your joy in Him is complete. Thank you for having responded to my call."

September 25, 2003

"Dear children! Also today I call you to come closer to my Heart. Only in this way, will you comprehend the gift of my presence here among you. I desire, little children, to lead you to the Heart of my Son Jesus; but you resist and do not desire to open your hearts to prayer. Again, little children, I call you not to be deaf, but to comprehend my call, which is salvation for you. Thank you for having responded to my call."

October 25, 2003

"Dear children! I call you anew to consecrate yourselves to my Heart and the Heart of my Son Jesus. I desire, little children, to lead you all on the way of conversion and holiness. Only in this way, through you, we can lead all the more souls on the way of salvation. Do not delay, little children, but say with all your heart: 'I want to help Jesus and Mary that all the more brothers and sisters may come to know the way of holiness.' In this way, you will feel the contentment of being friends of Jesus. Thank you for having responded to my call."

November 25, 2003

"Dear children! I call you that this time be for you an even greater incentive to prayer. In this time, little children, pray that Jesus be born in all hearts, especially in those who do not know Him. Be love, joy and peace in this peaceless world. I am with you and intercede before God for each of you. Thank you for having responded to my call."

December 25, 2003

"Dear children! Also today, I bless you all with my Son Jesus in my arms and I carry Him, who is the King of Peace, to you, that He grant you His peace. I am with you and I love you all, little children. Thank you for having responded to my call."

January 25, 2004

"Dear children! Also today I call you to pray. Pray, little children, in a special way for all those who have not come to know God's Love. Pray that their hearts may open and draw closer to my heart and the Heart of my Son Jesus, so that we can transform them into people of peace and love. Thank you for having responded to my call."

February 25, 2004

"Dear children! Also today, as never up to now, I call you to open your hearts to my messages. Little children, be those who draw souls to God and not those who distance them. I am with you and love you all with a special love. This is a time of penance and conversion. From the bottom of my heart, I call you to be mine with all your heart and then you will see that your God is great, because He will give you an abundance of blessings and peace. Thank you for having responded to my call."

March 25, 2004

"Dear children! Also today, I call you to open yourselves to prayer. Especially now, in this time of grace, open your hearts, little children, and express your love to the Crucified. Only in this way, will you discover peace, and prayer will begin to flow from your heart into the world. Be an example, little children, and an incentive for the good. I am close to you and I love you all. Thank you for having responded to my call."

April 25, 2004

"Dear children! Also today, I call you to live my messages even more strongly in humility and love so that the Holy Spirit may fill you with His grace and strength. Only in this way will you be witnesses of peace and forgiveness. Thank you for having responded to my call."

May 25, 2004

"Dear children! Also today, I urge you to consecrate yourselves to my Heart and to the Heart of my Son Jesus. Only in this way will you be mine more each day and you will inspire each other all the more to holiness. In this way joy will rule your hearts and you will be carriers of peace and love. Thank you for having responded to my call."

June 25, 2004

"Dear children! Also today, joy is in my heart. I desire to thank you for making my plan realizable. Each of you is important, therefore, little children, pray and rejoice with me for every heart that has converted and become an instrument of peace in the world. Prayer groups are powerful, and through them I can see, little children, that the Holy Spirit is at work in the world. Thank you for having responded to my call."

July 25, 2004

"Dear children! I call you anew: be open to my messages. I desire, little children, to draw you all closer to my Son Jesus; therefore, you pray and fast. Especially I call you to pray for my intentions, so that I can present you to my Son Jesus; for Him to transform and open your hearts to love. When you will have love in the heart, peace will rule in you. Thank you for having responded to my call."

August 25, 2004

"Dear children! I call you all to conversion of heart. Decide, as in the first days of my coming here, for a complete change of your life. In this way, little children, you will have the strength to kneel and to open your hearts before God. God will hear your prayers and answer them. Before God, I intercede for each of you. Thank you for having responded to my call."

September 25, 2004

"Dear children! Also today, I call you to be love where there is hatred and food where there is hunger. Open your hearts, little children, and let your hands be extended and generous so that, through you, every creature may thank God the Creator. Pray, little children, and open your heart to God's Love, but you cannot if you do not pray. Therefore, pray, pray, pray. Thank you for having responded to my call."

October 25, 2004

"Dear children! This is a time of grace for the family and, therefore, I call you to renew prayer. May Jesus be in the heart of your family. In prayer, learn to love everything that is holy. Imitate the lives of saints so that they may be an incentive and teachers on the way of holiness. May every family become a witness of love in this world without prayer and peace. Thank you for having responded to my call."

November 25, 2004

"Dear children! At this time, I call you all to pray for my intentions. Especially, little children, pray for those who have not yet come to know the love of God and do not seek God the Savior. You, little children, be my extended hands and by your example draw them closer to my Heart and the Heart of my Son. God will reward you with graces and every blessing. Thank you for having responded to my call."

December 25, 2004

"Dear children! With great joy, also today I carry my Son Jesus in my arms to you; He blesses you and calls you to peace. Pray, little children, and be courageous witnesses of Good News in every situation. Only in this way will God bless you and give you everything you ask of Him in faith. I am with you as long as the Almighty permits me. I intercede for each of you with great love. Thank you for having responded to my call."

Additional Medjugorje Resources

To be "fed" monthly by Our Lady's messages to the world, you can subscribe to the monthly newsletter "The Spirit of Medjugorje" by sending a free will offering along with your name and address to P.O. Box 6614, Erie, PA 16512. It can also be read on-line at www.spiritofmedjugorje.org. We also offer an 8-page "beginner's guide" that can be distributed. The suggested donation for 25 copies is $6 to cover the printing and postage. It is also available on tape for a suggested donation of $3 to cover the cost of the tape and postage.

*Hopefully this book has given you an introduction to Our Lady of Medjugorje and Her messages. For further information, we suggest you consult the hundreds of books and websites on Medjugorje. We present to you here favorites as determined by an informal survey with the members of the International Internet Medjugorje Prayer Group, which has ties to Ivan's prayer group in Medjugorje. (This survey was taken before Volume I of **The Best of "The Spirit of Medjugorje"** was published. We strongly recommend it for stories of the earlier days.) The members determined the following to be their favorite books on Medjugorje in this order:*

Visions of the Children - Janice Connell
Medjugorje the Message - Wayne Weible
Final Harvest - Wayne Weible
Medjugorje the Mission - Wayne Weible
Queen of the Cosmos - Janice Connell
Pilgrimage - Fr. Svetozar Kraljevic
Pray with the Heart- Fr. Slavko Barbaric
Medjugorje in the 90's - Sr. Emmanuel
Letters from Medjugorje - Wayne Weible
Medjugorje Day by Day - Fr. Richard Beyer

Suggested Medjugorje websites:
http://www.medjugorje.hr (The official Medjugorje website)

http://www.medjugorje.org (One of the most popular Medjugorje websites, has links to other sites too)

http://www.medjugorjeusa.org (This site was designed with the "doubting Thomas" in mind.)

http://www.childrenofmedjugorje.com (Excellent audio tapes by Sr. Emmanuel can be ordered on this site.)

Caution should be used in purchasing credible resources since there are some books and videos on the market that are "New Age" material. When in doubt seek advice from proper sources at the above websites.

About the Author

The author, who is a mathematics teacher by profession, received the gift of writing and editing on a pilgrimage to the village of Medjugorje in Bosnia-Herzegovina in 1998. A stranger walked up to her the first day there and told her she should be taking notes at the talks since she was a teacher. Since this man had no way of knowing that she was a teacher, she began taking notes at all the talks from that point on. When she came home, a lady from her parish gave her a copy of "The Spirit of Medjugorje" newsletter and told her to write up her testimony and send it to the editor, and it was published a month later. She continued to write, and in two years became co-editor. In 2002, after the editor suffered a heart attack, she began editing the newsletter. She has published a "beginner's guide" to Medjugorje for those who know little or nothing about Medjugorje. Over 20,000 have been distributed. "The Spirit of Medjugorje" monthly newsletter is distributed to 50 states and 35 foreign countries, and is published on the internet at www.spiritofmedjugorje.org. In 2005 she published Volume I of *The Best of "The Spirit of Medjugorje."*

The author also has been published in the Catholic best-seller, *101 Inspirational Stories of the Rosary.* and also *The Fruits of Medjugorje: Stories of True and Lasting Conversion.*

The author's mission in life is to spread the messages of Our Lady of Medjugorje to the world. Her articles have been used in many other publications, including ones in Canada, Australia, England, Poland, New Zealand, and Wales.

Printed in the United States
96566LV00003B/61/A